UNITED IRISHMEN

MAINSTREAM SPORT

UNITED IRISHMEN

MANCHESTER UNITED'S IRISH CONNECTION

CHRIS MOORE

MAINSTREAM
PUBLISHING

EDINBURGH AND LONDON

First published in Great Britain in 1999 by
MAINSTREAM PUBLISHING COMPANY (EDINBURGH) LTD
7 Albany Street
Edinburgh EH1 3UG

This edition 2000

ISBN 1 84018 348 9

Cover photograph © John McAviney

A catalogue record for this book is available from the British Library

Typeset in Perpetua
Printed and bound in Great Britain by Cox & Wyman Ltd

This book is dedicated to Manchester United fans everywhere
– especially those dedicated followers, like myself, who do not
live in Manchester and find themselves keeping the faith in the
face of harsh and often cruel abuse for following our heartfelt
love of the Red Devils. Having endured 26 years of misery
under Scouse domination we are as entitled as anyone else to
rejoice in the current success and to wish the Scousers another
16 years of misery under our domination. A football team is
for life! Manchester United is the religion – we are the
keepers of the faith! It is also dedicated to my two-year-old
grand-daughter Aimee in the hope that with a little help from
her mother, my daughter Louise, she will escape the Scouse
influence of her father Stephen.

Contents

Acknowledgements

This book was a labour of love.

Of course, it would not have been possible at all without the co-operation of 10 of the 11 players selected for my fantasy United Irishmen team. Harry Gregg was the first to agree to be interviewed and became a great source of encouragement – as did Frank Stapleton. Of course, others helped in the production of this book. Debbie Orme typed up some of my early interview transcripts – the remainder completed by my Liverpool-supporting wife Fiona who, in spite of her loyalties, was a source of tremendous encouragement. Then there was Gavin McClelland in the Sunday World picture library in Dublin who very quickly and efficiently saved the day when it came to finding suitable photographs of my footballing heroes. Ace Sunday World photographer Conor McCaughley was another source of inspiration and help. Photographer John McAviney kindly took the time to produce the picture of my shirt for the front cover. And finally, thanks to my two sons Steven and Jason who were supportive as always.

Preface

Tears ran down my cheeks. The television images of the smashed aircraft lying in the slush of a German runway seared into my consciousness. Matt Busby lying in a polythene tent in hospital. In another hospital bed not too far away lay Duncan Edwards fighting for his 21-year-old life. Then came the words of some of those fortunate to have survived – Harry Gregg. Bill Foulkes. The names of the players who died were read out, accompanying pictures of them as living heroes to the thousands of fans who followed the fortunes of the famous Busby Babes. It was the first time I had cried for the dead of Munich. Their lives were lost on 6 February 1958. My tears fell on Monday, 26 October 1998. It was my 48th birthday.

The pictures on the television set were generated by a birthday video I received that day from my children Jason, Steven and Louise – the *Official History of Manchester United Football Club*. The video was to be my inspiration as I worked on a chapter for this book. But it compelled me to turn away from my computer monitor to sit engrossed as the history of my favourite club unfolded. As you will read if you get beyond these first few pages, the Munich disaster was – for personal reasons – the beginning of my love affair with the greatest club in the world. But here I was sitting in tears more than 40 years later. Overcome with grief. I had little understanding of it. Why now? Why 40 years late? What does this sudden breakdown say about my state of mind? Am I going crazy? I searched for a rational explanation and this is what I came up with. The tears may have been prompted by a story from trainer Jack Crompton. Crompton described the moment when Matt Busby first returned to Old Trafford, walking with the aid of sticks. But when the great man got to the narrow passageway leading to his office, the sticks were discarded and he used the walls on either side to support him as he forced himself to walk to his desk. 'Courage' was the word Crompton used to describe this act of defiant determination by Busby. It was too much for this grown man to take. So it was that more than four decades after Munich I found myself overcome with emotion. Of course, the fact that I was only seven when the crash occurred might go some way towards explaining why there was no instant grief. Whatever my lack of emotion at the time, the tragedy of the team that died that day was to impact forever on my life. It was the beginning of my love affair with Manchester United.

As the tears began to dry, I realised I was particularly vulnerable at this moment. You see, I was writing the chapter on Tony Dunne who had a catalogue of stirring stories about the Munich and Busby legacies at Manchester United. Naturally, my emotional barrier was already weak in admiration at the manner in which Busby managed his players and created fantastic teams that fired the imagination – even after the tragic loss of his young Babes. If nothing else I suppose it provided an insight into the depth of emotional affiliation United fans have with their club. I am no different from thousands upon thousands of others. John Platt is a member of Carrickfergus Manchester United Supporters' Club in Northern Ireland. He told me of a recent event at the club whilst supping a few pints. It appears he was asked to name the players killed in the air disaster. John set off reciting the names of our dead heroes. Quite unexpectedly he broke down in tears before completing the names of all those who perished. He, like me, could offer no explanation for this breakdown. Following Manchester United is a religion. Staying with your team through the good and bad times gives us followers our faith. Hence, during our darkest 26 years without a League Championship we United supporters gave everything we could to encourage our team. Twenty-six barren League years. Think about it for a moment. Think about how United still managed to have the best support in English League football. There has to be some rationale for our extreme feelings for United. I have no idea what it is. All I do know is that life without football in general, and Manchester United in particular – such as during the close season – is just not fulfilling. There is a void.

Since I was seven I have learned to live with the disappointment of the old and anticipation of the new. For 41 years of my life I have travelled this road over and over. For 26 successive seasons without a League title, the disappointment never tempted me to lose my faith. I have not been alone in this endeavour. The name of Manchester United is known throughout the world. This universal appeal has given our rival supporters a stick with which to beat us. None more so that those bitter blue bastards who for some narrow reason seem to believe they own the copyright to the name Manchester. Thankfully, the great city of Manchester has not depended on their activities on a football pitch to carry the torch for the metropolis. The origins of true supporters of a club cannot be restricted by artificial geographical boundaries of the mind. My love of United was not pre-ordained by parental or other external influences. It came from the heart.

It was a human reaction to a tragedy that, for one member of my family at least, represented a painful but personal involvement with the great Busby Babes. It was my uncle Bobby Brolly's concern about the fate of his friend Harry Gregg that captured the attention of my seven-year-old heart and mind. Today the bond is stronger than ever. Manchester United are for life – not just in circumstances of tragic death. No one legislated for my feelings. Living in Northern Ireland but supporting a team based hundreds of miles away across an expanse of sea did not give this seven-year-old Co. Antrim boy any cause for second thoughts. United entered my life then and remain there today. I am not a 'day tripper'. I have jumped on no bandwagon. My devotion to the cause of United is no different from that of any of the seven-year-olds in Manchester who decided to follow the Red Devils – except, of course, that they had more opportunity to go to the games or to choose another club in Manchester. However, few seven-year-olds would meet the prerequisite of the Bitter Blues, namely that you must have a chip on your shoulder.

Not even being unable to see the Red Devils in action was a deterrent. It did not impinge on my devotion to the cause. It may have taken me until 1971 to finally visit the Theatre of Dreams. It may have been that United lost that day 1–0 to an Osgood goal for Chelsea. But nothing could shake or alter the make-up of the red, white and black blood coursing around my body. The result was not the only disappointment that day. I knew the ground so well from photographs and television images that, crazy as it may seem, I expected people to know me. Old Trafford was no stranger to me yet I seemed to be a stranger to it. It is difficult to explain. In any event, my Chelsea-supporting companion on this first trip to the Theatre of Dreams insisted we buy seats in the main stand. I really wanted to be on the terracing of the Stretford End. Every game since that day was watched from the Stretford End until the Taylor Report outlawed terracing.

Whilst the majority of my visits to the Old Trafford shrine were made from Northern Ireland, two periods of living in England brought me closer to the football love of my life. The first was in Sheffield during the seventies and that wonderful Second Division campaign of exciting, attacking football viewed from the fantastic atmosphere of the Stretford End. That was when football crowds were passionate, volatile, noisy, committed and, most important of all, prepared to contribute to the cause of the team by singing until their throats closed over – red hot, sore and silenced. The kind of raucous roar that Fergie so covets for nineties United. My second spell in England was in Manchester itself and it is not by coincidence that my first season as a season-ticket holder produced the first Championship-winning side in 26 years. Even though I moved back to Ireland, I have maintained my season-ticket interest. I am currently a member of two syndicates in Belfast with four season tickets. There are three others in each of the two groups – all United fanatics like me. Grown men who lose all sense of reason when displaying their passions for the greatest club football side in the world – nay, the universe.

Speaking of my Irish friends who also follow United brings me around to the fundamental purpose of writing this book, United Irishmen. When it comes to the Red Devils, Ireland *is* United.

Not only the clubs' supporters, but a tremendous wealth of playing talent as well – Ireland has contributed to the United cause. Just about every successful United team has had Irish blood in the line-up. Certainly in the five decades of my lifetime, it can be said that every one of our successful teams has enjoyed the contributions of Irishmen from both parts of the island of Ireland. The teams of the fifties had players like Johnny Carey, Jackie Blanchflower, Billy Whelan, Joe Carolan. Harry Gregg joined United in 1958 and continued into the sixties along with players like Shay Brennan, Tony Dunne, Johnny Giles, Pat Dunne, Noel Cantwell and George Best. The seventies gave us the involvement of Jimmy Nicholl, Sammy McIlroy, David McCreery, Gerry Daly, Mick Martin, Chris McGrath and Tommy Jackson. In the eighties Ireland was represented by Frank Stapleton, Kevin Moran, Paul McGrath and Norman Whiteside. The most recent highly successful teams of the nineties have witnessed the contributions of Denis Irwin and Roy Keane. An examination of the records during my researches for this book revealed a relatively small number of players who had starred in the famous red colours of United. You think about it for a moment. Try to guess how many Irishmen have played first-team football at Old Trafford. One hundred? More? Less? The actual number of players who have made it into the first team and played in recognised competitive games is 55.

It is from this select band of players that I have chosen my fantasy eleven 'United Irishmen'. Of course, it will not meet with the approval of all United faithful here in Ireland and beyond, but in making my choice I took into serious consideration only those players I have watched perform for United. This meant facing some difficult choices. Eyebrows will undoubtedly be raised about my exclusion of the great Johnny Giles. I took the view that as Giles made his name as a world-class player after leaving Old Trafford he did not meet my criteria. His name was in my original list, as was that of Johnny Carey. But I decided it would not be possible for me to justify the inclusion of players from the past. My team had to be based on those players who played in my lifetime.

As a consequence of that rationale, my *United Irishmen* team is as follows:

Harry Gregg

Jimmy Nicholl

Denis Irwin   **Kevin Moran**   **Paul McGrath**   **Tony Dunne**

Sammy McIlroy   **Roy Keane (Capt)**

George Best   **Frank Stapleton**   **Norman Whiteside**

This would be a formidable side – even by today's standards, a side to compete in an entertaining fashion in any league. In a recent poll of United fans to find the 50 Greatest-Ever Players for United – conducted by the Manchester United official magazine – seven of these Irishmen made the top 50. George Best led the way at No. 2 to 'King Eric' at No. 1. Next was Norman Whiteside at No. 11; Roy Keane at No. 17; Denis Irwin at No. 24; Sammy McIlroy at No. 26; Harry Gregg at No. 37; Noel Cantwell at No. 43 and Paul McGrath at No. 45. So it is a team heavily laden with talented characters. That is to say, a team composed of individuals with strong personalities, each with a passion for life and living it to the 'full'. When asked for his comments on this selection, Roy Keane told me: 'I think it would be a great team . . . soccer team as well as drinking team!' Indeed! But in a sense, that would be the strength of this side. For although each and every one of these players has his own very individual style of play, they all have experience of using those particular strengths for the benefit of the team. The one common bond is that every single one of them is a winner. Individually they have that desire to win, that hatred of defeat. Collectively, that is the single most significant factor to unite them in battle.

This book was made possible by the co-operation of the players selected for my fantasy eleven who were prepared to speak to me about their years at Old Trafford. They told of the highs and the lows and some humorous moments as well. They also endured my questions about games that stick out in my memory, games that gave me and thousands of other United followers great pleasure. I asked each of the players to fill in a questionnaire and now publish the answers of those who chose to complete the task. You will also notice towards the end of each chapter a section called 'Reason to Believe'. This is a brief account of my selection of that particular individual for inclusion in the *United Irishmen* team. During my chats with the players, our conversations covered a wide range of topics, including the following:

- the famous 5–1 win in the Stadium of Light when George Best tore Benfica to shreds
- the ten-man victory in the 1985 FA Cup final
- the glorious night of European triumph when we beat Barcelona 3–0 to overcome their first leg 2–0 lead
- the end of the 26-year League Championship famine in 1993 and the Double-Doubles that followed
- our European Cup win against Benfica at Wembley in 1968, of course.

This book is a tribute to the fallen at Munich and to all the Irishmen who have worn United's colours with such pride, passion and commitment to keeping the red flag flying high above the rest. Welcome to stirring stories about Manchester United's 'United Irishmen'.

We are just one of those teams that you see now and then,
We often score six, but seldom score ten,
We beat them at home, we beat them away,
We kill any bastards who get in our way.

We are the pride of all Europe, the cock of the north. We hate Scousers – and Cockneys of course (and Leeeds),
We are United without any doubt, we are the Manchester boys!

Laaaaaaaaa Laaaa Laa, La-la, La-la-la, Laaaa-la . . . .
Oooooooooooh!!

ONE

Harry Gregg

(GOALKEEPER)

Manchester United: 1957–58 to 1967–68: 247 games

DEBUT: 21 December 1957 v. Leicester City at Old Trafford. (Won 4–0)

TEAM: **Gregg; Foulkes, Byrne, Colman, Jones M., Edwards, Morgans, Charlton (1), Taylor T., Viollet (2), Scanlon (1).**

Outside it was a violent Atlantic Ocean that pounded the rocks around the tiny harbour – sending sea spray stretching ambitiously heavenwards, only to be blown off course by a wind strong enough to deny the sea's quest to reach the stars. The citizens of Portstewart, on Northern Ireland's north coast, huddled against the cool autumn conditions as they went about their normal Sunday routine of buying papers, milk and bread or drinking coffee and eating ice cream in the safety and warmth of promenade cafes. Inside the closed dining-room of the seafront Windsor Hotel, a 65-year-old man, who had earned a living reaching for the stars and become one himself, paced up and down between tables to illustrate how he developed the art of goalkeeping – seemingly drawing inspiration from the very walls around him, heavily laden as they are with the framed black and white photographic memories of the days he stood guard over the nets at Old Trafford and much further afield for his beloved Manchester United and Northern Ireland.

When Harry Gregg stood to his full height, he imposed himself on the room – the furniture dwarfed in comparison. The carpet faced erosion on a scale worse than anything the sea outside might threaten as he animatedly described the second of George Best's stunning strikes in the Stadium of Light in Lisbon on 9 March 1966. That was when Manchester United – the underdogs – overwhelmed, no stuffed, Benfica, in a remarkable 5–1 victory. The room filled with his passion for football, the game he graced as a Manchester United superstar between 1957 and 1967. This Benfica match was one I secretly listened to on a transistor radio under my pillow as a 15-

year-old under orders to go to bed and sleep. But how could you sleep when your team was fulfilling one of your dreams – a night of genuine pleasure between the sheets! Now, 31 years later, I was sitting opposite the man who was between the posts on that memorable night – one of the eleven United heroes.

Harry Gregg recalls his 'pass' to David Herd that left him with the simple task of heading the ball into the path of the 'Belfast Boy', George Best. Best then touched it once, then a second time as he threaded the ball at speed between a group of defenders before sweeping it into the Benfica net. 'That *was* a pass,' Gregg enthused as he explained to me how he used to tell United wingers to watch him closely once he gathered the ball from general play. 'I told them if I walked to the right of the penalty box bouncing the ball, then the natural reaction of the opposition right-back was to move across the pitch with me; if I moved to the left then their left-back would do the same. Do you see what I am saying? They would have been watching the ball travel across our goal in my hands. So if I moved to the right, the ball was going to go left – the opposite direction to which I was facing. I told the wingers to hug the line because their marker would have drifted inside. Then I would turn and deliver a drop kick right to them. It was this kind of thinking that created the second goal in the Stadium of Light.'

On this occasion, according to Gregg, it was the Benfica centre-half Germano who was pulled out of position – leaving an unmarked David Herd as Gregg's target for a drop-kick pass.

'I picked the ball up,' Gregg remembered as clear as yesterday. 'Nobby Stiles nearly had a heart attack as I went to reach for the ball and it bounced and hopped, and I was dead lucky just to grab it with one hand. I looked up and there's the big centre-half with the bald head – he had stayed in his own box, stayed at 'home', as we say. Davy Herd was up there, unmarked. I bounced the ball twice and I drop kicked it – from my box towards the right side of 'D' on the edge of their penalty box. Davy Herd headed it down and Bestie ran on to his knock down and, well, you know the rest . . . '

This conversation was taking place on the afternoon of 14 September 1997. Blackburn Rovers were at home in the Premier League to Leeds United. Harry wanted to watch the match live on Sky and so I was informed we had less than two hours to talk. Kick-off time passed by and we were still in the full flow of rejoicing in warm memories of United successes and failures. On television, as the game raced to a 4–3 scoreline by half time, our conversation raced to cover his memorable and distinguished, but surprisingly medal-less, United career. The match was almost over by the time I bade him farewell. I flinched as I stepped out into the angry Atlantic breeze, happy in heart at having just spent an engrossing four hours with the man who was unwittingly – but nevertheless inextricably – linked to my boyhood choice to become a devotee of Manchester United.

Harry Gregg was born in the small Co. Derry village of Tobermore on 27 October 1932. He had dreams of playing professional football, dreams he may have shared with my uncle Bobby Brolly. Gregg practised for hours on his own and did well enough to play for Northern Ireland schoolboys in 1947, then was a Youth international, represented and played for Northern Ireland at amateur international level and played for the Irish League before finally becoming a full international. 'You should never be ashamed of a dream,' Gregg told me. 'I used to go into a field in the dark with a ball and live my dream of doing things as a professional player. Every night with my brothers I would do a series of exercises – 40 press-ups, 40 sit-ups, and never smoked or drank. I was obsessed with being a professional.'

As a teenager he was caught breaking into the ground of Irish League side Coleraine one Saturday afternoon. He wanted to watch Coleraine's reserve side take on Linfield Swifts, the reserve team of the mighty Linfield, the Northern Irish equivalent of Glasgow Rangers. The Coleraine manager Jim White knew Gregg, living as he did just a hundred yards away. Rather than have him thrown out of the ground, White asked Gregg to play!

'I played in borrowed boots,' Gregg recalled, a smile forming banana-shaped on his face. 'I let in four goals. Coleraine paid me fifteen shillings and I never heard from them again.'

But the Linfield Swifts boss liked what he had seen and a few weeks later two Linfield representatives arrived at Gregg's front door seeking his signature. Thus began his goalkeeping career. Prior to making this step he had played for Ballymoney Young Men, alongside my Uncle Bobby. The two became close friends. It was this friendship which, through tragedy, brought Manchester United into my heart.

I remember the day so clearly, even though I was just seven years of age. It was my 'everyone-knows-what-they-were-doing-when-President-Kennedy-was-shot' moment. Except, he hadn't been yet and, besides, this moment I am about to describe in 1958 was much more important than the events in Dallas. I was at home in Ballymoney, Co. Antrim, a small market town with a population of just a few thousand souls. On this day I'm thinking of, I could do little but look on in bewilderment as they huddled in a corner of our living-room, talking in whispers, adult stuff not meant for the ears of a seven-year-old. But clearly something dreadful had happened – there was a great sense of foreboding about the manner of the huddle and, of course, the hint of tears from my uncle Bobby confirmed the worst. He was my first hero figure, uncle Bobby Brolly, my mother's brother, my first role model. He was a footballer who had played for Derry City in two Irish Cup finals and who finished his career playing for Cliftonville, the only 'amateur' team in the Irish League at the time. I'd once seen him play for Amateur Ireland at Coleraine Showgrounds against a team in red – it could have been Wales, or Spain, or Switzerland, it didn't matter really.

My greatest pleasure in visiting his house was to gaze lovingly at the international caps in his cabinet – God was I envious. He's in my earliest childhood memories, is uncle Bobby. I have this picture of him swinging me between his legs, kicking a ball against the coal bunker at the rear of our house, before my own legs could be relied upon to get me safely around the back garden. Anyway as I witnessed his distress on this particular day, I may not have understood exactly what was going on – I just knew it was not good, because he passed on that distress to my folks. Little did I know in my childish innocence that the drama unfolding before me would forever impact on my life. Uncle Bobby had arrived with news of a plane crash. This plane had crashed during take-off after it had stopped to refuel on the journey back from Belgrade in Yugoslavia. A close friend of uncle Bobby's had been on board. The friend was Harry Gregg.

This was a tragedy on a large scale. It was, of course, the Munich Disaster on 6 February 1958. There were many deaths and for a time no one could be certain if Harry Gregg had survived. Thankfully he did and uncle Bobby's demeanour improved, my parents smiled again and now, nearly 40 years later, I was fortunate to be able to sit talking face-to-face with one of my early United heroes. Of course, there had been many opportunities for me to meet him before now, but I have always had this feeling that I go to football matches to be entertained by players. When they are not playing they are not part of my life and do not need the likes of me hanging on their coat-tails.

Gregg could be extremely animated and passionate when talking about the game which still dominates his life. He has no airs and graces because he does not suffer from an overlarge ego. Getting him to speak about himself is like drawing teeth. Of course, there is one very sad chapter in his life of which he has not spoken until more recent times, when the public focus was on the 40th anniversary of the Munich air disaster. For 40 years Gregg has secreted inside him the ghosts of that dreadful day in 1958, preferring to suffer in silence, unwilling to articulate publicly the extent of pain he suffers from the tragic loss of so many good friends. Throughout those four decades, the world has spoken in loud whispers to acknowledge the heroic work of the big Northern Irish keeper. He twice risked his own life to climb into the still-smouldering wreckage, first to rescue a baby, and then to return her expectant mother to safety. Bugger the risk of an explosion. 'Get back you daft bastard – it's going to explode,' yelled Captain Thane as he ran about the charred remains of his aircraft with a fire extinguisher. To hell with personal safety. Harry Gregg got on with doing what he hoped others would have done for him, had they heard the sounds of life inside the remains of the fuselage. He had the same attitude to death and adversity in the 'real' world as he had on his world stage – the football pitches he graced and where he scorned personal safety when diving at the feet of marauding forwards. Taking risks for the team. Football is a team game. Life is a team game.

Thirteen nights after Munich, Gregg was back in action for United against Sheffield Wednesday in a fifth-round FA Cup tie. In front of 60,000 they won 3–0 and thus began a Cup campaign all the way to Wembley and with such a tremendous wave of public sympathy that Gregg felt sorry for opposition teams. However, it wasn't too many years before some opposition fans replaced that groundswell of sympathy with a disgusting attempt to offend and provoke. Even to this day some try to provoke United's followers by outstretching their arms to imitate an aeroplane, accompanied by the words, 'Who's that dying on the runway . . . ' Gregg himself could not believe what he heard behind his goal at some games. The first time he became aware of it was when he heard a low whisper grow into a loud whisper. 'I could barely hear it at first,' he remembered, 'but then as it got louder I understood what they were chanting. "You should have died at Munich . . . you should have died at Munich."' Even such severe and distasteful provocation could not move Harry Gregg. He continued to keep his grief private. He looked on in silence as he heard stories about what had happened at Munich, even though he was often angered by distortions, misrepresentations, truths, half-truths and untruths. His silence honoured the dead. He lived with Munich every day but only his desire to help the aircraft's pilot, Captain Thane, clear his name drew any response. It took Thane four inquiries in eleven years to establish finally the cause of the crash as slush on the runway, not his failure to notice ice on the wings. Harry Gregg rejoiced at Captain Thane's success.

Yes, Harry Gregg knew the reality of Munich – yet it was only when he himself finally disgorged the truth of those terrifying few moments on the runway at Munich that we, the population at large, finally could understand. Harry Gregg told his story on television and in newspapers. At last we learned the truth from the man himself about exactly what happened that day and what his role was in the aftermath of the tragedy. Many, me included, listened close to tears. We could feel the Big Man's pain. We could see it in his eyes and face. It was at one and the same time, compelling viewing and yet an uncomfortable intrusion into private grief. Harry Gregg wondered why there was all this attention forty years on – what happened to all the other years in between? No one could give him a straight answer. But the pain of publicly reliving over and over again the events of 6 February 1958 has had a cleansing effect. After walking once again on the Old Trafford pitch on Saturday, 7 February 1998 prior to the game with Bolton Wanderers, along with other survivors and the families of those who died, Harry Gregg told me the ghosts of Munich had left him. 'You know what?' he asked, 'The memorial service at Manchester Cathedral and the ceremony at Old Trafford helped me to face the families who had lost loved ones. I realised then that that was why I could not exorcise the ghosts of Munich. I dreaded having to face the families of my team-mates who had perished.' But when they took Harry Gregg in their arms and embraced him, they restored his soul and finally removed some imaginary burden of guilt over his own good fortune that has haunted the reluctant hero of the Munich air disaster.

Northern Ireland International (25 caps 1954–64)
DEBUT: **31 March 1954 v. Wales at Wrexham. (Won 2–1)**
TEAM: **Gregg; Graham, McMichael, Blanchflower D., Dickson, Peacock, Bingham, Blanchflower J., McAdams, McIlroy, McParland (2).**

By the time Matt Busby signed Harry Gregg from Doncaster Rovers as the most expensive goalkeeper in the world at £23,500, Gregg had already made his mark as an international. Recalling his debut in Wrexham against Wales, Gregg's face exploded with the delight of someone who has just remembered a mischievous schoolboy prank. 'The best coach I ever had,' Gregg enthused, 'was the great Peter Doherty at Doncaster. Here was a man who could lift people at a team talk. How do you like this for a team talk? I'd never met the man before he took us for a team talk the day before my debut game. In the dressing-room he turned and spoke to Brian Makepeace who was a big, quiet, hard collier. "You have no chance in the air tomorrow," Doherty said. Then he turned to Charlie Williams, you know the comedian, who was our centre-half at the time – a great fella who was good in the air. And Doherty says, "Charles, you haven't got a chance in the air against this guy." I am sitting on my own listening to this, me, the f***ing goalkeeper and the defence around me is being told they have no chance against this fearless centre-forward – and then Doherty looks at me and says, "You, my boy, will come for everything!" Who was he talking about in such frightening terms? Only the "King"! – John Charles of Leeds United, the "Gentle Giant". It was his first game for Leeds at centre-forward. He had been a centre-half. I came for everything and prevented him from scoring. What Peter Doherty did was to give me licence to take command of my own penalty area and so, of course, when I made my debut for Northern Ireland against Wales, I already knew how to deal with the threat of Big John Charles. That was the secret of my international debut. Before a game King John used to say to me, "Keep your knees down and mind my teeth!" We went on to become big buddies in later years when I managed Swansea City and gave him a job.'

Peter Doherty had given birth to the Harry Gregg style of play and such was his influence that when Gregg arrived at Old Trafford there was public speculation about this swashbuckling goalkeeper's attitude to the game. In the days before there was talk about football fixture congestion and of rest periods between games, Gregg had played four First Division games within a week of making his debut for United. It began on 21 December 1957 against Leicester City (4–0) and was followed by Luton Town at home on Christmas Day (3–0), away to Luton on Boxing Day (2–2) and was completed with an away game against Manchester City on 28 December that finished 2–2. Following his 'Derby' debut, a cartoon appeared in the local paper in which Gregg was caricatured as a Totem pole. The accompanying caption asked: 'Have United bought a goalie or an attacking centre-half?' When he mentioned the cartoon to Matt Busby, Gregg was a little taken aback with the response. The 'Boss' said that this was precisely the reason he had broken the world record for a goalkeeper, before concluding the conversation with: ' . . . and when I think you have done something wrong, I will send for you.'

Gregg's attitude to the professional game has been heavily influenced by the late Peter Doherty. Doherty was the stylish inside-forward who played his football in England with Blackpool, Manchester City, Derby County, Huddersfield Town and finally, Doncaster Rovers – where as player-manager he nurtured the precocious talents of the young goalkeeper from his homeland. When Gregg signed for United, Doherty was in charge of the Northern Ireland team. He was building a side to qualify for the 1958 World Cup finals in Sweden – a team which, just a few weeks before Gregg put pen to paper for United, had beaten England 3–2 at Wembley on 6 November 1957. It was a good omen of things to come in Sweden. The unfancied Irish showed tremendous commitment and oozed team spirit as they sneaked up on the world of international football. Not for the Irish side the breast-beating boastfulness that has repeatedly dogged the Scots and English, of whom so much is so often expected and so little is actually delivered. The Irish arrived in Sweden without that baggage and their devil-may-care attitude under the leadership of Doherty, in partnership with skipper Danny Blanchflower, took them on a merry dance through the qualifying round to the last eight. Blanchflower epitomised the spirit by informing a group of baffled international journalists that the great Irish tactical plan was as follows: 'We're going to equalise before the other team scores!'

Danny's brother Jackie missed out on the fun because of his injuries from the Munich disaster – but those who wore the green were determined. Gregg played in the first three games against Czechoslovakia (1–0), Argentina (1–3) and West Germany (2–2). He was injured for the play-off against Czechoslovakia which was won 2–1 after extra time with Portsmouth's Norman Uprichard in goal. Uprichard faced extra time without the use of one hand and, in the quarter final game with France, both goalkeepers were injured. Although he was hobbling about the team hotel with the aid of walking sticks, Gregg's injury was deemed the less serious of the two and so he faced France. Given the circumstances, the inevitable happened – and Northern Ireland's interests ended in a 4–0 defeat by the highly rated French side with world stars Juste Fontaine and Raymond Kopa.

After beating the Czechs in the first game, the Irish went night-clubbing to celebrate and when they lost the next to Argentina, they were the underdogs again and no one expected them to advance much further in the competition. It was manifestly a successful method of shoring up team spirit. On a personal level, the World Cup campaign in Sweden was an outstanding success for Harry Gregg. He was voted the best goalkeeper in the finals!

Yet, remarkably, given these outstanding achievements in Sweden, Gregg still savours above all else that wonderful victory over England at Wembley as his most treasured international memory. 'It was something very special to beat the English, but to do it at Wembley was undoubtedly one of the highlights of my international career,' he said. On that famous night at Wembley, Gregg faced three of the United players soon to become his team-mates – Roger Byrne, Duncan Edwards (who scored one of the English goals) and Tommy Taylor. It was an even more memorable occasion for Gregg because of his pre-kick-off encounter with the English captain, Billy Wright: 'I was chosen for the Irish League for a game against the English League in Belfast in 1952. I think the English side was Merrick, Ball, Garrett, Wright, Froggatt, Dickinson, Finney, Broadis, Lofthouse, Pearson and Rowley. They beat us 9–0! Our centre-forward touched the ball ten times! Anyway, in November 1957 as we were waiting in the Wembley tunnel before the game, Billy Wright came up to me and shook my hand as he said, "You have come a long way son." He was a wonderful man.'

Gregg was at Wembley at this crucial period in his career courtesy of the man who managed him at international and club level, the man he regarded as his mentor – the footballing virtuoso, Peter Doherty. 'Peter Doherty was a genius, years ahead of his time,' said Gregg, speaking now in reverential tones. 'A genius. He used to say the great player, the true genius sees a picture. Bad players do not see pictures. And I found it was true. When I had my spell as coach at Old Trafford, there was one young lad who shone through and who was truly a genius. That was Norman Whiteside.'

But Whiteside was not the first of his fellow countrymen to make a big impression on Gregg during his decade in charge between the Old Trafford sticks. In the early sixties Gregg made his acquaintance with a certain Mr Best at the club's training ground. The story of the day that the 'Belfast Boy' came face-to-face with the man who was once regarded as possibly the best goalkeeper in the world is a fascinating insight into keeper psychology.

This is how he described his first Best encounter: 'I thought about the game as a player, even when I was a young man. Very few people caught me in a one-to-one situation. See George Best, he is the only c**t to have done me, through one-to-one with a goalkeeper. As a player in the Second Division, when a guy was through on his own all I did was that (points to picture on the wall showing Gregg diving at the feet of a forward) and lay down there, dived in where it hurts, at his feet. Does that sound simple? I did that because the guy has got to look at you. Now it is impossible to look at you and kick the ball. So he looks and he sees me doing that (Gregg demonstrates how he would drop a shoulder) and he's got to drop his head down and when he dropped his head I was diving in there and saying thank you very much and he was giving me the ball. So I was throwing a dummy before it was thrown at me. I did that against the best in the world – and that's how I met Bestie.

'I was carrying a shoulder injury and I went to see Johnny Aston at the Cliff training ground and asked if I could work with the kids and he said, "You be careful boy!" I play in five-a-sides. These kids were over on holiday, no lie. I did not know who this wee c**t was. But after two or three minutes this kid gets the ball. I am in small nets where you never get beaten and he f***ing does that (indicates a dummy hold) and I am on my f***ing arse and he's gone. Nobody does that to me. I did that to other people. Then he does it again. And a third time. I told if he did it again I'd break his f***ing neck, I'm tellin' ye. That's how I met George Best. Later that day Matt Busby met me and asked how I was doing. I said it's coming on (the shoulder injury). I asked if he had seen this wee lad from Belfast. He said no. He met me a couple of days later and he said, "I know the boy you mean."'

Any initial doubts Busby might have had about Best being too small were soon dispelled by his performances on the pitch – and anyway, by this stage

Gregg said he had already contacted the Northern Ireland team manager Bertie Peacock to inform him that United had 'found a genius'. In fact, Best's parents had spoken to Gregg about Best turning professional before he eventually put his signature on a United form on the Thursday before the 1963 FA Cup final against Leicester, which Gregg missed through injury, his place taken by David Gaskell in the 3–1 victory.

It was typical of the big Irishman's luck during his ten years at Old Trafford, so many disappointments through injury as cup games reached the final stages. Even though he was fit in time for the final, the 'Boss' decided not to change a winning team and so Gregg was left to watch from the sidelines. As far as the United faithful were concerned, Gregg was a star and today he still gets pleasure from the fact that for years after he had gone, the supporters regarded him as the measure of a truly great goalkeeper. Gregg was an entertainer and as Ivan Ponting notes in his portrait of Gregg in his book, *Manchester United – Player by Player* (Hamlyn, 1997): 'He remains the yardstick by which all United custodians are judged and it will be a momentous day when, finally, one matches him in every respect. Harry Gregg was a superb entertainer blessed with courage, pride and character in ample measure. But when it came to the luck of the Irish, his was nearly all bad.'

Gregg recalled the days when he played his football at Old Trafford. He said: 'Whenever you went into Old Trafford in those days the hairs on the back of your neck would stand straight up. Running out on to the pitch was an unforgettable experience. I always had a great relationship with the crowd and even though I was 34 years of age when Alex Stepney arrived, I did not feel like I was finished. I still regarded myself as the best. One of his (Stepney's) first games for United was the Charity Shield against Spurs at Old Trafford. Pat Jennings kicked the ball over his head to score and I have to say I got great pleasure out of sitting down near the Boss (Busby) and hear the crowd shout from the Stretford End, "We want Gregg!" There were other games where the crowd chanted my name when I wasn't playing. That kind of support from the crowd, especially the Stretford End was very important . . . and anyone who tells you any different is telling you a lie.'

In spite of an Old Trafford career so severely disrupted by a persistent shoulder injury Harry Gregg looks back on his days there with deep satisfaction. Like so many others who have travelled that route, he has been caught up in that mysterious United aura that captures so many hearts. 'When you play for Manchester United, you play for the Hollywood of football,' he told me, a stern, serious look on his face, but with a glint of excitement in his eyes. 'I would go into Old Trafford an hour and a half before a match. When I hit that stadium, as I said, I could feel the hair go up on the back of my neck, and I was a player! When I went back there as a coach that feeling had nearly gone. In the dressing-room you would compose yourself but then you walked down the tunnel and you forget it all. There was always . . . how does one describe the electrifying presence at Old Trafford . . . and I swear to you I missed that when I went back as a coach. But that feeling is back now. It is incredible. Alex Ferguson has brought back the excitement and the team he has created is the closest yet to the Busby Babes and their achievements.'

After leaving Old Trafford Gregg went into coaching and management – taking charge of Shrewsbury Town for four years from 1968. He enjoyed bringing on young lads like 'Big' Jim Holton and a determined striker called Alf Wood, who for a time interested Bill Shankly at Liverpool before he was sold on, against Gregg's express wishes, to Millwall. Then he spent three years at Swansea City (1972–75) before moving on to Crewe Alexandra between 1975 and 1978. He finished his management career in the English game with Carlisle United before returning to Old Trafford as coach during Dave Sexton's rule. It was the least happy period at Old Trafford for Gregg.

'I thought Dave Sexton had the most advanced football brain in Europe at the time,' said Gregg, 'and I went there to learn. But I learned nothing.'

Sexton's reign at Old Trafford is not remembered with fondness. He played 'crab' football – moving the ball and his players around the pitch sideways or backwards, but never in the kind of dervish-like forward motion so favoured by the Old Trafford faithful. Still it did give Harry Gregg a brief opportunity to work with some of the cream of United's young players – Whiteside and Mark Hughes. It appears that when the shy young Welshman arrived at Old Trafford for a trial, he did so without boots! Harry Gregg to the rescue: 'Jimmy Curran was still at Old Trafford as A and B team coach when he came to me on a Friday and he asked me if I would try out a new pair of Puma boots as I was on the staff. He wanted my boots for this wee quiet Welsh kid who was standing beside him, head bowed. Mark Hughes was getting a game at centre-forward in the B team. I asked him what size he wore. Same as me so I told him he could borrow mine with pleasure. On the Monday, Jimmy came back to me and reported that "the boy Hughes" had scored five! At lunchtime on the Monday, the young fella arrived with the boots all polished and cleaned and, with head bowed, he said, "Thanks very much Mr Gregg." You scored five on Saturday? "Yes, I did," he says to me – so I told him ability has obviously rubbed off the Gregg boots and told him to keep them. He wore them again and again and scored fives and threes. That was my introduction to Sparky. What a player!

They used to say to me when Sparky was 18 that he would be too fat around the arse and I said he is the nearest thing I had seen to Gerdie Mueller of Germany. Sparky had a great physique and was a very quiet, reserved individual although I know he sorted his problems out when he had to. He put Steve Bruce on his backside in the car park one time, and then just quietly got into his car and drove off home. No one messed with Sparky. He just chinned him with a punch. A great talent – one of those players who can excite a crowd. I still get great pleasure out of watching Sparky, no matter that he is playing for Chelsea now. (Some time after this interview Sparky moved on to Southampton.) He has been accused in the past of being crude and brutal . . . but that is a load of shite. That is a gift that man has got. That is a gift the boy perfected. He is another one who does not have to look for people. He knows where they are. Alex Ferguson buried him. No two ways about it, he buried him and he is going to stand indicted for playing Andy Cole.' Oops! Like me, Harry Gregg doubted the potential of Cole. Perhaps like me he has since been compelled to rethink. Personally, I acknowledged my error of judgement publicly in my United column in the *Sunday World* newspaper, 'Red Rage'. As usual, Fergie was right!

However critical Gregg might be in his assessment of Alex Ferguson's determination to stick by his faith in Andy Cole, the former United keeper has no hesitation in stating that the Scotsman has 'turned the club around' for the good. He told me he had great respect for Fergie and his magnificent achievements as manager at what Gregg still refers to as the greatest club in the world. Gregg acknowledged the way in which Ferguson set about rebuilding United from the organisation of the youth team and scouting system upwards. 'For far too long the tail was wagging the dog,' said Gregg of the running of United in the pre-Fergie days. 'Now everything under Alex Ferguson's control is making Manchester United great again.' Gregg applauds the signing of Eric Cantona as one of the greatest signing coups of all time. 'Cantona was just made for United,' he said, 'and I believe Alex Ferguson learned something from the experience of having Cantona around with all those brilliant young kids. And when Cantona was in trouble, Alex stuck by him in a typically loyal Scottish manner. He had signed the Frenchman and still had belief that he could do a good job for United.' When it came to training, 'le Dieu' made a dramatic impact, said Gregg. 'After training one day,' he said, 'Brian Kidd came over to Alex Ferguson and said the Frenchman wanted to stay behind to do a bit of work. He added that Cantona wanted six balls. At first Alex Ferguson thought, "Who the hell does he [Cantona] think he is?" But then when Eric began to stay behind, a group of the younger players stayed with him as he practised his ball skills – especially shooting from free kicks and bending the ball around walls and so on. Soon they were all staying behind. Normally in the British game, players turn up at 10.30 a.m. for training and leave around 12.30 p.m.. But Alex watched the reaction to Cantona's extended training and learned a vital lesson. Suddenly everything began to click into place and they were soon on their way to a League championship for the first time in 26 years. The impact of Eric Cantona and his mentor Alex Ferguson on the rejuvenation of Manchester United can never be overstated.' It is because of what they and the teams Alex built have achieved that Gregg gets those hairs standing on the back of his neck nowadays when he goes to Old Trafford for a game. He reckons Ferguson has built sides that honour the memory of the late great Sir Matt Busby.

Looking back at his many happy years with the Red Devils, Gregg reels off the names of great players from past and present. Asked to pick the 'greatest-ever' United team, he rattles off 13 names without hesitation – forgetting to name a keeper – and then gives up the task as being too difficult. But his list of names makes interesting reading. It was as follows: Denis Viollet, Denis Law, George Best, Bobby Charlton, Roger Byrne (Capt.), Duncan Edwards, Eddie Colman, Tommy Taylor, Mark Jones, Mark Hughes, Norman Whiteside, Roy Keane and Eric Cantona. By this stage he realised he had forgotten one or two and he started up again with Kevin Moran, Paul McGrath, but when interrupted and pressed on the glaring omission, he said he would like to keep goal himself! There was no argument from me!

REASON TO BELIEVE: Harry Gregg provides the foundations of the defence. United fans everywhere acknowledge that he set the goalkeeping standard for everyone that followed in his footsteps. But for a persistent shoulder injury, Gregg would surely have won some honours. It seems downright unjust that someone with such determination and domination of the penalty area finally departed after ten years without a single medal. Alex Stepney came closest to the standards set by the big Irish keeper until the arrival of Peter Schmeichel. There were other Irish goalkeepers at Old Trafford, of course, such as Ronnie Briggs, Paddy Roche and Pat Dunne, who won a League Championship medal in his one season in goal. But the reality is that there is only one man to keep goal in this team – and who's going to argue with my choice of Harry Gregg?

TWO

Jimmy Nicholl

(RIGHT-BACK/SWEEPER)

Manchester United: 1974–75 to 1981–82: 234 (13) games: 6 goals

DEBUT: 5 April 1975 v. Southampton at The Dell. (Won 1–0)

TEAM: Stepney; Forsyth, Houston, Young A., Greenhoff B., Buchan M.,
        (Nicholl), McIlroy, Pearson S., Macari (1), Daly.

HONOURS: FA Cup 1976–77
           Northern Ireland International (73 caps 1976–1986)

The six young teenagers left Old Trafford, their hearts beating faster than
they had ever known, their heads swimming with dreams of one day
fulfilling the promise they had shown to make them Old Trafford triallists
in the first place. After tea at their digs on the Chester Road, the six set
off for an evening stroll around Old Trafford in the company of the man
who had discovered their talents. Their 'Theatre of Dreams' was awaiting
them and was within walking distance. As they circled the famous stadium
they could be forgiven for wondering how many of them would one day
wear the famous red shirt of Manchester United in front of crowds of
50,000–60,000 souls. Only one of them did make it – but an incident on
that first night in Manchester might have ended that career before it had
begun. Their appetites whetted by the evening dander around the 'Theatre
of Dreams', the party stopped at the chip shop at the top of the Warwick
Road, later to be renamed the Sir Matt Busby Way. Jimmy Nicholl was a
happy-go-lucky 15-year-old on that July evening in 1971. He told me: 'I am
standing outside the chippy with Bob Bishop, United's scout in Northern
Ireland. The rest of our lads were inside. I saw these fellas coming out of
the Trafford Bar and walking across the road and they were staring at me.
Our lads were inside getting fish suppers. Bob says to the boys from the
bar, "Alright lads? Everything alright?" That was the worst thing he could

have done – speaking to them. As soon as they went into the chip shop and heard our lads ordering fish suppers, one of them nipped back across to the Trafford Bar. Then a gang came out of the bar and all hell was let loose. Wee Bob had all our expenses for the week in his breast coat pocket, about three to four hundred quid. We bombed down that road to get away. They didn't get the money. They left old Bob alone and he was already away down the road, you know. We got the whole shooting match about being Irish bastards and all the rest of it.'

Safely back at their digs, the landlady called the police and eventually one of the party, Jimmy as it happens, was asked to go to the Trafford Bar with the police to see if he could identify any of the assailants. The paradox of the situation was not lost on young Nicholl who found it amazing that the party of seven from Northern Ireland should find themselves involved in a violent incident on their first visit to Manchester and from men drinking in what is a Manchester United bar. As Jimmy put it: 'You come out of Rathcoole or Belfast where there was so much trouble and this happens on your first night in Manchester. (Laughing at the memory) It could only happen to us.'

The incident failed to dent the young Nicholl's determination to play professional football for his favourite club although he often wonders how his assailants from the Trafford Bar reacted when he began appearing in the first team at Old Trafford.

The remainder of the trial period passed off without incident. Frank O'Farrell saw enough to make him sign the young Belfast boy as an amateur in November 1971. Eleven months later he became an apprentice before finally signing a professional contract in March 1974. By the time he made his debut, United were playing their way out of the Second Division in the exciting team created by Tommy Docherty.

Jimmy Nicholl liked playing for 'The Doc' and unlike so many of his team-mates, he never experienced any of the famous 'fall-outs' associated with some of the more senior players and the flamboyant Scotsman. But then perhaps he had good reason to think well of the United manager. Like so many young Irishmen before and after him, Nicholl had genuine fears about how the violent conflict back home was affecting his family. As Nicholl remembers, it was the Doc who came to the rescue: 'He was the one who got my ma and da a house in Manchester and got them out of Rathcoole. I was only 16 when he helped get them out. I got the message from home about how things were beginning to cut up rough. I used to go home every month and got the message, don't come back for a wee while. After a game at Preston I went back to the Doc and said if I don't go back now I will be going back for funerals. Things were starting to creep into Rathcoole. I told them I was away and went off back home. The club told me to bring my ma and da back with me because the club had a house for them in Sale, a three-bedroom detached house in a cul-de-sac with a garage.'

It was not the first time or the last that the club showed a caring attitude when dealing with young players worried about their families living through the violence of the conflict in Northern Ireland. As you will read later, they did the same for Sammy McIlroy. But on this occasion, as Nicholl recalled, his family moved into a recently vacated home: 'Bill Foulkes went to America and it was Bill Foulkes's old club house. It had not been lived in for 18 months. At the time I was an apprentice living in digs in Stretford. Then came the message from United: "Nicholl get yourself back here and bring your ma and da with you — tickets are at the airport." When we arrived at Manchester airport the groundsman picked us up and took us straight to this house in Sale. I couldn't believe it, nor could my parents. A house in a tree-lined avenue and when we went into the house there was a woman. She said to my mum, "Mrs Nicholl, I have been told you have to pick whatever wallpaper you want, pick your paint, and me and the groundsman are doing the gardens and cleaning the house up for you." Absolutely brilliant. So, two or three weeks later they went back home and packed — got the removals on the boat and moved in to the house in Sale. Two uncles and two brothers and sisters and that was it. All we were doing was paying them rent right up until I left in 1982. Even though I was married with my own mortgage, they let my family stay there. What a thing to do when you don't know what way life is going to take you — particularly for my two brothers and sisters. That is United in the great scheme of things in football — absolutely brilliant. Since then we have bought my ma and da a house in Warrington and they love it there. So when anybody is critical of the Doc I say to them — listen to what he did for me and my family before I signed professional, when I was only 16.'

So with his family settled safely in England, the young Jimmy Nicholl was left to concentrate on his football career and was very soon repaying the Doc and the club for their investment in the Nicholl family. The highlight of his career came in 1977 in the FA Cup final against our arch rivals Liverpool. The Scousers were on course for a unique 'Treble' of the League title, the FA Cup and the European Cup. United were still only ten years into the 26 wilderness years and winning FA Cups was all that was on offer during these lean times.

FA Cup final: 21 May 1977 v. Liverpool at Wembley Stadium. (Won 2–1)
TEAM: Stepney; Nicholl, Albiston, McIlroy, Greenhoff B., Buchan,
    Coppell, Greenhoff J. (1), Pearson (1), Macari, Hill (McCreery).

This was the side that the Doc built. They offered hope. For once we seemed to have a genuine championship-challenging side. In their first season back in the First Division they had finished third and had reached Wembley in the FA Cup final only to lose in a disappointing game to an offside goal from Bobby Stokes. After that disappointment the Doc promised to come back next year and win it. His team were as good as his word and although they only finished sixth in the League, they had a very real chance to cause the Scousers very real grief – and they did inflict the pain of defeat! The United full-backs were star performers in this match. Nicholl on the right took care of Heighway and 19-year-old Arthur Albiston came in to replace the injured Stewart Houston and gave a magnificent 'man-of-the-match' performance. Nicholl began the move leading to the winning goal – picking out Lou Macari with a high ball which Macari headed into the path of Jimmy Greenhoff who managed to dump 'Kicker' Smith on his arse. The ball ran free and the oncoming Macari blasted in a shot. It hit Greenhoff on the chest and went into the net past a baffled Clemence. Macari later said he had been unaware of the ricochet off Greenhoff but added that had it not hit his team-mate, it would have ended up at Wembley Central railway station!

During the summer United fans were watching for news of who might sign for the Red Devils – someone who could provide the missing ingredient required for League championship glory. Instead we got a horror story that took United off the sports pages and put them on the front pages of every English daily – the Doc had been playing away! As soon as the FA Cup had been placed on a shelf in the trophy room at Old Trafford the media were presented with a gift-wrapped scandal. The United manager was having an affair with the wife of the club's physiotherapist Laurie Brown. The disclosure threw our club into turmoil and ultimately led to the Doc's dismissal.

Jimmy Nicholl was on a family holiday when he heard about events back home: 'I was out in Spain at the time and I just could not believe it. We knew nothing about the affair. We were sitting down at the pool when these Manchester lads told us that the Doc had been sacked. What? They said he was messing around with Mrs Brown! You are joking, I said. Just when we were looking forward to things going our way and building on our success. Nobody had any idea. When the players got together, sitting talking, we looked back and people began to say things like, "You remember the Doc that night at the dance when he was very subdued?" And he was, given that we had just beaten Liverpool to win the FA Cup. We thought he was just taking it all in. It definitely wasn't like him. So then, with hindsight, we knew there was something wrong. You begin to think about whether or not he knew something was going to happen, that he was going to get the bullet.

It was sad really, especially when you look at some of the things that go on these days.' Shocked and dismayed as they were, the team had to go on without their mentor. But for Jimmy Nicholl, winning an FA Cup final medal was to be his only tangible record of his Old Trafford career – the rest is down to memories!

The man behind the glass at the P&O European Ferries desk in Larne Harbour was adamant. There was no way I could get on the 6 a.m. sailing for Cairnryan, even though I was going as a foot passenger. The time was 5.45 a.m. on 16 January 1999. Even though the ship was still sitting at the quayside, he was turning me away. Quietly cursing the 'jobsworth' mentality, I set off for Belfast and the Seacat sailing to Stranraer at 7 a.m. The irony of this situation amused me on the journey. From the window of my office at home I can see Scotland – on a clear day of course. I have a view of the Ailsa Craig rock just off the Ayrshire coast at Turnberry and the ferry port of Larne! Yet here I was speeding in the opposite direction to keep an appointment with the Raith Rovers manager Jimmy Nicholl, who was bringing his team to the Scottish west coast for a First Division game with Stranraer.

With the later sailing I decided to take the car to ensure my arrival at the Raith Rovers team hotel in Portpatrick, a few miles down the coast from Stranraer. The view from the hotel reception area was stunning. The entertainment was provided by the angry white waves pounding the walls around the small harbour in Portpatrick. During the sailing, notebooks were checked and textbooks were noted on the Nicholl career. Stirring memories of Nicholl in action were evoked in preparation for our meeting. It occurred that one of my most enduring memories was of Nicholl's forays up the right wing and those crosses he whipped in at great speed and which left his foot with such a low trajectory that they were too often accidentally intercepted by opposition players. But these were the early precursors of the Beckham cross – a point put to the man himself shortly after we made our introductions and found a quiet corner for our chat. When asked whether his crossing ability was something he worked on or if it came naturally, Jimmy explained how two senior professionals at Old Trafford played a key role in the development of the Nicholl cross.

He told me: 'I don't think it was a natural thing for me 'cause I was never a right-back. Because you're always sweeper or midfield you don't have to cross too many balls. You see, they converted me to right-back. Frank Bluntstone was the youth team manager and I remember Frank taking me to one side. Frank had been an outside-left. He began to coach me on how to position myself to challenge a left-winger. He illustrated this by telling me how to get my belly position right first of all, and then I got thrown in to right-back, you see. So when you're saying about natural, it didn't come natural to me because it was a type of way of hitting the ball that I didn't have to know. But we used to do a lot of crossing and finishing, crossing and finishing.'

It was during this time that another 'old pro' was instrumental in further enhancing the Nicholl style of play – Jimmy Greenhoff. Just like Cantona in later years, Greenhoff used to stay behind when training finished to work on his ball skills. Soon the young Nicholl was staying behind as well: 'Talking about hitting balls, Jimmy Greenhoff was the best and for whatever reason he used to ask me if I fancied staying behind and kicking at goals. Of course I did. So Jimmy and me, we used to stay out on the park and he used to strike a ball in a particular way. I would say I didn't know how to do that and it was brilliant because he worked at it and showed me. Jimmy used to get the ball, you'll remember it yourself, he'd get a ball there, chest it, bring it down. He held the ball like that and he used to punch it with his feet. I could see him afterwards strike the ball that way, punch it to the front of his foot and it's a hard thing to do – the way he struck a ball was his own thing. You're working at it without being conscious of it. It was just somebody who wanted to stay behind and kick a few balls. I tell you, Jimmy Greenhoff was a 32-year-old when he came to Old Trafford. He was in the twilight of his career and still wanting to kick balls at 32.' Jimmy explained that he tried to school his young players at Raith Rovers to spend extra time with the ball to improve their skills and soon we were deep in conversation as we both reminisced about our past involvement with the famous Manchester United. He might have become a player, but we both spent our childhood years supporting the Red Devils, although for Jimmy that did prove to be rather awkward, as he remembered: 'I was a United supporter, yet the boys' club I played for were all Liverpool. In Rathcoole [a large housing development on the northern outskirts of Belfast] we used to go to a club on Friday night, pay our dues, see who we were playing on Saturday morning. On Saturday afternoons I played for the Boys' Brigade. But on Saturday mornings we would meet at this wee club and have a game of pool, game of darts, a football quiz. It was great. Now and again the lads that used to run the club, Chuck and Geordie Mitchell, would turn round and say, "Right, go back and get your coats, tell your ma and da we're taking you on the boat to Liverpool tonight to watch Liverpool." They were Liverpool men – but it didn't matter.'

Jimmy was soon to learn the meaning of the word diplomacy on one particular trip to Anfield when the visitors were Manchester United. 'I was stuck in the Liverpool end,' he told me, and did he cheer for the Red

Devils? 'No, not at all. Not whenever they were playing at Anfield and I was in with the Liverpool fans. Call it self preservation!'

It was while he was playing for the B.B. that United scout Bob Bishop made the approach which eventually led to that first memorable evening in Manchester with five other young hopefuls. In his early days at United, Nicholl played in midfield or the left wing. He has fond memories of his time in the reserve team after the Doc had taken over from Frank O'Farrell and was busy attempting to save United from relegation. 'Tommy bought all these experienced players to try to stay up in the First Division,' Nicholl reflected, a broad smile breaking on his face at the very thought of his early years at Old Trafford. 'He bought the likes of George Graham, Ron Davies, Jim McCalliog and Tommy Baldwin. It wasn't just exciting when I was in the first team, it was exciting growing up. Whenever I was in the reserves, when they got relegated with that squad of players, Tommy Doc just turned round and said well that's it then, I'm gonna bring in fresh new blood, young blood. He said he would work with what he'd got in the club – players like Sammy McIlroy, Stevie Coppell, Gordon Hill and Gerry Daly. So I'm in the middle of the park in the reserves at 16 or 17 years of age with George Graham on one side and Jim McCalliog on the other – great! George Graham was a stroller and Jim was a passer of the ball and I was doing all the running and they were doing the thinking. It didn't matter. A big red head and a big red face running up and down and they were doing all the passing, the talking, brilliant it was. Anybody coming through was getting an early education. You didn't realise it then but when I look back certainly progress must have been quicker, rather than trying to break through into the first team because you came up with your own age group.'

Breaking into the first team as a raw 18-year-old was not an easy task for Nicholl because of the affection United fans had for his rival for the right-back position, Scotsman Alex Forsyth. It was Forsyth who dominated during the promotion season – having been bought from Partick Thistle for £100,000 in December 1972 at a time when United were struggling to avoid relegation. Forsyth was popular with the fans because of his swashbuckling style and confidence in his own shooting ability which meant he would frequently, to the delight of the fans, have a 'rattle' from 20 to 30 yards out. The fact that he rarely hit the target did not seem to disappoint him or the fans. But when it came to the 'new' boy, at first there was a growing faction within Old Trafford that began to express their disapproval of his inclusion in the side by booing. There is no doubt that it began to impact on the youngster's performances. Nicholl had come through the youth team and was being lauded as a star of the future. Yet when he eventually began to show the kind of form that the Doc wanted from his right-back in the

First Division, he found he was also battling against the will of the fans. As it happens, this kind of experience was something from which he benefited enormously and which he was able to put to good use in his managerial career with Scottish side Raith Rovers. 'Supporters can take an instant dislike to a player,' Jimmy recalled, with obvious personal memories. He continued: 'Now I sit on the other side of the fence. I have been playing players over the last few seasons at Raith Rovers and supporters have decided there is no way they are going to accept this fella or that fella. Now because everything was not honey and roses for me, I can sympathise with them. I say to my players "listen never you worry about that, just you worry about your team-mates and what I think about you". Sometimes players ask you if you fancy leaving them out this week. I say never worry about that. You're starting to worry about supporters and comments and it's worse when it's two and a half, three thousand people, because you get one-liners. You don't get fifty thousand booing you. It's not as bad as individuals who you can hear and see, so I tell them to get out there now, because your team-mates know your contribution. So it was a good one for me to learn early on in my career. But I'm glad it happened, because now, on the management side of the game, it helps me. When somebody knocks the door and says I don't fancy it because . . . well, I always say to people going to Old Trafford or Ibrox or wherever they want to go; you all love getting cheered by fifty thousand people, but can you handle a game booed by fifty thousand people? And that was my early lesson, you see.'

The one person who finally helped the young Jimmy Nicholl come to terms with the crowd abuse was one of the 'senior' United players who approached Jimmy on a Friday night before a game when the team gathered at their usual hotel on the outskirts of Manchester. Jimmy picks up the story: 'I used to room with Sammy Mac. Wee Lou [Macari] came to my room one night. Brilliant he was. Everybody thought he was a wee rogue, ducking and diving and his horses and gambling and all, but see when it came to football he took it dead serious. He said to me, "How are you?" and I was having a bad time and my confidence was shattered and I'm talking about seven or eight weeks in a row. He says, "Why do you think you're playing?" I said to be quite honest with you I've no idea. I says I'm there and I'm giving the ball away and he says, "But how many kicks are you getting?" I said I'm getting a thousand kicks alright. "There you are, that's why you're playing." But if I'm giving the ball away? "It doesn't matter . . . what does matter is that you are making yourself available to receive the ball, making sure you are involved in the game. It is when you stop wanting the ball, when you walk into areas where you cannot receive the ball that you are gone." So he was telling me it was worse if you are not on the ball.'

The young Nicholl learned quickly not to hide on the pitch and that his boss, the Doc, appreciated the fact that he was constantly looking for the ball, wanting to be part of the action. Nicholl now understood it was for that reason that he was being chosen to play in the United team.

Lou Macari had spelled out the future attitude to Nicholl of professional football: 'If you're not on the ball it means . . . you think I never made any mistakes today but you only made half a dozen kicks. So you weren't in a position to cross the ball into a keeper's hands or slice it over the top of their bar. You just thought, well we done alright today, didn't we? The day after speaking to Lou I went out and I knew as long as I was getting as much of the ball as I could I was doing something right, it didn't matter. Now if I'd won the ball more than somebody else, I'm gonna make mistakes more than somebody else, so it was how you handle making the mistakes, how you handle getting booed by fifty thousand people for making those mistakes. Now the same mistake is unforgivable, so if I keep giving and giving it away, there'll come a stage when I'm not playing but at least I'm still on the ball and my whole attitude to the game just changed completely.'

United boss Tommy Docherty confirmed Lou Macari's reasoning to Nicholl but gave him a warning. This is how Jimmy remembers it: 'The boss told me that the first time I got into positions where I could not receive passes from team-mates, I would be dropped out of the team. Nowadays, that's a simple thing I say to our players, especially in the Premier League against Rangers and Celtic. I tell them we'll do well to get a result today but if I see any one of you, at all, walk into a position where you can't receive a ball from your team-mates, you're coming off.' That is precisely what happened to the young Nicholl as soon as he had got himself into contention for an extended run in the first team, battling for the title the season after promotion to the First Division. The Doc was as good as his word — although that is not quite how he explained it to Nicholl.

29 November 1975 v. Newcastle United at Old Trafford. (Won 1–0)
TEAM: Stepney; Nicholl, Houston, Daly (1), Greenhoff B., Buchan M., Coppell, McIlroy, Pearson (McCreery), Macari, Hill.

Manchester United had used the Second Division championship title as their 'get-out-of-jail' card and by the time they faced Newcastle at Old Trafford in November 1975, they were pushing hard to follow up with the First Division title. Tommy Docherty had stuck by his young dudes in the chase for further glories. But after the first five games of the season he dropped his right-back, Alex Forsyth, in favour of Jimmy Nicholl. The Northern

Ireland teenager then enjoyed a run of 17 consecutive games in the first team – 14 of them in the League, culminating in this match against Newcastle. In the next match United were away to Middlesbrough.

The United squad set off for the North-East not knowing what team the Doc was going to choose for the game. Shortly before kick-off, the boss took young Nicholl aside. The date was 6 December 1975 and Jimmy remembers it well: 'We were out on the pitch having a look at it. He says to me you have done a great job but the pitch is going to be very heavy so what I am gonna do, he tells me, is leave you out tonight and I am going to bring back Alex Forsyth. But don't worry son, he says, you'll play at Old Trafford on Saturday. I was alright then when he said that. After the game the first team went on and we stayed the night and were travelling back the following day when I realised that the first team were away to Sheffield United on the Saturday and it was the reserves playing at Old Trafford.' Nicholl bursts into a laugh: 'The Doc had done me! I came on as sub for Alex against Newcastle but never got back into the team that season.' Nicholl had made his full debut for United at home against Spurs on 6 September, a game won 3–2 by the Red Devils, and with typical Nicholl modesty he blames himself for giving away a goal. As he put it: 'I gave away a free kick for the first goal. Hoddle scored. But we won so I guess it was alright.'

As the Portpatrick hotel seemed to sway as the wind outside approached gale force, Nicholl made a remarkable confession about another game in which he claimed he was at fault for the winning goal. He was talking about the 1979 FA Cup final, his second appearance at Wembley in two seasons – winning in his first against the Scousers in 1977 to prevent them doing the 'Treble'.

FA Cup final: 12 May 1979 v. Arsenal at Wembley Stadium. (Lost 3–2)
TEAM: **Bailey; Nicholl, Albiston, McIlroy (1), McQueen (1), Buchan, Coppell, Greenhoff, Jordan, Macari, Thomas.**

This was to become known as the 'Five-Minute-Final'. Perhaps it should have been the 'Shamrock Final'. After all, there were eight Irishmen on the pitch that day – six of them in the Arsenal side. As you will read later (see Sammy McIlroy), I was there to witness United snatch potential victory from the jaws of defeat – and then moments later surrender that potential extra-time victory to the jaws of defeat. The winning Arsenal goal came as United continued to celebrate their resurrection with goals by McQueen and then McIlroy. I had just informed Jimmy that my eldest son Jason was at Wembley to see United for the first time that day. Jimmy responded: 'You went to see Arsenal. I blame myself for Arsenal!' Wow! So it was all down to Nicholl, was it? This was a fascinating admission and one I needed to have fully explained because in all the years of discussing and debating the famous 3–2 defeat, no one has ever pointed the finger of blame at Jimmy Nicholl. Gary Bailey yes. Arthur Albiston perhaps. But Jimmy Nicholl? No. Never. So, Jimmy, go on and explain yourself! You can start by telling me if you feel this way because Rix beat you going down the left wing to put in the cross for the winning goal: 'He didn't beat me going down the wing – I wasn't down the wing. I was like a bull seeing a red flag, me – do you know what I did? Everybody was pumped up and I was standing there – it was such a poor game – one of the most awful, shocking. You remember the experience of the Liverpool final and winning, the disappointment of the Southampton final and losing – playing for Northern Ireland. The whole Wembley thing and being such a young age at the time . . . I started thinking, "You have been here before", so now you start taking in the game. The Arsenal game was so bad and I'd contributed absolutely nothing to this game. When it was two each, I came flying in to the middle of the park. Wee Lou [Macari] standing there where that bag is [pointing to a sports bag about 10 yards away]. There's Brady where the chair is [about 12 yards away] and I'm standing here. As Brady's on the ball, I go flying at Brady. He just turned and he turned the opposite way to what I had anticipated and he knocked it out to Graham Rix. Wee Lou turned round and must have thought, where the hell is Nicholl, and wee Lou goes running out to Graham Rix and I'm standing in the middle of the park. He whips the ball over and Gary Bailey was near post and missed it. Arthur Albiston [United's left-back] said after the game he had just let the ball run across his body, thinking he would just take it out. He said he saw it go over big Bailey and as he turned with the intention of letting the ball clear the goal before he played it, there was Alan Sunderland. He had no idea Sunderland was there behind him. I remember people being critical of Gary Bailey and Arthur Albiston. Talking afterwards I thought if I'd stayed at right-back, Martin Buchan would have been in the centre where he should have been, wee Lou would have come over to help me, and Liam Brady mightn't have passed the ball to Graham Rix.'

I wondered aloud how the other players had reacted to Nicholl's remarkable confession. His response was as startling as his candour: 'I did not confess it because nobody looked at it. I have seen Lou Macari since but it has never been discussed. I was so pumped up to contribute something to a poor game in which I had contributed nothing. I thought it was 2–2 and here we go for victory. But later when I looked at what I did, it should not have happened. They would never have scored if I had just been composed and not let the whole thing, well, if I had been a bit more experienced. You look at it now, the whole set up, the whole play, and if I had stood at right-back the cross would not have gone in to the penalty area and we would have won the FA Cup in extra time. Of that there is no doubt.' They may not have known about it at the time Jimmy, but they do now! But then even at the peak of his powers as an international footballer, Jimmy Nicholl conspired to keep secrets from his colleagues and his boss!

Northern Ireland International (73 caps 1976–86)
DEBUT: **3 March 1976 v. Israel in Tel Aviv. (Drew 1–1)**
TEAM: **Jennings (Platt); Rice, Scott, Nicholl J., Hunter, Blair, Nelson, Hamilton, Spence, Anderson (McGrath), Feeney (1).**

Just six months after he made his first full game for United at home to Spurs, Jimmy Nicholl made his debut for Northern Ireland. On this occasion he played as sweeper, although the vast majority of his caps came in the right-back position. Many United fans thought he should be given a chance to play sweeper for the club but in truth the opportunities were limited by the dominance of Martin Buchan. However, Nicholl was fortunate in another respect in that he managed to play in two World Cup finals. Few Irish players get the chance to appear once in the World Cup finals but, under the experienced management of Billy Bingham during the eighties, a select band of Northern Ireland players enjoyed the privilege of two appearances. Nicholl had played his part in the famous 1982 victory over host nation Spain, when the unfancied Irish qualified for the quarter-finals, repeating the achievement of the 1958 squad. 'This was the highlight of my football career,' Nicholl told me. 'It was a marvellous result when you consider we were down to ten men for the final half hour or so.' But it was for the 1986 finals that Jimmy and another member of the Northern Irish squad maintained a big secret from the rest of the players and manager Billy Bingham. 'Lady Luck' conspired with fate to put Northern Ireland in the same group as Brazil, Algeria and Spain. It was a tough call!

World Cup finals: 3 June 1986. Northern Ireland v. Algeria in Guadalajara, Mexico. Attendance 22,000. (Drew 1–1)
TEAM: **Jennings; Nicholl, Donaghy, Worthington, McDonald, O'Neill J., McCreery, Penney (Stewart I.), Hamilton, McIlroy, Whiteside (1) (Clarke).**

Norman Whiteside got the 1986 campaign off to a good start with a goal after six minutes from a free kick. But it was a lacklustre game from two of the sides that had been the surprise packages four years earlier. There was to be no repeat of the heroics against the Spanish who managed a 2–1 victory, with goals in the first and 18th minutes stealing the initiative from the Irish who managed to pull one back in the 46th minute. As expected, the boys from Brazil sent the boys in green home after a 3–0 victory that marked the 119th and final appearance of goalkeeper legend Pat Jennings. Those were the events on the pitch during the finals – but it is on what occurred during the run-up to the games in Mexico that we want to concentrate just now. For it was while the Irish players were becoming acclimatised to the playing conditions that Nicholl and a team-mate became aware of the astute man-management of their boss Billy Bingham.

Bingham had taken his squad of players to Albuquerque in New Mexico, just a couple of hundred miles north of the Mexican border. Nicholl takes up the story: 'Billy Hamilton had a dodgy knee and I had a hamstring injury but Billy [Bingham] told us to come to Albuquerque and if we got through the ten-day training session he would take us to Mexico. We went and our legs were getting better. Billy had all his players locked up in their rooms at night to keep them out of mischief. One night I said to Billy Hamilton that I had been across the road at the Holiday Inn during the afternoon and they had a country and western group playing that night. Martin Harvey came around at eleven o'clock to check everyone was in their rooms. At a quarter to twelve me and Billy are out the door, sneaking through the car park keeping our heads low. We clamber up and over the perimeter fence, cross eight lanes of freeway and climb the fence into the Holiday Inn. We have one jug of beer, just one jug which gives us about three wee glasses each. We hear a bit of country and western music. Great night. After half an hour we leave the Holiday Inn – over the fence, across eight lanes of freeway, back over the fence to our hotel, sneak through the car park and get into our rooms through the patio doors. This established the routine for the remainder of the stay. Every night me and Billy performed the same escape trick and had a few beers. Throughout the ten days Billy had imposed strict rules on us and no one was allowed out for a few beers. During our evening meal on the night before we leave one of the lads suggests that someone go to Billy and ask if we can have a few beers. Sammy Mac [McIlroy] is the team captain – so he agrees to go and ask on our behalf. He tells Billy the boys have worked hard and as they are going away the next day, he asks if they could they have a drink? Billy agrees to a few beers but only in our hotel, not down the town. He also instructs Sammy to ask Nicholl and Hamilton if they think he [Bingham] is stupid. [Nicholl burst out laughing at this point!] When Sammy returns he passes on the message and then asks what the hell it means. I reply that I have no idea and that I am going to see Billy. When I arrive he is sitting with Rebecca in the restaurant and I ask him what he meant by his message. He repeats the question, "Do you think I am stupid?" I ask him what he is talking about. And he tells me that every night at a quarter to twelve Rebecca and him sat down in the restaurant for a cup of coffee and a "wee cake". Every night, he emphasised. He pointed at the dark glass that you could see out of but could not see in. He said that every night Rebecca and him could see two heads bobbing about furtively in the car-park before climbing the fence and crossing the freeway to the hotel over the other side. He was still there when we were coming back, watching every move. But he said he was keeping a particularly close look on our performance in training. He told me if we had missed out or been late just once, we would have been sent home. He also said if the number going to the Holiday Inn had grown to include three or four other players, we would have been sent home. But because we had gone over and done whatever it was we were doing and did not tell anyone else about the escape route and because we still did our work, he was prepared to overlook it.' Nicholl is in stitches as he concludes the story but he just manages to add: 'Is that brilliant man-management or what?' There's no doubt Jimmy Nicholl the manager has taken on board some of the skills he witnessed in people like Billy Bingham, Tommy Docherty and Dave Sexton. But it is unlikely his young players at Raith Rovers will learn anything from the affable Irishman when it comes to goal scoring!

English League First Division: 27 September 1975 v. Manchester City. Attendance 46,931. (Drew 2–2)
TEAM: **Stepney; Nicholl, Houston, McCreery (1), Greenhoff B., Buchan M., Coppell, McIlroy, Pearson, Macari (1), Daly.**

Jimmy Nicholl scored six goals for United but his first goal in a United shirt was in this game – a wonderful lob from 30 yards out over the top of Stepney's head! Yes, in his first-ever 'derby' game against 'Shitty', he managed to conjure up a splendid goal of the kind that would later feature on those cheap and nasty Danny Baker videos. It is a memory not exactly cherished by the embarrassed Nicholl. In over 230 games, Nicholl scored just six times. 'Sixteen,' he said when I mentioned the official statistic. No, Jimmy – SIX! He clearly remembered some better than others. 'I was playing sweeper against City one time,' he began reminiscing about an entirely different 'derby' game. 'We were getting beaten 3–0 at Maine Road and somebody got the ball in the inside-left position. It came across to me and I got a touch to it and then I just hit it as hard as I could and it went in, past big Joe Corrigan. But you know what? There was not one handshake, no celebration of my great goal because we were getting beaten 3–0. The game finished 3–1.' *That* game was played on 10 September 1977 in front of a crowd of 50,856. Perhaps Jimmy was simply trying to avoid discussing what he believes was his worst game ever for United. Interestingly, his blushes were spared. Fellow countryman David McCreery hit the equaliser in what was also his 'derby' debut.

So few were his successful strikes at goal that Nicholl can describe each one in detail. But then stopping goalscorers was his primary function on the football pitch. Nowadays in management with Raith Rovers he aspires to create a team built on the attacking principles he witnessed at first hand in the Doc's teams. Remarkably, he has a weekly routine that takes him down to Manchester to study the present training and coaching methods employed by the 'Wizard' [Alex Ferguson]. Nicholl has preserved his links with Manchester United in an unofficial capacity as he explained to me: 'I train on Tuesday mornings in Kirkcaldy and then go down to Manchester on Tuesday night to watch a United reserve game or junior game. On Wednesday morning I watch United train and then go and see another game on Wednesday night involving one of United's teams before driving back north to Scotland to be ready for training again on Thursday morning. So it allows me to take in two games, go and watch a United training session and also see my ma and da.'

But as Jimmy has discovered during his managerial career with Raith Rovers, then Millwall and back to Raith for a second period, nothing is guaranteed. Sadly, five months after our meeting Jimmy Nicholl and Raith Rovers parted company. Hopefully he will soon find a new club to benefit from the experience he gained whilst playing for the club Harry Gregg has described as the 'Hollywood of football'!

REASON TO BELIEVE: Jimmy Nicholl gets my vote as a sweeper. Of course, he played most of his Old Trafford football at right-back, but I always thought he could read the game well and in my opinion was impressive when he got the few opportunities he did during his career with United and as an international with Northern Ireland. His best qualities were his ability to control the ball, predict attacking plans before they occurred and a wonderful ability to pass accurately. Initially, as a young player, he left himself open to the criticism that he was rather quick to commit himself in the tackle, but he soon learned to hold off and to use his body to shield the goal he was guarding. After leaving United, he played for Rangers, Sunderland and West Bromwich Albion before becoming player-manager at Raith Rovers, for whom he continued playing into his 40th year.

JIMMY NICHOLL: THE QUESTIONNAIRE
BORN: Hamilton, Canada – 28 December 1956.

Which junior clubs did you play for?
Whitehouse Primary School then Rathcoole Secondary School. Later I played for 7th Newtownabbey Boys' Brigade and Glymower Wolves Boys' Club.

Which club(s) did you support as a boy?
Linfield and Manchester United.

Was it always your ambition to be a professional footballer?
Yes.

Do you recall the moment you first realised you were signing for United and describe your reaction to being taken on by such a big club?
I do. It was a great feeling because there were so many young lads on trial and the numbers were whittled down to twelve apprentices. Nine of them were English and we had to be really determined to get an offer of becoming an apprentice.

You made your debut for United in Division Two (1974–75) as a substitute away to Southampton on 5 April 1975. Can you describe your feelings on that day? Did you know you were going to play?
I didn't know if I was going to get on or not but Martin Buchan got injured and I went on to replace him with about 25–30 minutes to go, I think. Peter Osgood was centre-forward and I got elbowed about two minutes after I went on.

You played 234 games – which one stands out in the memory and why?
There were many semi-finals against Leeds and Liverpool. Then there was the final against Liverpool, and Oporto at Old Trafford when we won 5–2 and I scored. Also the League Cup game against Newcastle United at Old Trafford when we won 7–2 and I scored my favourite goal.

The best manager you played for at Old Trafford – and the worst?
Tommy Docherty was my favourite. I also liked Dave Sexton. And just because Ron Atkinson didn't rate me doesn't mean he was the worst.

The highlight of your football career?
The answer has to be Spain v. Northern Ireland in the 1982 World Cup. We won 1–0 when down to just ten men. The host nation on their home

43

ground in Valencia. Great effort on the night and an enjoyable evening afterwards.

Your worst moment at Old Trafford and why?

Realising Ron Atkinson didn't rate me and when John Gidman came, knowing I was going to have to leave one day – sooner rather than later.

Which individual was the biggest influence on your career – firstly as a player and secondly as a manager?

Paddy Crerand was the first influence when in United youth and reserve teams. Then Tommy Docherty and Jimmy Greenhoff. Lou Macari was also a help. As a manager – myself, although I have had a lot of help from people in the game.

Your best game for United?

I really enjoyed the Oporto game when I scored the second or third goal just before half-time. We were 4–0 down from the first leg in Portugal and lost eventually 6–5 on aggregate. The atmosphere at Old Trafford was brilliant.

Your worst game for United?

My own goal against Manchester City on my 'derby' debut. I hit it over Alex Stepney's head from 30 yards. David McCreery got the equaliser to make it 2–2 and it was his 'derby' debut as well.

Your greatest ever United team?

Schmeichel; Irwin, Bruce, Buchan, Dunne, Coppell, Charlton, Robson, Best, Law, Greenhoff J. I have chosen only players I have seen play for Manchester United.

You were at Old Trafford at a time when there were many players from Northern Ireland and the Republic of Ireland. Did this add to the enjoyment of playing for United or did it cause difficulties?

It added to the enjoyment because everybody got on great.

Best player you ever saw in a United shirt?

Without a doubt, George Best. I just think he had everything. He could dribble, shoot, head, pass, was two-footed, brave, he could tackle and wrap his leg around the ball and then quickly get back on to his feet.

The most difficult opponent you faced?
Willie Johnston of West Bromwich Albion and John Robertson of Nottingham Forest. Both were good two-footed players and clever on the ball.

You made your international debut in 1976 against Israel. Describe your feelings on that day.
One of my favourite days. We drew the game and I played sweeper. I had a decent game in that position.

The best game for your country . . . and the worst?
[The best was] the game I scored in against Sweden in Belfast to help us qualify for the World Cup finals. The worst was against Iceland, away, when we lost 1–0 in a World Cup qualifier. A shocking result and performance.

How did you regard the Man Utd fans?
I had to work hard to get them to accept me after Alex Forsyth and although I didn't convert them all I thought I did alright for them.

Why do you think they remained so loyal throughout the years when they so desperately wanted a League title but had to watch for 26 years as Liverpool dominated?
It is just the magic and the image of Manchester United from the fifties that draws them to the club. I am glad Alex Ferguson has finally achieved it for them.

Did the fans' desire for a League Championship ever put pressure on the players? Do you think it might in some way have contributed to the failure to win the title for 26 years?
At times, but the biggest hurdle playing at Old Trafford was knowing just how good the players in the fifties and sixties were and trying to please the supporters that watched those players play.

Your views on the team selected for this book?
Delighted to have been selected and playing with some great players. I agree that you have put me in as sweeper, as I look back and sometimes wish I had played my football in that position. Good team that would take some beating and a cracking night out afterwards.

THREE

Denis Irwin

(FULL-BACK/THE MOST DECORATED SOLDIER IN ALEX FERGUSON'S RED-AND-WHITE ARMY/MASTER OF CONSISTENCY)

Manchester United: 1990–91 – present: 414 (13) games: 27 goals

DEBUT: **25 August 1990 v. Coventry City at Old Trafford. (Won 2–0)**

TEAM: **Sealey; Irwin, Donaghy, Bruce (1), Phelan, Pallister, Webb (1), Ince, McClair, Hughes, Blackmore.**

HONOURS: **League Championship 1992–93; 1993–94; 1995–96; 1996–97; 1998–99**
FA Cup 1993–94; 1995–96
League Cup 1991–92
European Cup-Winners' Cup 1990–91
European Cup 1998–99
Republic of Ireland International (53 caps, 2 goals)

It was 4 January 1994 B.B. That is to say, Before Beckham. Irwin stood over the ball on the edge of the Scouse penalty area, just at the 'D'. He took a few paces forward and with his right foot sent a high, then dipping and curling shot past the hapless Grobbelaar into the top of the Scousers' net. Twenty-four minutes gone and we are 3–0 up against the 'Dirties' at Anfield. Neighbours may have wondered if murder was taking place in our living-room, such was my verbal appreciation of Irwin's wondrous free kick and I was later left wondering what our neighbours might have done if murder were actually to take place! My Liverpool-supporting wife Fiona sat with her nose buried in a newspaper during my joyous celebrations. United goals against the Scousers are a joy to behold. Every one a nail in the coffin of their arrogance. Every goal involved a scream of 'Yeeeeeeeeeeeeessssssssssssssssssssssss', followed by a leap in the air as high as the ceiling would let me go. After my third re-entry from my third triple somersault of the evening I reached for the telephone lying on the floor beside me. My Liverpool-supporting father-in-law, Derek Boyd, was waiting for me this time. The call was answered before the first ring had even finished and he screamed something very rude down the line, something questioning my parentage in conjunction with his reference to the lineage of the Manchester United team. It was the third time I had called that evening so I could empathise with his pain and discomfort. But it was Derek who began this 'game' some three or four years earlier when the Scousers had something to shout about. Tonight it was 'our' turn to torment our arch-rivals, although in truth their star was already beginning to wane, leading to today's situation when they are simply not on the same level. On this January evening, call one came after nine minutes when Bruce headed United into the lead. Call two was made eleven minutes later when Giggs struck a sweet curling lob over Grobbelaar. The third, as I have explained, was just four minutes later when Irwin's free kick gave us an unexpected three-goal lead. The reason for these calls? As I have said, it was a game played out with Derek over a number of seasons. The trick was to call each other when one or other's team scored, or when the result of a game became known . . . but you had to let it ring twice before the other party answered and then you hung up. It was a bit of fun although if you don't follow a football team passionately you will probably regard it as a bit of childish behaviour between two grown men, one in his forties and the other in his sixties.

For the remainder of the game I sat with my hand beneath the cradle of the phone waiting for his call, should Liverpool score. I didn't have long to wait. Clough got a goal in the 25th minute – just 60 seconds after Irwin's strike. Strangely, there was no call from my father-in-law. Nor was there a call in the 38th minute when Clough struck again. Even when that bundle of blubber, Razor Ruddock, headed the equaliser in the 79th minute there was no call. What the hell was wrong? I kept my hand under the cradle for some time after the match finished just in case he was trying to lull me into a false sense of security. After all, I had done that to him in the past – even calling from as far afield as the United States when I was there on business trips, or from one of the Greek islands while on holiday. But this was the last time we ever played the telephone game. It has never been mentioned or discussed since.

But what a game that Man Utd–Liverpool clash was. I have it on tape and sometimes put it on while I am working in my office at home to entertain me. At the time I considered it to be one of the greatest games I had watched 'live' on television. Games between United and Liverpool are special. During the 26 years Liverpool dominated English and European football while we struggled to match our past glories, we tended to regard these games as our 'cup finals'. In much the same way they now are reduced to that very same scenario due to our dominance in the nineties. Long may it continue I say. But what has not continued much since that famous night is the Irwin free kick – but as a glance at the team will reveal, there was no such thing in 1994 as David Beckham – and Mr. Irwin was not just as old!

FA Premier League: 4 January 1994 v. Liverpool at Anfield. (Drew 3–3)
TEAM: Schmeichel; Parker, Irwin (1), Bruce (1), Pallister, Keane, Ince, Kanchelskis, McClair, Cantona, Giggs (1).

So why does Mr Irwin not take a free kick these days? Not even occasionally? After all he undoubtedly has a talent. Admittedly he takes penalties from time to time. But why not give him a free kick occasionally if only to confuse our opponents by providing a bit of variety? It was one of the first questions I put to United's most dependable and reliable performer of the last ten glorious years. We were meeting in the Republic of Ireland's team hotel on 9 February 1999 on the eve of their friendly game against Paraguay. According to the man himself, it is not just the arrival of Beckham and his incredible talent that has brought about this particular change to Denis Irwin's contribution on the pitch. This is what he told me: 'I think as you get older you probably don't have the same strength in your legs, plus I had a couple of knocks on my knee as well, mainly with ligament pain as well. I was off for eight weeks, obviously with the one at Feyenoord and a couple before that. Sometimes you can be out for a while even though you play on. But you feel it in there [pointing to the knee area] when you hit free kicks the way Becks and me hit free kicks. So sometimes you have to be careful. I think when I had those spells out of the team, Becks just took over and eventually it seemed to go on and on.' Have you ever noticed when Beckham takes a free just how much his left ankle bends and touches the ground at a 90-degree angle? Denis says that is required to get the 'necessary whip on the ball'.

Face to face, Denis Irwin looks much younger than he does on television or in photographs. Both he and Roy Keane had agreed to be interviewed for the book although I had only spoken to Roy Keane on the telephone and it was Captain Keano who had assured me he would get Denis to meet with me as well. United's midfield maestro was true to his word and once we had finished our interview he said he would send Denis up to see me. Denis duly arrived holding in his hand my completed questionnaire sent ahead many months earlier by post to Keano. Just like his Cork colleague, Denis Irwin was articulate and extremely friendly. The overwhelming impression was of a modest man who was not afraid to speak the truth and give his opinion on a wide variety of issues.

Staying with the issue of his age, Irwin was candid about his future with United. He has consistently confounded observers with his ability to see off all the young dudes like the Neville brothers, John Curtis, Wesley Brown and Michael Clegg. They have all been pressing for a first-team place. Irwin recognised that he could only sustain the fight for maybe another season and he said: 'Well, I think Gary is a very strong player. I think he has a lot more mental strength than his brother, physical strength as well. I think Philip will come on in time. Wes Brown, obviously he is a hell of a player. I think when he fills out a bit more he probably will be a centre-half for United. He is young and he has a lot to go for. John Curtis, again, he has come in as a right-back, he's played a couple of times at left-back, so he'll have to look for his position opening up. I mean, probably at the most I'll have next year at the club and I think that'll be me. Then I have to go somewhere else. That's the way it is in football. It's part and parcel of football, you have to move on some time. I am 33. So we'll see about that, but the quality in the full-back section is definitely very strong. There's always been pressure there. Ever since I was there they have always had good full-backs competing for places in the team. It's just that in the last two or three years that's got stronger and with Wes coming on to the scene in the last few months, it is just getting stronger and stronger. You can only play at the highest level for so long. I don't think there's that many players, I think the exception has been the Arsenal full-backs [Lee Dixon and Nigel Winterburn] at the moment who go on and play until they are 34 or 35.'

Irwin seems to be determined to go on playing for as long as possible and he points out that he has based this attitude on conversations he has had with former United players: 'At the end of next season I will be two months off 35. I have spoken to players – the likes of Kevin Moran – and they say you should play as long as possible. You could play to 37 or 38 and you still have a hell of a road in front of you so you might as well play for another couple of years. I think you'll find in the modern game now that players will retire earlier basically because they'll have more money and they will be able to retire. I think the pressures in the game now – compared to four or five years ago – the pressures are unbelievable in the game and by the time they get to 33 or 34, they will be able to pack it in and I think they will do.'

Probing just a little bit deeper about this age problem by mentioning the fact that Peter 'The Great' Schmeichel has announced his retirement because he is finding it tougher to recover from each game, I discover that Irwin clearly identifies with the Dane's problems. He tells me: 'As you get older, you definitely get more tired and take longer to recover. Where you used to feel it on the first day, you start to notice tiredness on the second day after a game and you feel stiff. Big Peter has a big frame and he is throwing it about. Sometimes when he plays Wednesday, Saturday, Wednesday, he takes a couple of days to get over it. He feels that with playing in Europe he can only play once a week. But he feels he will get a couple of years playing abroad at a higher level than he would do here. I have never thought about going abroad. The Bosman rule has come in a little bit late for me. You can see people, like MacManaman, taking the opportunity to go abroad.' Mind you, even the Liverpool fans will tell you that McManaman's departure will be of no great loss. We will just have to wait and see how long the Spanish fans will tolerate his great runs across the pitch into dead-end situations! He never really posed any threat if you stayed on your feet and pushed him crab-like across the pitch. My opinion, not that of a certain Mr Irwin, who comfortably dealt with the threat of the likes of Steve McManaman so easily over the years, often being overlooked when the plaudits were being heaped upon the goal-scorers and goal-makers in the United team. But in typical self-effacing manner, Denis Irwin said it is natural that the forwards steal the glory and no, it does not 'get to him'. He put it this way: 'They are up there to be shot at. I mean, Coley [Andy Cole] is up there and is having a good time now and is having a lot of things written about him in the press. Go back two years ago and he was getting hammered a little bit in the press because he was probably missing a few chances. The day we lost to West Ham – well we didn't lose the game, we drew with West Ham but we did lose the League and he had a couple of chances. You know, I think they are up there to be shot at a bit more than us. We are probably just cogs in the machine, the full-backs, and I think the main strength of the team has always been right down the middle.'

Getting back to the 3–3 draw with the Scousers on the January night in question, it was for me an outstanding game played in front of a packed Anfield in what was a tremendous atmosphere. Then Denis reminded me of another reason to recall the game: 'It was remembered more for Bruce Grobbelaar saying, well he didn't say anything at all actually. But that was one of the matches that came up when he allegedly threw a couple in. I don't know if he could have saved any of them, but I think he made a tremendous save from Keane in the second half. The thing is we were 3–2 up, Clough scored two goals just before half-time, but we should have scored plenty of goals even after half-time. I just remember it because there is such good rivalry between the two of us.' The players are obviously aware of the great rivalry between the fans – but does that great rivalry extend to the players? Irwin says that games against Liverpool are 'slightly different

. . . they shouldn't be . . . but they are because of the rivalry'. Naturally, that rivalry is all the more severe because of United's 26 barren years – a point Denis agreed with: 'Yeah, but it's only been about eight years they've been living under ours . . . and long may it continue. But if we beat them it is three points. If we beat Leicester City it is three points, so it shouldn't really be that way, but it is just the way the game is, I suppose.'

FA Cup semi-final: 8 April 1990 v. Oldham Athletic at Maine Road. (Drew 3–3)

TEAM: **Leighton; Martin L. (Robins), Gibson C., Bruce, Phelan, Pallister, Robson (1) (Wallace (1)), Ince, McClair, Hughes, Webb (1).**

REPLAY: 11 April 1990 at Maine Road. (Won 2–1)

TEAM: **Leighton; Ince, Martin L. (Robins (1)), Bruce, Phelan, Pallister, Robson, Webb, McClair (1), Hughes, Wallace.**

You will quickly notice that his name does not appear on either of these two United team sheets but 1990's semi-final games marked the beginning of Denis Irwin's career at Old Trafford. The Wizard (Alex Ferguson) liked what he saw in the No. 2 shirt for Oldham. United went on to win the FA Cup that season, beating Crystal Palace in a replay to save the Wizard's career at a time when the first rumbles of discontent could be heard among fans after Fergie's four trophy-less seasons. Two months after the semi-finals Irwin was a United player, signed for what turned out to be a bargain at £650,000. Born in Cork on 31 October 1965, Irwin had arrived in England as an apprentice at Leeds United in 1982 before becoming a professional in 1983. After just 72 games for the 'Sheep-shaggers', he moved on to unfashionable Oldham in 1986 when they were in the old Second Division, pre-Premier League days. He made 167 League appearances for the 'Latics' before joining the Wizard at Old Trafford in June 1990 at the age of 24.

As a child growing up in Cork – playing his junior football for Everton A.F.C. and in the Cork Schoolboys' League – Irwin harboured no ambitions to play professional football. Gaelic football and hurling were of more interest to him: 'I just wanted to play Gaelic football. When I was growing up, you see, my heroes would have been Jimmy Barry Murphy and Charlie McCartland. I used to watch *Match of the Day* but the coverage then was really poor in the seventies and eighties. Cork were fairly handy with the hurling and the football . . . going back a few years now. I played football at Croke Park a couple of times, not for Cork now, but with the college. And I played for the 'Bars, St Finbars. Jimmy Barry Murphy used to play for them so I played for them in under-age hurling. That was more my scene at the time. Certainly back in those days, Gaelic football and hurling were the predominant sports down in Cork. Probably though, since Jack Charlton took over the Irish soccer team, soccer has taken over as the big sport down there. Hurling is not as bad as you think.' Irwin's last few words were directed at me because during our conversation I recounted my first memory of seeing a hurling match in the village of Dunloy, a few miles up the road from my home at Ballymoney in Co. Antrim. The abiding memory is not so much of what is regarded as the fastest team game in the world, but of one of the players being led past this impressionable young lad with his nose hanging off, having been thumped in the face by one of the hurling sticks. It was a harrowing sight that confirmed within me a determination never to be tempted to try playing the game. Irwin's first season with United was as a right-back, but when Paul Parker arrived the following season he made the switch to left-back. His first season was an enormous success for by May 1991, Irwin picked up his first medal in the classic European Cup-Winners' Cup game at Rotterdam against the mighty Barcelona.

European Cup-Winners' Cup final: 15 May 1991 v. Barcelona in Rotterdam. (Won 2–1)
TEAM: **Sealey; Irwin, Blackmore, Bruce, Phelan, Pallister, Robson, Ince, McClair, Hughes (2), Sharpe.**

This was the beginning of a remarkable run of success for Irwin. Put simply, it was the first of ten medals, making Irwin the most decorated soldier in Ferguson's red-and-white army alongside Ryan Giggs. Of course, but for the foolish refereeing of David Elleray, Irwin would and should have had three medals in the historic treble-winning 1999 – but instead he got just two, having to sit out the FA Cup final against Newcastle. His crime in the game against Liverpool at Anfield was to give away a throw-in and Elleray took exception to that apparently! Irwin should be known as Irwin 'Eight'. In his ten years as a United player he regularly gives eight-out-of-ten performances, with a fair splattering of 'Man-of-the-Match' performances for even higher scores. Yet, have you ever seen Peter Schmeichel give him a verbal bashing? No? Denis has that difficulty too: 'To be fair, I don't think he has shouted at me that many times. I would ignore him anyway. It wouldn't bother me. Pete's been a wonderful goalkeeper for us. It's hard to pick somebody out and say he won the League for us, but the year we caught Newcastle up, he was outstanding. The Newcastle game at St James's Park, and other games, went a long way to winning us the League.' Now Manchester United face the future without the 'Great Dane', who played the final game of his United career in the Nou Camp Stadium on 26 May 1999.

European Cup final: 26 May 1999 v. Bayern Munich. (Won 2–1)
TEAM: **Schmeichel; Neville G., Irwin, Johnsen, Stam, Beckham, Butt, Giggs, Cole (Solskjaer (1)), Yorke, Blomqvist (Sheringham (1)) (Not used: Van der Gouw, May, Neville P., Brown, Greening)**

Four days after missing out on FA Cup glory at Wembley, Denis Irwin gave his normal classy display in the biggest game of his career. In 1968 United had three Irishmen in their European Cup-winning side – Brennan, Dunne and Best. In 1999 there were two Irish European Cup-winning medallists, although only one was on the pitch. Keane had to sit out a ban because of his booking in the Juventus semi-final. But Irwin did Ireland proud. Two minutes after giving Bayern Munich the lead, Basler broke clear of the United defence. He was striding purposefully towards the United goal. But before he could transform the threat into a match-winning action, he had the ball removed from his control by yet another consummate tackle by Irwin. Danger snuffed out in typical Irwin style. No fuss. No foul. No goal. While Gary Neville flapped about in the right-back spot and all too often left his team-mates in danger with 'hospital' balls or simply gave the ball away with bad passes, the left-back area of the field was under Irwin's control from start to finish. Irwin 'Eight' again!

When talking to Denis in Dublin in February he had a very clear desire to secure European Cup glory: 'I think victory in the European Cup is long overdue . . . I am running out of years so I need it this year! There's no doubt that it is the players' and the club's ambition to win the European Cup. I think last year we lost out in the League a little bit because of it. I don't think that will happen this year. I think we were all hurt at the end of last year because we ended up winning nothing, especially the League. Then there was the way we lost to Monaco – we lost the plot for a while. The team seemed to peak in January away in the Cup at Stamford Bridge [United were 5–0 after 75 exquisite minutes and eventually won 5–3] and never seemed to recover those heights again.' Even in February, the challenge of winning the 'Treble' was being whispered and even though United had been in position several times during the nineties to win three domestic trophies in one season, they had never succeeded. They faltered famously in the 1997–98 season when chasing the League and Cup double, both surrendered to Arsenal and yielding European Cup glory to Monaco. Irwin's reading of the potential for a unique 'Treble' in 1999 struck a chord in my heart: 'It would be very hard, I would think. It is a big treble, the proper treble as well. It would be very hard to do. Now we have the squad capable of doing it. We have a lot of players there to use in this rotation system. I prefer to play your first eleven and then if somebody gets injured someone comes in. But I think the manager prefers to rotate the players. It didn't work last year, I don't think. I think just in the last two months or so he's kept more or less the same team except for the last week or so. So I think he'll go more this year for a more settled side.' Yeah, rotation systems should only come into play when compelled by injury or suspension. The Wizard, at times, seems to be reluctant to continue with a winning team. Yet the famous Liverpool sides of the seventies and eighties were only altered when it was forced upon them. Tactical team changing is not a favourite of mine although how dare anyone criticise the Wizard in 1999, now that such an impressive array of silverware is perched in the greatly enlarged Old Trafford trophy room. Apparently United retrieved some unused shelving from the Maine Road trophy cupboard!

I mentioned the Tony Dunne attitude to winning the European Cup in 1968 when the enormity of the relief at having won the tournament was like having a millstone removed from the neck. Denis had this response: 'I wouldn't say there is that kind of pressure. I think maybe if we won it you might say, phew, thank God that's over with but it is definitely the one everybody wants to win. The manager wants to win it. There are going to be comparisons with the team that won in 1968. Until we win the European Cup you could never really say we were as good as them . . . that's the pinnacle. We might have more League titles than them or FA Cups, or the European Cup-Winners' Cup, but this is *the* one to win.'

Well, victory in Barcelona has answered that question. And on Sir Matt Busby's birthday as well! It puts Sir Alex Ferguson's team up there on a par with the great '68 side. Mind you, the argument to describe the 1999 version of the team as the greatest in United's history is very compelling given the unique nature of the 1998–99 season which saw the players tackle a rigorous 62 games – and that does not include international matches. The '68 team played a total of 53 games and 42 of those were in the League. They played only two games in the FA Cup – losing a third-round game to Spurs in a replay. That meant they won the European Cup by playing only nine games, against Hibernian Malta, Sarajevo, Gornik Zabrze, Real Madrid and Benfica.

In 1998–99, United had played eight Champions' League games before Christmas in the 'Group of Death', which included high-class opposition in Bayern Munich and Barcelona. Another five games were played between March and May, again with victories over top-class teams like Inter Milan and Juventus before the final victory over Bayern Munich. That was 13 European games. Next season they face even more European games. So the team of '99 has done it the hard way and is worthy of the 'greatest-ever United team' title!

Even Denis Irwin has become a fan of that great team! As a kid he supported Wolves and Cork Hibs. Now, as he contemplates life after Old Trafford, he has reason to bring expression and meaning to his life as a United fan: 'I have played there for nine years now and hopefully I will a tenth year next year. My little boy, Liam, that's all he knows. I tried to tell him I played for Oldham, he just doesn't understand or just dismisses it. I live in the area and I am settled in the area and if I am bringing my little boy to a match, then Old Trafford will be the first place we will want to go to.' From my limited experience of speaking to United players, it seems they all leave Old Trafford at the end of their careers there as United fans. Denis Irwin has always had a good rapport with fans but he does have concerns about the kind of 'sterile' atmosphere which persists on occasion at Old Trafford: 'The game as a whole has changed with business and commercial people have come a lot more into the game. Obviously the all-seating has taken away a bit of the atmosphere down there . . . the atmosphere down there before we first won the League was unbelievable in the 1991–92 season and especially the 1992–93 season when we won the League. The atmosphere down there was really unbelievable. But it has gone all-seater since then and it hasn't been any help because there's now a lot of business people and the commercial people coming to games, to the boxes and all that, so it takes a bit away from it.'

So there you have it. The players do notice the fact that the middle classes may bring financial security to a club but the singing classes are required to make an atmosphere. Denis even expressed the hope that with the new Old Trafford extension to bring the ground up to a 67,000 capacity, United will think carefully about how to distribute the extra spaces in an age where some fans are being priced out of the ground by the season ticket regime. He said: 'You do need a season ticket nowadays. But surely when they put in this new extension they will think about that and give the extra seats to the ordinary fans. I think they will do.' Denis Irwin – a man of the people!

Republic of Ireland International (53 caps 1990–present)
DEBUT: **12 September 1990 v. Morocco at Dublin. (Won 1–0)**
TEAM: **Bonner; Irwin, Staunton, Whelan, O'Leary, McCarthy, Houghton, Townsend (Sheridan), Quinn (Cascarino), Kelly D. (1), Kelly M. (McLoughlin).**

Denis Irwin's first international cap came just a few months after he had signed for United and less than four weeks after he made his debut for the Red Devils. Jack Charlton obviously respected the talent-spotting skills of the Wizard! If he was good enough for Fergie, he would be good enough for the Republic of Ireland. However exciting it was to become an international, Irwin's memory of his debut is tempered by the opposition on the day: 'My first game for Ireland was against Morocco at Dalymount Park and it wasn't really all that exciting. They had just come back from the World Cup where they had done so well – but it was my first game and it was special in that sense, although it was a poor match and it was over before I knew it.'

But greater glories lay ahead as the Irish, with Irwin on board, plotted their way to their second successive World Cup Finals in the United States in 1994. It was to become the high point of Irwin's international career – particularly that wonderful victory over Italy!

World Cup finals: 18 June 1994. Republic of Ireland v. Italy in New Jersey. (Won 1–0)
TEAM: **Bonner; Irwin, Phelan, Keane, McGrath, Babb, Houghton (1) (McAteer), Townsend, Coyne (Aldridge), Sheridan, Staunton.**

This was such a tempting morsel that disgraced Irish Bishop Eamonn Casey broke cover to see it for himself. The Bishop had fled Ireland many months earlier when news broke that he had fathered a child many years earlier and had deliberately set about concealing the facts of the matter. Ireland was scandalised by the revelations from the mother of the boy. One newspaper report of this crucial World Cup encounter described the scene as Casey entered the Irish end of the stadium. With his ticket in his hand he was carefully trying to seek out his row and seat number among the thousands of Irish supporters when one wag in the crowd shouted out: 'Dad! Dad! I am over here!' According to the report, the crowd burst into gales of laughter as the red-faced Bishop tried to maintain his dignity as his posterior was placed firmly into his seat.

On the pitch, the only red faces belonged to the fancied Italian side. A superb Ray Houghton goal gave the Irish a magnificent start to their campaign. Irwin, as usual, was a model of efficiency when it came to dealing with the Italian attack. He did not put a foot wrong as the Charlton-inspired men in green held on to their winning margin. It was the most outstanding achievement of Irwin's international career: 'The excitement of the World Cup is so memorable. The night we qualified up in the North – which was a bit rough that night . . . we only got a draw, but the fact that Spain beat Denmark on the same night made it special . . . the fact that we got over to the World Cup was tremendous. I'll never get another chance to go to another World Cup but every professional player wants to play at the highest level and that is the highest level. It wasn't a great World Cup for me, I only played two matches, got suspended and didn't play in the last one [Ireland lost 2–0 to Holland]. So it was a bit of a mixed one for me. But the fact remains that I was over there and the Italy game was tremendous!' Houghton had scored in the 12th minute of play.

Sadly, as the Irish players listened to the half-time team-talk from Jack Charlton in New Jersey, back home in Northern Ireland a gang of sick scumbags was snuffing out the lives of six football fans in a country pub. Just before half-time two strangers came into the bar and had a drink. They left at half-time and shortly after that gunmen burst through the doors of the bar at Loughinisland in Co. Down and opened fire on the crowd gathered inside to watch the game. The UVF admitted responsibility for the sectarian attack. Obviously in their vision of loyalty to the British Crown it was acceptable to murder indiscriminately, even if it meant using sport as an excuse. The message from the UVF seemed to clearly mark out their ideology: 'Fenian football teams must not win games – and if they do they must bear the consequences!' It is that kind of sick, depraved thinking that contributed to over 3,000 deaths during 30 years of conflict in my homeland. Two months later both loyalist and republican murder gangs declared ceasefires and today in 1999 mass murderers are being released early from jail. Their lives will resume but nothing can bring back the dead or relieve the suffering of the families of the 3,000 who died during the past three decades. The paradox is that in a society so bitterly divided as Northern Ireland, sport has so often been a unifying force bringing Catholics and Protestants together. The Irish football team in New Jersey was horrified to learn of these tragic deaths. For Denis Irwin and his fellow players, it totally removed the shine from what had been a magnificent sporting achievement.

REASON TO BELIEVE: Choosing the full-backs was a nightmare. Shay Brennan and Tony Dunne were a terrific partnership and it was tempting to continue with that pairing, especially given that they had won the European Cup together. Now, of course, since the events in Barcelona just a few weeks ago as I write, Irwin has added a European Cup medal to his impressive collection. In a previous age, Brennan was a converted left-winger who became exceptionally efficient, if not flashy, as a defender. He used his left-wing knowledge to read opponents' options accurately as they tore down the wing towards him. Like Dunne he had his uncanny habit of displaying a wonderful 'power-of-recovery' ability. Like Irwin, Brennan exuded a calm exterior when on the ball. Brennan's 'weakness' was his ability in the air and although Denis Irwin lacks height, he somehow manages to win more than his fair share of aerial contests. It was impossible to ignore the consistency of our 'Mr Dependable' of the nineties. Another reason Irwin shaded it over Brennan was because of his shooting ability. Irwin was a reliable goal-scoring free kick specialist before the arrival of the famous Beckham benders. He is 'Mr Cool' when it comes to taking penalties. No doubt I will get slagged off for neglecting to recognise Brennan's attributes. In the final analysis, Irwin just shades it over one of the best full-backs to appear in the red, white and black of Manchester United. Brennan won two League Championships and, of course, a European Cup-winners' medal. However, Irwin has won ten medals in his time at Old Trafford. He should have had 11 but for the sad refereeing of David Elleray. Irwin was dismissed for conceding a throw-in during the sad Scousers' 'Cup final' at Anfield in May which was drawn 2–2, thanks to the dodgy penalty Elleray gave to the 'Bayern Munich' flag wavers, not to mention the equally disgusting sending off. Thus the Irishman was denied his rightful place in the Wembley final against Newcastle.

DENIS IRWIN: THE QUESTIONNAIRE
BORN: **Cork – 31 October 1965.**

Which junior clubs did you play for?
Everton AFC, then to Cork Schoolboys' League.

Which club(s) did you support as a boy?
Wolves and Cork Hibs.

Was it always your ambition to be a professional footballer?
Not really. At that time Gaelic football and hurling were the main sports so to play for Cork would have been higher on the agenda.

Do you recall the moment you first realised you were signing for Manchester United? Describe your feelings that day.
I remember Alex Ferguson taking me onto the pitch while my agent [Eddie Gray] talked to the chairman. It was then that I realised how big a club it was.

Spurs were keen to sign you at that time. Was there any doubt in your mind? Why did you choose United?
I wasn't aware of any interest outside of Manchester United. I was letting my contract run out at Oldham but Manchester United came in early June, one month before my contract ended.

You made your League debut against Coventry City at Old Trafford in a 2–0 victory. Describe that day.

It was different for me because we met at noon, three hours before kick-off. At Oldham it was two o'clock when we met up. It was a full house and it was quite a feeling. It was a nice sunny day and I think we won quite comfortably. I set up both the goals, one I think for Steve Bruce and the other for Neil Webb. I think it was a good debut.

What differences are there between playing at United and playing for Leeds and Oldham?

Leeds was still quite a big club but was only playing in the Second Division. Oldham was a small homely club also playing in the Second Division. So the size of Manchester United compared to the others was the main difference.

In your first season you won the Cup-Winners' Cup. Where does that stand in your long list of accomplishments?

It still rates up there as one of my best achievements. It was my first year at the club and therefore my first trophy in professional football. It was also a great night in terms of the atmosphere.

You've scored some brilliant goals. Which one is your favourite and why?

The goal against Wimbledon in the FA Cup. We won 3–0 and I think it was the last goal. We kept the ball for some time. I played a 1–2 with Incey, did a couple of turns, which is unusual for me and swung my left foot.

The best manager you have played for – and worst?

I've learned a lot under every manager. Joe Royle and Willie Donachie were good at Oldham. But I've learned more under Alex Ferguson and Brian Kidd. Their knowledge of the game is so great. I respect even manager because it's not an easy job.

The highlight of your football career so far – when, where etc?

May 1991 – The European Cup-Winners' Cup versus Barcelona in Rotterdam. 1992–93 – winning the League after the club had waited 26 years, and playing Blackburn at home when we had already won the League was an unbelievable and unforgettable experience. 1994 – the first 'double' and playing in the World Cup finals.

Your worst moment(s) at Old Trafford and why?

Losing out in the League – Leeds 1992, Blackburn 1995, Arsenal 1998.

Losing to Leeds was the biggest disappointment. Also we've lost an FA Cup final and a couple of League Cups.

Which individual has been the biggest influence on your career?
It's very hard to pick just one individual. So I've picked a few but the last nine years or so I've learned the most about football. My dad. Keith Mincher, the youth coach at Leeds United. Joe Royle and Willie Donachie (turned my career around). Alex Ferguson and Brian Kidd.

Your best game for United? When, where and against whom?
It's hard to say or remember. In big matches I can remember maybe the 1996 FA Cup final versus Liverpool.

Your worst game for United? When, where and against whom?
Again it's hard to remember. In big matches I think versus Everton in the 1995 Cup final.

Pick your greatest ever Manchester United team. Give a few comments to explain if possible.
The Double-winning team of 1994. It had everything – toughness, individuality, pace, defensively strong and good going forward. Schmeichel, Parker, Bruce, Pallister, Irwin, Kanchelskis, Ince, Keane, Giggs, Hughes, Cantona.

Best player you ever saw in a United shirt?
Schmeichel is a hell of a goalkeeper. Brucey was very underrated but was a very clever player. Keano and Incey were very strong in midfield. Sparky was there when you needed a 'get-out-ball'. But Eric was so individually clever, he gave us an extra dimension.

The most difficult opponent you ever faced? Give an example of the game, the year and the competition if possible.
John Barnes – 1990 versus Liverpool at Anfield. We got beaten 4–0. He had vision, pace, was powerful and had great passing ability. He also scored plenty of goals. For a winger he had more than most.

You won your first full international cap in September 1990 against Morocco in Dublin. What was that like?
It wasn't a great match. We won 1–0 at Dalymount Park in front of a very average crowd. I think David Kelly scored.

The best and worst games for your country?
The best occasion was versus Italy in New York in the World Cup finals. What a feeling and I think we did well defensively. The worst was the following match in Orlando versus Mexico. It was too hot and it was hard to concentrate as much as normal.

What was it like playing in the World Cup finals?
Every professional footballer wants to play at the highest level and the World Cup is just that. It was a great feeling even though I had a mixed World Cup. I have some great memories from U.S.A. 1994, especially the Italy match.

How do you regard the Manchester United fans?
They've always been brilliant. I think I joined the club at the right time. Obviously it's become more commercial with more hospitality and business people going so it may have lost a bit of atmosphere.

Has the success of the nineties, in which you have been involved, raised the pressure on the players, as the fans demand more trophies? If so, how do you cope with it?
There's no doubt there's more pressure in the game. Every match is seen and analysed. The demands on players these days are much greater than even three or four years ago. Every player has different ways of coping. I get away from it by spending time with my family – my wife Jackie and three kids, Liam, Lauren and Katy.

What are your views on the team selected for this book?
It looks good enough to me. I played with some and heard about the others. Manchester United has always had a great tradition with Irish players and fans.

Having won all domestic trophies as well as the Cup-Winners' Cup, does the European Cup represent a top personal goal? And how heavy does it weigh upon the team's shoulders?
Answer: I think everyone knows it is the one trophy Manchester United would like to win above anything else. We've been so close over the last couple of years. Last year I think we forgot about the League in pursuit of it. We are a lot more focused in everything this year. All good things come to those who wait, as the saying goes. Personally, I've waited long enough. I'm running out of years so it would be great if we won it soon, ie, this year!

FOUR

Tony Dunne

(LEFT FULL-BACK/MASTER OF RECOVERY)

Manchester United: 1960–61 to 1972–73: 529 (1) games: 2 goals

DEBUT: **15 October 1960 v. Burnley at Turf Moor. (Lost 5–3)**

TEAM: **Gregg; Setters, Dunne, Stiles, Foulkes, Nicholson, Quixall, Giles, Viollet (3), Pearson M., Charlton.**

HONOURS: **European Cup 1967–68:**
League Championship 1964–65; 1966–67
FA Cup 1962–63
Republic of Ireland (33 caps 1962–76)

Tony Dunne jogged past Matt Busby on his way to a warm shower after a tough training session. The 'Boss' started jogging alongside him. 'Saturday,' says Busby. 'Oh yeah, Boss,' says Tony. The Boss laid it on the line. At least that is the meaning Tony Dunne took from the following rather one-sided exchange: 'Fella playing left-back on Saturday, he looked like Tony Dunne but it was . . . this fella was a little bit selfish, just playing for himself a little bit. Cut his man off, the ball never saw the outside-left. He was having trouble down the middle and this fella's very selfish. Tony Dunne would have been across covering the back and let the winger get it all day, but because of so much trouble on Saturday, this fella can't think proper. He'll be dropped this week. He'll be out of the team this week. Hoping Tony Dunne comes back this week. How's mum and dad? Are they coming over for a game soon? Have a word with Les, he'll get the tickets. Ann alright?' By this stage a dazed Tony Dunne was trying to get away from Matt Busby as the Boss concluded the conversation with a final, 'Hope to see Tony Dunne this week.'

Tony Dunne had just had his buttons pressed by Busby the psychologist. 'I was f***ing glad to get away from him,' said Dunne, relishing the telling of the story. 'F***ing dizzy I was. So then you're working your bollocks off in training 'cos it's going through your head. Selfish, f***ing master at it. Master. He was an education.' And so it came to pass that Matt Busby got his wish to renew his acquaintance with the 'proper' Tony Dunne the following Saturday.

The dark eyes that gave Tony Dunne his handsome good looks are now smiling in Irish, even though he has long since taken on a strong Lancashire accent to regale callers at his golf-driving range in Altrincham, about five miles from the Old Trafford stadium he once graced. For two years I lived just around the corner, totally unaware that United's most accomplished left-back since the Munich disaster was running a driving range. That in spite of the fact I quite often played the very course where he is located. Anyone who has memories of this Dublin-born full-back going up and down the left wing for Manchester United in the halcyon days of Best, Law and Charlton will not be surprised to learn that Tony Dunne worked hard at being a success. My lasting memory is of a defender who could cleverly hold up his winger or shepherd him into a corner where he could do no damage. Even if someone did manage to dump Dunne on his arse, the little fella would be up in a flash to get back and win the ball with his second attempt. He was a master of recovery. But it did not come naturally. Dunne made a vital discovery on his first day in a United shirt.

On Dunne's debut against Burnley at Turf Moor, he faced future team-mate John Connolly. The Burnley winger gave the 18-year-old Dublin debutant a roasting he was never to forget. 'The closest I got to him was when we came off the field and he shook my hand,' Dunne recalls, his face breaking into an enormous smile. 'John Connolly, who is still a very close friend of mine, set my standards for me that day. He ran me ragged and left me to face up to the reality that I could go one of two ways – raise my standards or accept failure at this level. We lost 5–3. I learned that if I was going to be a success I had to shut my corner off to give me another bite at the cherry. I wanted two bites at the cherry.' In order to get two bites at the cherry, Dunne began doing his own sprint exercises when training finished. It irked Matt Busby, Dunne doing his own training sessions. 'Running,' as he puts it, 'every f***ing way I could while others were flicking the ball about. Anybody can flick a f***ing ball up. I mean, Albert Scanlon, he was terrific – banging a ball against a wall, keeping it up and then putting it round his head. But when it came to playing, he couldn't f***ing play – he didn't have this John Connolly thing of coming inside, seeing the f***ing goals and going for them, cut-throat style.' Busby often approached Dunne at training to say 'you're training too hard'. Dunne insisted on going to the back of the Old Trafford pitch on his own and putting his body through a series of sprint exercises. Busby would tell him he didn't have to do this and that he could have 'tomorrow off' if he wanted because of the extra work he had done. But Tony Dunne was adamant he needed this regime of body punishment if he was going to make the grade as a First Division star. It certainly worked. In the great United teams of the sixties, it is all too easy to remember the 'three Kings of Europe' — Best, Charlton and Law. But the Irish defenders of the United faith at that time, Shay Brennan and Tony Dunne, were two of the finest full-backs in Europe. Indeed, in choosing this team of 'United Irishmen' for this book, there was a compelling argument raging in my head to keep the Brennan–Dunne partnership in place. But it is difficult to overlook the fact that Denis Irwin has been United's 'Mr Consistency' during their domination of the nineties.

Tony Dunne, however, was in a class of his own. He was outstanding and, what is more, he was dedicated to the cause of Manchester United. Mind you, ask him about what was surely his finest hour, as a member of the successful European Cup team in 1968, and brace yourself for a stunningly candid response. 'At the end of that game I just said thank f**k for that,' he explained in the fashion of someone who has just endured the unnecessary, self-inflicted pain and exhilaration of a rollercoaster ride. 'I was just so glad this pursuit of European glory was finally concluded. Most people celebrated that night, but it was a flat night for me.'

This overwhelming feeling of relief was undoubtedly the consequence of Munich and Busby's 'Holy Crusade' to win in Europe. This was the legacy of a man who fought so hard to take his team's talents into Europe in the first place — against the advice and might of the unwilling English football hierarchy. The legacy of a man with a vision of the future which saw Britain's best competing against the best in Europe and beyond. The legacy of a man who wanted to honour the team that was on the verge of European 'greatness' before it was decimated in runway slush at Munich Airport. Busby felt he owed it to the dead players and club officials to become the Champions of Europe and it became his obsession. As a consequence, this European fixation percolated down through the club. It touched everyone associated with United and, in Tony Dunne's recollection, it placed a great burden of pressure on the playing staff at Old Trafford. Hence victory in the 1968 European campaign brought about the heady mix of joyous celebration and sheer relief at the extra-time defeat of Benfica. The ghosts of Munich had finally been laid to rest and for some, like Dunne, the main sensation was that of not having to carry that cross any longer. He explained how the 'Euro-Dream' dominated life at Old Trafford: 'Winning the European Cup was bred right through the club, all the way through. It wasn't like playing football as playing football, it was like something that was within Busby – that the whole thing was to win it. Sometimes you knew he [Busby] was placing European victories over and above the League campaign. Every time you were playing in Europe you could tell he was different, so much pressure – you could always tell it was that and the crash coming together and he was a bit frightening at times. He'd come in and say things he wanted you to do but you knew you could not do them. He would stress that he wanted you to go out there and sort this thing for him. "Once you've done that, we'll win the game," he would say. And you're thinking f***ing hell, how can I sort it? You're not so sure, but he's f***ing sure. But when he says it to you, you think you've got to do it. You'd waken in the morning like that. Quite nervous and everything because that's when the pressure is put on you. And that's the way it was all the time – he'd never ever leave you alone. I used to do my routine and he'd say, "You're nervous? You want to see their f***ing outside-right." Then he'd say, "You have to be the last man Tone – that's you." I'd say no. He'd say, "You have to be the last man, end of story."'

So it was. 'Tone' was the last man, unless he wanted the Boss pressing his buttons again some morning after training. If he felt the urge to push forward and help in the attack during these all-important European games he had to remember he was expected back to be the last man especially for the one-twos because in Dunne's own words 'he knew I was the fastest'. So in this perverse sense of logic, Busby was recognising the hard sprinting work he often told Dunne he did not need to do.

As Dunne puts it so delicately: 'Going to the European Cup Final, the pressure was on again. And *that* was f***ing pressure. He [Busby] kept at it so much so that I think he put incentives up to win it, but he was ignoring the league.' Incentives? Not of the financial kind, according to Dunne. Busby thought that wearing a Manchester United shirt was enough. He would be horrified, no doubt, by today's attitudes in a period when it is the players who hold the power. Perhaps the best way to illustrate Sir Matt holding on as tightly to Manchester United's money as if it were his own is to hear Dunne describe how the Sunderland manager Charlie Hurley wanted to bring United's left-back to play for Sunderland at Roker Park. Hurley promised the move would treble Dunne's wages. But the congenial Irish full-back was too frightened even to broach the subject with the Boss. At the time Sunderland players were receiving £2,000 to £3,000 for finishing third from bottom, but United stars, according to Dunne, were getting just £1,000 to win the League. 'Not to finish second or third,' Dunne emphasised, 'to win it. Liverpool were exactly the same. For Busby it was do or die! Like taking blood out of his body.'

On the eve of what was to be Busby's – and Manchester United's –

greatest night, Bill Foulkes called to see Dunne in his hotel room. Dunne looked upon Foulkes as United's gentle giant and as a great servant of the club, someone who had survived the pain of the Munich disaster and who had fought hard to restore the team to top spot in England. In fact, rather fittingly, it was Foulkes who scored the winning goal against Real Madrid in the European Cup semi-final. United won the first game at home 1–0 but were trailing 3–1 by half-time in the return game. Sadler scored to level the aggregate score. Then Best went on a twisting run down the right wing, crossing for Charlton or Kidd to have a shot at goal. But there, waiting, was Foulkes, who obviously thought it was his birthday or something. It was Foulkes, therefore, the giant defender who was on hand to side-foot the ball into the Real Madrid net to secure United's victory and his place in history. Of all his nine goals during his long career (679 games in all), this undoubtedly was the most important. So when Bill Foulkes called to see a nervous Tony Dunne on the night before the biggest game in their careers, Dunne was happy to listen to the big centre-half who had lived through some of the most historic events in United's history. When Foulkes told Dunne United were destined to win the European Cup the next evening, Dunne nodded politely. But he did not really believe it. 'I never had that f***ing feeling,' he tells me during our chat. 'Never,' he repeats before adding: 'I think you can be lucky sometimes. The best teams in the world have to be lucky, 'cos otherwise you never win.'

Clearly, Lady Luck was with Bill Foulkes, Matt Busby and the thousands of United fans all over the world when the teams lined up on 29 May 1968 at Wembley.

TEAM: **Stepney; Brennan, Dunne, Crerand, Foulkes, Stiles, Best (1), Kidd (1), Charlton (2), Sadler, Aston. Won 4–1 (after extra time)**

On that balmy May evening, John Aston became the forgotten 'Man-of-the-Match' with an outstanding example of wing play which was eventually overshadowed by the facts of victory over Benfica. Yes, Lady Luck may have been smiling down on the glorious 'Red Devils' as we were crowned the 'Kings of Europe' in extra time with a 4–1 scoreline. But success was not achieved with luck alone. There was a fair sprinkling of brilliance from Alex Stepney, that huge dose of fantastic wing-wizardry by John Aston and goals from Bobby Charlton (2), George Best and 19-year-old birthday boy Brian Kidd. Tony Dunne might have regarded this as just another game to be won, but it really was a very special occasion – a watershed in our history. To the United faithful – and undoubtedly to the soon-to-be-knighted Sir Matt Busby – the 1968 side was there to conquer Europe for the lost heroes of

1958. Dunne played his part. He was bought from Shelbourne for £5,000 to do exactly that. To fill the boots of the late, great Roger Byrne. Byrne, along with all the other players who perished at Munich, was destined to dominate Europe. At 28, United captain Byrne was regarded as 'father' to the younger members of 'Busby's Babes'. Although right-footed, Byrne made the left-back position his own after periods in the first team on the left-wing and at left-half. He was one of the earliest proponents of the attacking full-back who often linked up with Duncan Edwards to establish United attacks down the left side of the pitch. After Byrne's death, the left-back position was filled for a time by Ian Greaves and then for a longer run by Dubliner Joe Carolan. By the time Dunne arrived at Old Trafford in 1960 the battle for the left-back position was with Cork-born Noel Cantwell, a cornerstone of the defence in the new-look United as it was rebuilt following the Munich disaster.

Dunne soon made the position his own and thus began the famous and successful partnership with Shay Brennan in the right-back role. In truth, though, Dunne was the first candidate at left-back to begin to emulate the style of the great Roger Byrne. He says he feels honoured that so many people compared him to Byrne. 'People have been quite complimentary,' he told me, 'and put me in with Roger Byrne's standard and I don't mind that. But *they* [the Busby Babes] set the standards and that was the period of time I played during which my life was f***ing hell sometimes because you were trying to emulate them. So you'd win the European Cup for them, you wouldn't win it for yourself. But it's a nice thing to say we won it.'

Dunne recalls the constant reminder of Munich as he made his breakthrough into the first team, playing alongside survivors like Charlton, Foulkes and Gregg. As a 19-year-old rookie, Dunne was in awe of these great players. 'I thought they were close to the people that we were trying to f***ing emulate,' he recalled of those early days, 'and yet they were turning up every day wearing football boots. I would look at Bobby Charlton and wonder, "does he ever think about it?". All this goes through your mind and he's probably not even thinking about it, but you're thinking it must be twice as hard for him. But Bobby on the field was, well, I never saw anybody so Man United in my life. I mean in the early days when the crowds weren't great as we were rebuilding in the early sixties and Bobby would be talking about hoping we get a big crowd tonight. I think he was more worried about Manchester United getting money to rebuild itself. No matter what Bobby said or did I was never that bothered about it, I was just in awe of him, as I was with Foulkesy and Gregg as well.'

There was another player Dunne was to be in awe of – but it was not someone from Munich past. No, this player was definitely the future. An

Irishman called Best, from the northern side of the border dividing Ireland. Tony Dunne was in the side at Old Trafford when Best first appeared in a 1–0 victory over West Bromwich Albion. Like just about everyone else in this United Irishmen team, Dunne views George Best as the greatest player he ever saw in a United shirt. 'George Best was simply brilliant,' Dunne says, his eyes lighting up with passion and enthusiasm at the very memory of the tricky young Irishman from Belfast who was to become known in every corner of the globe for his football – long before his reputation for other activities ever took hold.

When the dressing-room banter turned to the international achievements and ambitions of the first team, Dunne was glad to have this gifted young Belfast man to use as a 'big stick' with which he could beat the others. It seems Charlton and Law were the international kingpins. Scotland and England were, apparently, the only two major football nations on the planet! 'The Scots thought they had the greatest team in the world,' Dunne recalled, 'and it is well known that the Scots hate the English and they thought Bobby Charlton was a wanker and couldn't play. The arrogance of them. We never had a real international team, the Northern Ireland team did brilliantly in the '58 World Cup but the Scots always felt they had the best players in the world and once they threw the name of Denis Law at us, that was my trigger. I used to say: "The best player in the world?" And they'd ask who, and I would say: "George Best . . . and he's f***ing Irish." I told them when they wanted to mention football, they needed to talk about Bestie.'

Republic of Ireland International (33 caps 1962–1976)
DEBUT: **8 April 1962 v. Austria in Dublin. (Lost 3–2)**
TEAM: **Kelly (Lowry); Dunne, Traynor, Saward, Hurley, Meagan, Hale, Giles, Cantwell, Curtis, Tuohy.**

Like Best, Dunne's international career suffered because he was Irish. Neither Northern Ireland nor the Republic of Ireland was exactly a world power in football. One of the consequences of this international ineptitude was that Best and Dunne never graced World Cup finals. Indeed, few Irish players ever get that opportunity. Tony Dunne made his debut for Ireland in Dublin on 8 April 1962 against Austria. The Irish lost 3–2. Johnny Giles and Noel Cantwell were the other United players on the pitch that day. Dunne made his final – and 33rd – appearance for his country on 13 October 1976 against Turkey in Ankara. The outcome was a 3–3 draw. The point of this, however, is to show that in 14 years Dunne made just 33 appearances for his country. He knows there should have been many more caps. With even a cursory glance at his international statistics, you do not have to be a rocket scientist to work that out. Dunne says he was chosen for his country at least one hundred times. But he says, without any acrimony by the way, that it was Matt Busby who cost him greater international honours. 'I should have had at least a hundred caps,' Dunne said ruefully. As an example, Dunne mentioned events following a home game against Arsenal. 'Shay Brennan, Noel Cantwell and me were going to the Republic and we'd booked the plane,' he said. 'I got my gear and I'm running out after the game and just as I came out Matt Busby's standing right at the door, blocking my exit. Cool as you like he informs me that the taxi has gone. I said, "What? We've got an international tomorrow." He just said that Noel and Shay had gone.'

Now dear readers, we might now justifiably ask ourselves why Matt Busby was so against Tony Dunne playing for his country? Surely, every club realises success with its playing staff attracts international team managers and thus the release of players becomes a recognition of the club's coaching abilities and is something in which they must take pride, albeit accepting the potential risks of international injuries. Tony Dunne was candid enough to cast light into this dark corner. His story goes some way to explaining why Matt Busby was so cagey over his international appearances. It is only when you hear this second strand of the story that you begin to understand where Matt Busby was coming from. Bear in mind, the events you are about to read of occurred after Dunne's return from a previous international match. It is also worth remembering that at this time the entire Manchester United team had achieved international recognition, three of them for the Republic of Ireland. According to Dunne, the Irish, like many other small nations, were working on a small budget and, for instance, according to Dunne, the Irish did not have a physiotherapist. In any event, the players brought their own boots and on this particular occasion Dunne arrived in Spain with long studs in his boots having played on a wet pitch for United in the First Division. One of the Irish team officials was asked by Dunne to provide short studs for the game on a dry pitch. Tony Dunne takes up the story: 'I asked this fella who worked at Bohemians [League of Ireland club] if he could get me some small studs and put them in it. So just before we played he brought me boots in. The referee had already inspected everyone's boots except mine because they were so late. Anyway, I put them on and I don't think anything about it 'cos the referee is not going to examine my boots. But when I get on the pitch I can feel the nails in them and I was pulling my toes back to avoid the pain. Running was very difficult. When I came off at half-time my feet were bleeding. So the boots came off. I discovered what he had done — he'd cut the f***ing studs in half! He told me they didn't have any short studs. I put a pair of rubbers on for the second half but the damage was done. When I came back to Old Trafford I went to see United's physiotherapist Ted Dalton. My foot was tight on the muscle with holding the toes. I asked him to have a look and I said I did not want him to mention this to the Boss. In the end he f***ing did tell on me because I was limping. So Busby came in and the first thing he said was "I hope you're alright for playing tomorrow." I said, "Oh yes I am." He said, "Let me have a look at your foot." I said it was alright. He said, "Let me have a look at it." He went absolutely spare. He said again, "You play tomorrow because I need you, but you may never play for that f***ing team again." Little wonder Sir Matt was so reluctant to let his talent go.'

But letting Tony Dunne go was exactly what Tommy Docherty did when he took over the stewardship of United in December 1972. By this time, of course, the team that peaked with victory in the 1968 European Cup final was showing signs of being terminally ill. Matt Busby had retired and then temporarily replaced his replacement, Wilf McGuinness, before retiring a second time with the arrival of congenial Irishman Frank O'Farrell. Dunne survived these early management skirmishes but had begun to witness the team's decline at the beginning of what was the period of uncertainty which eventually culminated in relegation to Division Two in the mid-seventies.

During this time, Dunne saw changes in George Best. Dunne described it as Best having 'stopped playing as a winner'. He told me: 'You could tell immediately he wasn't a winner – he had become a showman, a great showman. But there is a difference between a showman and a winner. George was a winner for about six years. He always wanted to be a winner but I just felt that it got to a stage when it was becoming a little harder and he settled for the other, the showman. You see, when he settled for the other he killed off three or four players who were playing with him.' Naturally, the three or four other players being left because of George Best's showmanship were not inspired, impressed or indeed even amused.

There is no doubt George was a brilliant entertainer as well as a match winner. Whilst the older hands in the United team could overlook his 'greed' on the ball when he was liable to produce a match-winning goal, they became less tolerant when they thought they witnessed the demise of the 'killer' instinct. As Dunne put it: 'George took to beating the same man ten times. The crowds loved it. But by this time you looked across and Denis has made about five runs – Bobby's made four – nothing's happened. Kiddo's made runs – nothing's happened, and they're looking at me saying "Tony" and I'm saying, "It's nothing to do with me, he's got it." By the time Best crossed it they're all walking out of the opposition penalty area – four players had been taken out of the game by one of our own!'

Dunne's appraisal will no doubt ruffle a few feathers of Best's legions of fans, but let us be clear there was no bigger fan of the 'Belfast Boy' than Dunne himself. He enjoyed waxing lyrical about the 'best' player in the world: 'He knew he could play. There was nothing he couldn't do. But Denis [Law] was pulling his f***ing hair out. George played at Villa one night, and he must have beaten the fella, without exaggeration, nine times, one fella, nutmegged him, pulled it back and the crowd were going wild. The defender was absolutely knackered, fair dues to him, but all he'd done was take the piss out of people who kicked him. Somebody whacked him and George just wanted to show the guy that it wouldn't work with him and he was like a matador, come on, come to me. George Best was f***ing good. And that's how he was. And that was the change. It still didn't make any difference to George Best, 'cos the crowd loved him, 'cos every now and then he was likely to score two goals, but you were playing it, like . . . the Denis Laws and the Brian Kidds were becoming redundant because it was all happening through him. They used to moan at me – Bobby Charlton, Denis Law and Brian Kidd. Then Bobby would come and push me to get the ball off me, just to make sure that George didn't get it. The way they saw it was that if I gave it to George, you weren't going anywhere else. And that's when the game was changing. That's when Busby ducked – he ducked a little bit – well fair dues to him, I think we all would – who'd want to get rid of George Best? And he could've gone anywhere George and he was just getting to the stage where he'd become the entertainer, he hadn't kept what Pele had kept, that f***ing will to win. He knew he could do anything. But when he got the first taste of the crowd he was like Spartacus. I'm behind him and I'm watching him and thinking "F**k, here we go again."'

Meanwhile, in the dressing-room, how did the offended players address the issue with Bestie? According to Dunne, the dressing-room could be hot and heavy as the 'offended' shouted at Best. It was along the lines of, 'George, for f**k sake give them the ball.' Or Denis Law shouting: 'Give him a f***ing ball of his own!' Best did not take any notice. But Dunne was also quick to point out that this was not the way United played. In his view, 'We always played where we had to work hard for one another to give us a spell in the game where we could play. We worked hard, teams we had to play against – like Chelsea – we used to say "If you stand around picking your nose they'll see you off – they're not half as good as you, but they'll run like f***ing mad." So for about twenty minutes you're going to have to forget you play even, you get it, you give it, but you'll have to run as hard as them for twenty minutes. But when the game turns into a game there's only one f***ing winner.'

Clearly, by the time Frank O'Farrell took charge of team affairs at Old Trafford, one of his biggest dilemmas was how to deal with a wayward and discontented George Best. Mind you, in his first full season in charge he could not have asked for better. By Christmas, United were five points clear at the top of the League having played 23 games with only two defeats, away to Everton (1–0) and at home to Leeds (1–0). The run to the top included an exciting 3–3 draw in the 'derby' at Maine Road in which Sammy McIlroy made a scoring debut, his goal assisted by his 'mentor' George Best. But then disaster!

On New Year's Day 1972, United stepped out against West Ham United at Upton Park. Tony Dunne remembers the occasion well.

1 January 1972 v. West Ham United at Upton Park. (Lost 3–0)
TEAM: **Stepney; Dunne, Burns, Gowling, Edwards P., Sadler, Morgan, Kidd, Charlton, Law, Best.**

This was an embarrassing defeat for the League leaders in front of nearly 42,000 spectators and, of course, it was not the first or last time the Hammers had upset our quest for League Championship glory. On this occasion, however, the United team had been 'nobbled' from within, according to Dunne. There was no mincing of words when it came to describing the O'Farrell reign. 'Frank O'Farrell was probably the nicest fella I ever met in my life,' he said, 'but the worst manager I ever played under.'

Sitting on top of the First Division pile was a very encouraging sign for all United fans, unaware of the plans O'Farrell was plotting behind the scenes. According to Dunne it was at this crucial point of the season that the manager decided it was time to introduce the team to the 'zone' system. This was without doubt, said Dunne, the craziest tactical move O'Farrell could make. Dunne said: 'He came in to zone marking – f***ing zone marking – telling an Irishman about zone marking. We got beaten 3–0. I said it was Sadler's fault. He said it was mine. I said he should've been marking the proper f***ing zone. Zone markings – that's your area, if the player runs out of the zone, you don't follow him, he goes into someone else's zone and they pick him up. So I said what if they've got two or three players in the one zone? He said that doesn't happen. We got beat 3–0. I said I can't play like this. I was quitting. It was a very strange thing – it ran into a bad time then, some of the good players could see it – George and that. They weren't really playing the game at all. It was a frightening thing that – 'cos you thought all that lovely fun you used to have trying to win things and now it's survival. I mean we were winning the League and Alan

Gowling and Bobby Charlton and Willie Morgan in midfield, playing really well you know, and then he brought them tactics in.'

If it was survival O'Farrell was seeking, then patently the plan failed him. The West Ham defeat was the first in a run of seven such results that concluded with a 2–0 beating from Spurs at White Hart Lane on 4 March 1972. O'Farrell had snatched defeat from the jaws of victory in the League championship chase.

Evidently Dunne was missing the influence of Sir Matt. His view of O'Farrell's term of office with Malcolm Musgrove as coach is coloured by what 'went before'. Dunne told me it was 'unfortunate' for O'Farrell that he inherited players who had, to use Dunne's expression, 'played with a man who was very simple in his thinking and who never asked you to do any one thing with a ball'.

Worse was to follow. When asked to elaborate, Dunne went on: 'If you get the ball to your feet and somebody's five yards and he's free, you give it to him. If he's 20 yards away, you give it to him, but if you've got a ball in front of you and the manager's told you only to give it to one man, well, it is a problem.' Dunne did not like being told before he went onto the pitch what he should do with the ball. As someone with a brain cell or two, he resented being told to purge all logical thought and do what he was told. He went on: 'We had Ian Storey-Moore, a wonderful player I had played against so I knew how he used the ball. If you ran at him he would run it all the way back to give it to his goalkeeper. If I was playing against him, Busby used to say, "You know how to play him Tony," and I would say, "Yeah, boss." So I knew Ian Storey-Moore. I knew his game. He wasn't one who would turn quickly for you. You'd get a feeling of him on your back and you wouldn't even have to tackle him, he'd run back all the way and he'd pass it back. So when he was playing for us I knew this. But now I was being told every time I got the ball to give it to Ian Storey-Moore. I'd say, "what if someone is just five yards away?" He'd say, no, just give it to Ian. So I'm playing Liverpool . . . I said, don't you think Chris Lawlor is going to f***ing let me give it to him all the time and he'll stand with his back to him and make him come back all the way. So every time I pass it to Ian he's going to end up coming past me. "Tony, just do as you are told," was the response.'

When it actually came to playing against Liverpool, Dunne said Lawlor approached him as they left the pitch at half-time to say it was time for the United man to 'knock a few inside' because the Scouser was complaining of being run up and down the wing 'like a f***ing madman'. Coach Malcolm Musgrove was beseeched to give Dunne licence to do what he felt was best on the pitch. The order to pass the ball to Storey-Moore was rescinded. The end for O'Farrell came on 16 December 1972 when his team was slaughtered by an average Crystal Palace side. Tony Dunne played in the humiliating 5–0 defeat at Selhurst Park although he was replaced by substitute Denis Law. The team that day makes interesting reading: Stepney, O'Neil, Dunne, Young, Sadler, Buchan, Morgan, MacDougall, Kidd, Davies and Moore. European domination had long since vacated Old Trafford. The Best-Law-Charlton-inspired era was at an end. Manchester United was in turmoil as they travelled to London for this fixture. O'Farrell had placed George Best on the transfer list eleven days earlier on 5 December following the player's unapproved nightclubbing disappearance to London the previous day. Then on 14 December United chairman Louis Edwards announced that Best would resume training – thus, presumably, removing him from the transfer list. O'Farrell was less than impressed by this development and after the 5–0 debacle at Palace there were rumours that he was contemplating resignation over the club's handling of the Best affair. He needn't have worried. The United board sacked him three days later on 19 December – along with coach Malcolm Musgrove and chief scout John Aston. On the same day Best announced his retirement from football in a letter to the club. Scotland manager Tommy Docherty was given permission by the Scottish FA on 22 December to travel to Manchester for talks. He accepted the appointment. However, it was later claimed that Docherty had been at the Palace game and at half-time in the boardroom he was offered the job. Under Docherty's stewardship Dunne made only three more League appearances for the club as the Doc set about rebuilding United by signing his own 'tartan army'. George Graham was purchased from Arsenal and full-back Alex Forsyth from Partick Thistle.

Dunne's last appearance for United was away to Ipswich on 17 February 1973 – a game lost 4–1. The man bought to replace him, Forsyth, also played that day at right-back. Dunne knew within himself that his playing days at Old Trafford were over but he faced something of a dilemma given that, with one year of his contract to run, he had been granted a testimonial by O'Farrell. The new manager was less than helpful when it came to finding a dignified manner for Dunne to leave the club after 13 years. 'Docherty just wanted rid of me,' Dunne recalled, a bitter tone creeping into his voice. 'He just threw me out and it was a f***ing nasty way he did it.'

According to Dunne, the arrival of Tommy Docherty suited Sir Matt Busby. Busby had not got on well with O'Farrell and felt his influence at the club diminish during the Irishman's reign. But with the arrival of the Doc, the two Scotsmen became pals. As a consequence, Dunne said, the Doc and Busby were united when it came to dealing with the long-serving left-back. For Dunne, it was a really sour end to his career with United. 'I said to Tommy that all I wanted to do was to play in the reserves, have my testimonial and then, if not needed, I would shuffle along,' Dunne recalled of those bitter days. 'I thought that was reasonable. But he said no, no, no. He said if you're staying here you'll have to stay at home and we'll send your wages to you. He told me I had a reputation at the club and if he was putting people out there to play they would be under pressure.' According to Dunne, the Doc did not accept the argument that the public could be trusted to make up its own mind about whether he or Alex Forsyth was playing well enough to be in the team. Dunne approached Busby. 'By now old Matt was trying to get his way back in,' said Dunne. 'It had changed him because it wasn't football now he was dealing in, it was survival and it was a f***ing different kettle of fish and he was moving back into his quarters. I went to see him. He said, "Tony, you're not finished yet." I said it was one of those things that happens and that I didn't think I was finished yet but I accepted the manager's decision. But I pointed out that I had my testimonial year, as he knew, and then I had to harp back to the past. I said I was embarrassed to say this to him, but reminded him that he had said he would help me. I reminded him of saying to me, "Don't mind the newspapers, don't mind the stars, you're the best left-back I've got and you do the job for me, I'll look after you." And he said, "I'm not involved in the club any more." I was f***ing shocked. They wouldn't even sell a ticket for me.' Even worse was the fact that although Dunne was the third most senior professional at the club and even though he had been planning his testimonial, United suddenly decided to give a testimonial to Denis Law. They wanted Ajax to play during the summer of '73, but when that was not possible they moved it to the autumn and it was played just a matter of a few weeks before Dunne's. 'The way the club handled these two testimonials was hurtful to me,' Dunne told me. 'Normally for testimonials they send out raffle tickets in the Development Association envelopes and in those days that usually raised about £3,000. But when I approached them about doing it for my testimonial, they said they couldn't because they had just sent out tickets for Denis Law's.' In the end, Dunne got the offer of help from a friend at Manchester City and they put up the opposition for his game. A crowd of 17,000 turned up and Dunne said he got a cheque for £8,000 – of which he was charged £1,500 by the club for the stadium and the policing. It was a very bitter conclusion to a 13-year career.

There's no doubt Tony Dunne was still the best left-back at the club when he left for Bolton Wanderers in August 1973. Between 1973 and 1979 he managed to make 170 appearances for the Trotters. He did not score for Bolton, but he is officially credited with two for United. Rather than end his chapter on a 'sour' note, it is worth learning from the determined Dubliner what he recalls about those two glorious goal-scoring moments. The first comment he makes is to claim that he actually got three goals! His first came in the 1965–66 season away to West Brom in a thrilling 3–3 draw and the second was in a 2–2 draw away to Newcastle in the 1967–68 season. This is what Dunne had to say about his goal scoring achievements: 'For the first goal at West Brom, I played a one–two with somebody and because I was so quick I just kept going and the door opened up and I just hit it. The goalkeeper was looking upwards and the ball went downwards for that one. The second one at Newcastle was a cross. I just whacked the ball and it's always windy up there in Newcastle and the keeper had come upfield and he was left there as the ball went in. I did hit another one when we played Stoke in the cup and it was really foggy near the end of the game. I got right down to the line and whacked it across. I thought I had scored and everybody else thought I scored. But when we went in David Herd said he got a touch to it. I said I didn't care who touched it as long as we won. And it was 1–0!' No one should be surprised that Dunne was prepared to accept David Herd's claim on the goal. It typifies the unselfish nature of Tony Dunne's commitment to the United cause during his wonderful 13 years.

REASON TO BELIEVE: The left-back position belongs to Tony Dunne. If there was something of a dilemma in choosing his full-back partner – the Brennan v. Dunne decision discussed elsewhere in this book – I have never seen anyone with Dunne's fantastic powers of recovery. It was his benchmark that he could always find a way of getting a second tackle in even after he had been dumped on his arse by a marauding winger. He always used the ball well, preferring to pass it ten or twenty safe yards rather than be tempted into a cross-field 40-yard pass with greater potential to surrender possession. In simple terms, Dunne had no serious rival.

TONY DUNNE: THE QUESTIONNAIRE
BORN: Dublin – 24 July 1941.

Which junior clubs did you play for – and during what years?
St Finbars and Shelbourne in the League of Ireland.

Which club did you support as a boy?
St Patrick's Athletic [League of Ireland].

Was it always your ambition to be a professional footballer?
No.

**You made your United debut in a sensationally high scoring game –
away to Burnley and United lost 5–3. What are your thoughts about
making your debut and your thoughts on the outcome?**
John Connolly gave me a roasting and I thought if they are all like him I
might as well go home now.

**Did it take you long to settle in at Old Trafford? Which players did you
form close friendships with?**
When I came over from Ireland I was closest to a lad called Willie
Donaldson from Northern Ireland. He was from Northern Ireland and we
were in the same digs. Willie went to South Africa. He was a good lad, was
Willie.

Do you still have friendships with former colleagues?
I am still friendly with the lads. Still see them occasionally and play golf
with Bill Foulkes and David Herd and some of the others. I see Alex Stepney
now and again. I still see John Connolly as well.

What were your first impressions of the club?
Well, I was in awe of the thing. It just looked like one massive big place
to me, ten times bigger than anything I had seen before. It was the first
time I had seen real professional footballers close up. It was awesome. It
just takes you over, you were like a little boy.

The highlight of your Old Trafford career?
I had 13 great years as a United player. There were many great moments,
too many to chose just one.

The lowest moment at Old Trafford? And why?
Leaving the club the way I did. No shame in leaving, it was just the way I
did.

Your best game for United? (When, where and against whom?)
It had to be the European Cup game against Gornik Zabrze away in front
of 105,000. We had won the first leg 2–0 at home. In the second leg I
ruptured my heel just before half-time. It was just blubber and at half-time
I went to take my boot off and they told me not to because I would never
get it on again. They gave me a couple of tablets and a cup of tea. Busby

said you're going to have to sit out for the second half. I said I would do my best on the wing. He said never mind the wing. The winger doesn't know you're injured. We held out although they got one goal back 20 minutes from the end. I was in agony. But Matt was soft-spoken and overpowering and you didn't want to let him down.

Your worst game for United? (When, where and against whom?)
The first game for United was the worst game . . . I was chasing John Connolly all over the park. It set my standards.

Which individual has been the biggest influence on your career?
It has to be John Connolly because of the damage he inflicted on me on my first appearance.

Pick your greatest ever Man Utd team.
It would have to be: Gregg, Irwin, Buchan, McGrath, Byrne, Charlton, Edwards, Colman, Best, Law, Connolly.

Best player you ever saw in a United shirt? And why?
George Best. There was not anything he couldn't do on a football pitch.

The most difficult opponent you have faced?
John Connolly.

You made your international debut against Austria in 1962. Describe your feelings on that day.
It was probably a little less awesome than appearing for Man Utd. But it was something everybody wanted to do and it was nice to introduce yourself to internationals you had seen over the years. Bit nervous. But they were good lads.

The best game for your country – and the worst?
The best were when you won, the worst when you lost. I always hated hearing someone say you played great when you got beaten. I would rather hear them say we played badly but won.

How do you regard the Man Utd fans?
They were superb. Magic. One of the great things about them at one time was their singing. They used to sing before a game. They would sing all the players' names and chant and give you a great feeling of it was happening for you, it was happening to win. You had this feeling you had to get it

right for these people. And if you were going in on top of a situation you could feel this crescendo of noise. It was absolutely magic. I was fortunate they never gave me stick, well, if they did I never heard it. I thought they were good to people having a bad time.

Your views on the team selected for this book?
I would move Jimmy Nicholl up into the middle. He was good enough to play there. I never thought Norman Whiteside did anything in that position, midfield. But I did think he was a big man up-front. If you had four chances in the box, he would be on the end of three of them. Slow in everything but up-front! It was very bad thinking on their part. Norman could have stayed at the top – holding up the ball, in the box dangerous and always got a great touch on him. Great player up-front. He was big enough to roll them over. So I would put Norman up front with Frank Stapleton, a great header of the ball who also was quick. George? Well, he is simply the Best.

FIVE

Kevin Moran

(CENTRAL DEFENDER/BLOOD DONOR)

Manchester United: 1978–79 to 1987–88: 282 (5) games: 24 goals

DEBUT: 30 April 1979 v. Southampton at The Dell. (Drew 1–1)

TEAM: **Bailey; Albiston, Houston, Sloan, McQueen, Moran, Coppell, Paterson, Ritchie (1), Macari, Grimes.**

HONOURS: **FA Cup 1982–83 and 1984–85**
Republic of Ireland (71 caps 1980–94)

The 'Blood Donor' sat behind his desk tackling business with his customary zeal and yet there was not a drop of blood in sight. Not like his playing days when tackling was his business and when the cause of defending the good name of Manchester United led him to spill his own blood. The telephone lines were hot. He fielded the calls, apologising to yours truly for the interruptions. I understood. Business, after all, is business. Manchester United is still big business to one of its most devoted old foot soldiers. He still looked fit enough to play, his appearance smart and 'bandage-free' as he sat comfortably in the boss's chair behind a large desk. Dressed in a crisp white shirt and tie, he looked every inch the entrepreneur.

Kevin Moran became known affectionately to United fans as the 'Blood Donor', the man who would, if necessary, die a thousand deaths with as many stab wounds. During his decade at Old Trafford he probably leaked more blood in the United cause than any other player in our history. Fear was neither a word nor a concept familiar to Kevin Moran as he used his body as a human shield to defend the honour of Manchester United. Given the circumstances on the day, I was fortunate to get a half-hour with this former United hero at his office in Wilmslow.

It was the morning of 9 December 1998. The vital European Champions' League game against Bayern Munich was to take place that night at Old

Trafford. The understanding was United had to win to be certain of progress from the 'Group of Death' into the quarter-finals of the competition. The game itself was not as exciting as what was going on in the minds of the fans who were confused, to say the least, as both teams seemed content from about the 75th minute to play out a 1–1 draw. Clearly they knew something we did not. For us fans it was only as we left the stadium that the public address system finally got around to confirming our qualification for the next stage of the competition. Anyway, it was Kevin Moran's business to get his clients from all over Europe to Old Trafford in time for the 'hospitality' and the game itself.

Since he retired from playing for Blackburn Rovers and the Republic of Ireland in 1994, he declined opportunities to remain in the game as a coach or potential manager. Instead he chose to make use of his business and commerce degree to set up a business with another former United hero of the eighties, Jesper Olsen. Proactive Sport Management has its base in Dublin with the other office in Wilmslow and it looks after the Irish rugby and football teams as well as a number of international Scandinavian footballers. In addition, the company organises corporate hospitality packages and sets up major golf tournaments and horse racing meetings. Through his contacts Kevin also acts as agent for a number of players. Andy Cole may be one of them – he was arriving at Moran's offices as I was leaving. This [1998–99] season above all others, Andy Cole has played with fire in his belly and has become a very accomplished talent in a side that won all before it.

Passion and commitment were Kevin Moran's watchwords. He was fearless in defending United's honour against all comers. He played football with the same determination that made him a winner for the great Dublin Gaelic footballing side of the seventies. In this respect Kevin Moran is quite unique. He played in three All-Ireland finals, winning the Sam Maguire twice. For United he played in two FA Cup finals – winning on both occasions. But ask him which of these four winners' medals means most to him and he has to take a long pause before committing himself to an answer: 'I won an All-Ireland medal in 1976 and another in 1977. I came over to United in February 1978. They allowed me to come back and play in the All-Ireland in that year – and although we got to the final again, we lost this time. United at Wembley? This has some tradition about it, you know. In soccer terms it's like the pinnacle but then you've got Gaelic football and the highest you can obtain in that is to get to an All-Ireland final and play there. I suppose in some ways there must be no greater feeling, I think, than the fact that having been born in Dublin and playing for your own county is a greater sense of pride obviously, like you're playing for your country. If I was born and raised in Manchester and a Manchester United supporter all my life I would probably have that same sort of pride. I am not saying that there wasn't – but you know what I mean. I suppose the Dublin thing was that bit more special because of my background.'

Most people will remember Kevin for the 1985 FA Cup final against Everton when he made history by becoming the first player ever to be sent off in a final. But Kevin says it has not marked him: 'No, not at all, I wasn't even marked by it after the game. I've said it before, it has never bothered me. It's never bothered me because we won the game. If we had lost the game I think, well I don't know what would have happened because I would have thought it would have a bigger effect on me then. Then I would have looked at it and blamed myself because possibly if I hadn't got sent off we would have won the game. I'd have stayed on instead of putting the team down to ten men and you would have thought that way. But even the fact that I got sent off – okay, it's not the nicest thing to do. But the fact that we won the game totally eliminated any unhappiness or sadness as regards the sending off. I was not different from anybody else afterwards.'

FA Cup final: 18 May 1985 v. Everton at Wembley Stadium. Attendance 100,000. (Won 1–0)
TEAM: **Bailey; Gidman, Albiston (Duxbury), Whiteside (1), McGrath, Moran, Robson, Strachan, Hughes, Stapleton, Olsen.**

However, what is certain is that Kevin Moran did feel different during that portion of the game he was forced to watch from the bench after his sending off in the 78th minute for what looked like an innocuous foul on Peter Reid. Referee Peter Willis was the man who made a name for himself by this act of treachery against United in general and Moran in particular. As Willis astonished 100,000 fans in the stadium by producing a red card from his pocket to wave at Kevin Moran, it was the last time the two men were ever to see each other face to face. The act of being sent off was a sickening blow to the soft-spoken Dubliner who told me: 'I went through a whole range of emotions. When I got sent off I honestly believe I was totally numb, I do not remember anything. I was just numb on the bench. I was watching the game alright but I was not taking it in. I was just devastated at being sent off. But after Norman [Whiteside] scored I remember jumping up and then that was it. After that I was no different from any supporter, hanging on to every ball. So I do remember the game from the goal on.' Every United fan remembers the Whiteside goal. As we learn later in the book, Whiteside claims he deliberately practised precisely that type of shot during training sessions! In among the Everton fans with my ten-year-old son Steven [also described in the Whiteside chapter] we could hardly believe what we were seeing as Moran got his marching orders. Naturally, the Scousers were delighted and convinced this was the moment which would turn a rather disappointing spectacle in their favour. Obviously they would think that. But the ten-man United team galvanised itself against the Scousers of the blue hue and scored an historic victory which prevented them from completing a 'treble' of European Cup-Winners' Cup, League Championship and FA Cup.

At the end of extra time Moran was unsure of whether or not he would get a medal. Paul McGrath has gone on record stating that as he had delivered the short pass that led to Moran's sending off for the foul on Peter Reid, he was prepared to hand over his winners' medal to his fellow countryman. Moran laughed when I told him of this offer by McGrath and then he described just how confused the situation had become when it came to the presentation ceremony: 'I got the impression that Big Ron said to me you can't really collect your medal. Obviously no one knew what was going to happen because it hadn't happened before. But Big Ron says to go on up the steps anyway. I was under the impression that I couldn't be handed it there and then but that it would be waiting in the dressing-room for me, or at least something like that. So I went up and to be perfectly honest with you, if I'd held out my hand I would have got it . . . I walked after the rest of the lads and went up and all that, shook hands, and I half-said no I don't have to get the medal. I think I shook hands with whoever was there to present the trophy, the Duke or whoever it was. But it didn't bother me that I wasn't getting it then because I knew I was going to get it afterwards.'

Kevin Moran was born in Dublin on 29 April 1956. He is married to Eleanor and the couple have four children – Darragh (13), Rachel (10), Shauna (7) and James (2). As a child he harboured ambitions of becoming a professional footballer. 'I think every kid had this ambition,' he told me. 'I was no different to anybody else. So ambitions to play for Manchester United? Definitely! But I think I was brought up as a Liverpool supporter. One of my other brothers was a Manchester United supporter so in my family everyone had to have a different team and United was already gone!' Ask him where his allegiance is nowadays, if it is still with the Scousers and he will be very quick to inform you: 'Ah Jesus no! The Liverpool thing went out the day I signed for United!' Good job too!

It was also a good job for United that the young Moran lived in changing times. By the time he was going to secondary school in Dublin, the Gaelic Athletic Association had removed a rule preventing GAA members from playing 'foreign' games such as football or rugby. As Moran recalled: 'I think most of the kids my age played Gaelic football. If you went to a Christian Brothers' school you played Gaelic football and then outside of that you played soccer for the cup team and that is how I played it. You mixed the two games together because by then the ban had already been lifted.' Anyone who has played Gaelic football will tell you how physically demanding it is. For those who have never seen Gaelic football, let me explain, it is played with a round ball at great speed. Like rugby, players can use their hands. In fact, they can use their hands, feet, head, shoulders – any part of their anatomy to play the ball and the object is to score either goals or points. The goals consist of tall posts as in rugby but with football nets beneath the bar. A goal is worth three points and a ball put over the bar but between the posts, as in a rugby conversion, is worth one point. Physical contact sport it definitely is. Not a game for the faint-hearted. It can be an aggressive game in which boys soon become men. Kevin Moran learned how to deal with the physical aspects of the game and so when he came to United he was not afraid to put his body in danger in order to protect the United goal.

He signed for United in February 1978 – eventually making his debut 14 months later away to Southampton, the day after his 23rd birthday. It was the first of nearly 300 games for the Red Devils over the next decade. Ordinary mortals like me tend to think we would remember every game we ever played in United colours – forgetting that for the professional who trains most days and who plays maybe as many as three or four games in a week, it becomes impossible to recall every detail. Certainly, in my dealings with the players interviewed for this book, it has become apparent that they have very real difficulty remembering particular matches. Of course, there may be a variety of reasons for this – ranging from the 'too many to remember' category to the more modest players who feel it is not for them to choose their 'best' or 'worst' performances. So it is just as well that I remember games where these individuals have made an impact on my mind either by their superb individual performance or as part of a magnificent team-game. In the case of Kevin Moran it is tempting only to recall those occasions when he spilled blood for the cause. However, I prefer to remember a couple of games in which he played a significant part in a particularly memorable team performance. I did press Kevin quite hard to persuade him to give any clue as to which of those games stick out in his mind and he has chosen two that coincide with my choices. In no special order, Kevin said he particularly remembered the European Cup-Winners' Cup quarter-final against Barcelona when United recovered from being 2–0 down in the first leg at the Nou Camp stadium to win 3–0 at Old Trafford. He also singled out his FA Cup win with United in 1983 – when he got two games at Wembley and where he remained on the pitch for the entirety of each performance – unlike the 1985 final. He also mentioned the victory by the Republic of Ireland over England in Germany during the 1988 European Championship Finals. But to begin with, I want to recall a game that Kevin has overlooked – one in which he played a significant part, albeit after he left the field of play!

Milk Cup final: 26 March 1983 v. Liverpool at Wembley Stadium. Attendance 100,000. (Lost 2–1)
TEAM: **Bailey; Duxbury, Albiston; Moses, Moran (Macari), McQueen, Wilkins, Muhren, Stapleton, Whiteside (1), Coppell.**

A wedding prevented me from watching this game right through but from the highlights I saw on television later and from the media reports, the turning point came in the 70th minute. Up until this point, United had been largely under the Anfield 'cosh' but had defended magnificently and had managed to hold on to the 12th minute lead given to them by a brilliant Norman Whiteside goal. The Scousers enjoyed enormous territorial advantage for long periods but even the Ian Rush goal-scoring machine failed to make the most of his chances. Then just when it looked as though the Gods were smiling on the United defence, it happened. The man who, along with Gordon McQueen, was managing to withstand everything the formidable Liverpool attack was throwing at them, Kevin Moran, fell to the ground. He was hurt. We knew he was hurt because he did not get up quickly. Kevin Moran does not feign injury. Eventually he limped off the pitch. Lou Macari placed his diminutive frame on the pitch. But it was to no avail. Within five minutes of Moran's departure the long-awaited Liverpool equaliser came from Alan Kennedy. When I played with Kennedy in a charity game in 1997, he told me that his side anticipated a quick and easy victory after Moran's departure. The Irishman had been a thorn in the sides of Kenny Dalglish and Ian Rush. Even better from a Scouse perspective was the injury in about the 80th minute to our other defensive superstar, Gordon McQueen. He was clearly unable to continue in defence so he moved into the forward line and Frank Stapleton came back into central defence alongside Mike Duxbury. United fought bravely and might have some justification for claiming a penalty in the dying stages of the match when the injured McQueen was mercilessly felled by Liverpool 'keeper Bruce Grobbelaar. As it was, Ronnie Whelan hit the winner in extra time and the best team won on the day. Norman Whiteside was in tears and the United fans were absolutely gutted! Never worry though – Kevin Moran, Norman Whiteside and the rest of the United team were soon to be back at Wembley to win the FA Cup against Brighton just a few weeks later. Mind you, Brighton fought hard to win – putting up a performance that belied the fact that they were about to be relegated from the First Division. The first game was finely balanced at 2–2 in extra time when Gordon Smith had his opportunity to write his name into the history books. In the last minute, he was put through in the six-yard box with only Gary Bailey to beat. He failed to make this his moment of glory. Bailey saved and United went on to win 4–0 in the replay five days later. Kevin Moran picked up his first United FA Cup-Winners' medal on 26 May 1983 on Sir Matt Busby's 74th birthday. The team that won the cup was as follows: Bailey; Duxbury, Albiston, Wilkins, McQueen, Moran, Robson, Muhren, Stapleton, Whiteside, Davies. This was the team that was to lead us into Europe the following season to give us one of our most celebrated nights of European glory at Old Trafford. It was on 21 March 1984 that United scored a wonderful victory over Barcelona at Old Trafford. Two–nil down from the first leg, they won 3–0 with two goals from Bryan Robson and the winner coming from Frank Stapleton. But it was the team fielded in the semi-final against Juventus that gives us time to reflect on what nearly was.

European Cup-Winners' Cup semi-final. (First Leg): 11 April 1984 v. Juventus at Old Trafford. Attendance 58,171. (Drew 1–1)
TEAM: **Bailey; Duxbury, Albiston, McGrath, Moran, Hogg, Graham A., Moses, Stapleton, Whiteside, Gidman (Davies (1)).**

Second Leg: 25 April 1984 v. Juventus at Stadio Communale. Attendance 64,655. (Lost 2–1)
TEAM: **Bailey; Duxbury, Albiston, Wilkins, Moran, Hogg, McGrath, Moses, Stapleton (Whiteside (1)), Hughes, Graham A.**

They should have been mentioned together in the same breath for years to come. Moran/McGrath. They should have been our defensive foundation stones for a Championship-winning team. Instead, we had to wait for nearly another decade before we got Bruce/Pallister. It remains a totally baffling fact that these two failed to strike up the kind of partnership that should have been within their grasp. They played often enough together for the Republic of Ireland team and with considerable international success and recognition for their troubles. But it just did not seem to gel at Old Trafford. Moran had been at United for just over three years when McGrath was signed. McGrath made his debut against Spurs at Old Trafford in November 1982 – replacing Moran who had been playing in defensive partnership with the ageing duo, Gordon McQueen and Martin Buchan. As

McGrath tried to secure a regular first-team place, the records show that he only got into the side when Moran was injured or dropped. Mind you, their first appearance in the defence together was hardly an inspiration to manager Ron Atkinson. Just before the end of the 1982–83 season, Big Ron paired McGrath and Moran together for a visit to Highbury. United lost 3–0. It is interesting to note that Laurie Cunningham played one of his five games for us during this transitional period. But more importantly, that was the first McGrath/Moran outing. McGrath was dropped for the next game against Swansea City but was back in the side for the next game at home to Luton when he scored two of United's three goals. For most of the time thereafter, it was a case of one or other in the side, usually taking each other's places. There were short spells when they combined to defend United's goal, but in truth they were far too rare an occurrence.

The failure of the McGrath/Moran partnership at club level is something that baffles Moran to this day: 'It just never did come together. More and more of these things disappointed us in many ways. We were there long enough to have a great partnership but we just hit injuries all the time between us. I had problems with the likes of, say, a hamstring. It was not so much the knocks, because they keep you out of one match, so it's not a problem, but when you're out for a pulled hamstring it could be four weeks, five weeks. Then maybe you get a pulled muscle here or there and unfortunately Paul had the same sort of run of injuries. He had problems sometimes with his knee. Sometimes it would be something else and I remember thinking at the start of the season that we would try to start with the attitude, "Let's keep it going." It was a case of touching wood. But then you look afterwards at what happened to United. They had the Bruce/Pallister partnership and the Bruce/Pallister partnership was founded very much on two excellent players, two great players. But they were able to play week in, week out. I think they missed four games in five years, it was phenomenal, so it was, and that brings up a tremendous partnership which I know I could have had even better with Paul. He'd get injured, someone else would come in, then we'd get back together again. If you looked at the number of times we played together even though we would have been automatic choices at that particular time. I know now I would say the best run we ever had together was maybe 14 consecutive games if we even reached that, I don't know. So it's a shame.'

They did, apparently, have a good partnership off the field! By the time Alex Ferguson arrived in 1986, the writing was on the wall for what the new manager had identified as the McGrath, Whiteside, Robson and Moran group of drinkers. Frank Stapleton told me he thought that under the Big Ron regime, the manager allowed too much leeway to his players and that

that in itself might have been a contributory factor in United failing to clinch a League Championship title. But it is not an argument that Moran could bring himself to endorse: 'Yeah but there was nobody more relaxed than Liverpool. So what's Frank saying? Because there were a few having drinks and all that? Well, Liverpool used to do that ten times more than Manchester United did. I know that was the fact. But the game is changing now. The game has changed dramatically now so it's easy to look upon it now saying it, and making comparisons between now and then. You can't do it because the game has changed significantly in that particular way – players don't go out as much as they did in the past. But I can tell you now I know for a fact that the Liverpool team at that particular time and era was a hell of a team for going out and enjoying themselves. And yet it didn't hinder their progress in Europe or anywhere for that matter.' In Moran's view such behaviour was good for team morale, bonding players together. But he was a little coy when asked directly if he went out drinking with the 'usual suspects' at United and if he was ever told that he was doing too much of this or that. He responded with a wry smile: 'There wasn't a question of . . . it was highlighted once or twice really and again it's something blown out of proportion, it really is and because the lads used to enjoy it – they always did it at the right times – they never did anything at the wrong times, you know what I mean. There was never a situation when they weren't there to perform and I suppose when you look at it in many ways, if you ask anybody throughout the eighties name your best three consistent players – Whiteside, McGrath and Robson would be the three. And if that wasn't the case then you could easily say no wonder they're not performing because they're out on the tear, but that wasn't the case.'

Moran left in August 1988 when he moved to Sporting Gijon in Spain for a season before coming back to spend five seasons helping rebuild Blackburn Rovers. Ferguson had bought Steve Bruce from Norwich City and McGrath, Hogg and Moran, briefly before he left, had to battle it out to partner him. The players did not know it at the time, but the end of the League Championship wilderness years was in sight. Moran left a United squad that felt it was good enough to win the title but yet somehow managed to spurn its opportunities. Kevin could offer no definitive reason for this failure: 'I can't put my finger on it, really, looking back now. I don't know, I just felt at the time that we could always beat the top teams and the big teams and we'd fall against some teams at the bottom, if you know what I mean. But the team at the bottom we'd draw at home and be expected to beat them and all that. We weren't able to just carve out those one–nil results that I remember Liverpool used to do an awful lot of, really. Even so we had opportunities when we went in to the 1985–86 season, when we were ten points clear. So from positions like that we should have, we should have won it, and I think more than anything else, talking to the likes of the players like Norman, Paul and all the rest of them, that rankles with me more that we never won a championship at Old Trafford.' In any event, a season after Moran left, Ferguson got rid of McGrath to Aston Villa and sold Whiteside to Everton, leaving Robson as the sole survivor of that group of players. But just like Robson, the McGrath/Moran partnership still had the legs to survive for many more years.

Republic of Ireland International (71 caps 1980–94): 6 goals
DEBUT: **30 April 1980 v. Switzerland in Dublin. (Won 2–0)**
TEAM: **Peyton; Langan, Hughton, Daly (1), Moran, Lawrenson, Grealish, Waddock, Givens (1), McGee, Ryan.**

One day after his 24th birthday, Kevin Moran arrived on the international scene. A crowd of 20,000 watched him help the Irish side to a comfortable two-goal victory over the Swiss. As with his United career, the record books reveal long gaps between caps, suggesting that the injury problems were already also interrupting his international career. By the time McGrath made his international debut in February 1985, Moran had just 18 caps out of a possible 31 international matches since his debut five years earlier. By the time he made his 19th appearance, McGrath was winning his seventh cap in what was their first appearance together for Ireland against Denmark in Dublin. They lost 4–1. But soon they were to be a formidable defensive duo for Ireland. Between McGrath's first game in 1985 and Moran's final international appearance in 1994, the Republic of Ireland played 84 games and the McGrath/Moran partnership featured in 40 of them. So for Ireland it was an enduring partnership with some outstanding memories of European Championship and World Cup success. As far as Moran is concerned, the highlight of his international career came in 1988.

European Championship finals: 12 June 1988. Republic of Ireland v England at Stuttgart. (Won 1–0)
TEAM: **Bonner; Morris, Hughton, Whelan, Moran, McCarthy, Houghton (1), McGrath, Stapleton (Quinn), Aldridge, Galvin (Sheedy).**

Irish football, north or south of the border, has always struggled on the world stage. In a sense this is only natural given the limited resources available. It took an Englishman, Jack Charlton, to put football on the map in Ireland and to give an entire nation reason to believe, to be proud of their professional footballers. Inevitably, it is the English League which provides the best training and coaching opportunities for the Irish, the Welsh and for a great many Scots. A consequence of this is that individual clubs will have a rich variety of players of different nationalities on their playing staff. Players at United of Irish origin would engage in a rather intense form of banter with their English-born colleagues. No doubt there would have been some betting on the outcome of games between the two nations. On this occasion the Irish lads would have won any bets rather handsomely. That is to say, 'Robbo' would have had to hand over some of his hard-earned cash to Kevin and Paul. Because Irish football success seems to go in cycles with one or other part of the island doing well at times when the other is doing rather poorly, there are those who believe Ireland should be united and have just one international team. It works in other sports, most notably rugby. But in football, it leaves the Irish open to jibes from their club mates of being the poor relation. Kevin, however, does not remember the Irish being the butt of changing-room humour: 'No, because there was a general feeling, I think, if you look throughout the period that we played in, '82 was the time that Northern Ireland qualified for Spain. It was the year that Northern Ireland did very, very well in Spain. They beat Spain themselves one–nil and went on to another stage over there. So they had a very good team then, Northern Ireland. There was more talk about combining the two teams at the time, I would have thought, than anything else. The general feeling over here in England among players was that we had an awful lot of good players. They were amazed that we didn't do better than we did, so it wasn't as if they regarded us as rubbish or something like that. It was far from it, it was just a question of, "I can't believe with the players youse have you don't do better."'

Of course, it was easier for the Irish to hold their heads high in club locker rooms if their team did well and in Stuttgart, the Irish did exceptionally well. Playing for Jack Charlton and rescuing the fortunes of Irish football, they achieved some stunning results and this defeat of England was one of the rungs on the ladder of success for the Republic of Ireland side. 'There are lots of different games at international level to look back on with pride,' said Kevin, 'but probably beating England was the highlight of it because it really brought it on to the scene. It was the first championship we qualified for and the first game of that championship was against England as well. It was a massive game, playing against the players you play with and play against . . . week in week out in England. I think in many ways the significance of beating them at a neutral ground was a huge bonus. You know we played really well in that particular tournament even though that wasn't our best performance but result-wise and occasion-wise is probably the one that stands out for me more than anything else.'

This game took place just two months before Moran packed his Old Trafford bags for a sojourn in the sun of Spain, leaving behind confused United fans who were uncertain of the future without the 'Blood Donor'. Fans who were soon to witness the demolition of the 'nearly' team built by Atkinson.

The same fans had clearly built up a rapport with Moran and he clearly recalled one particular incident when he was being led off injured, and bleeding no doubt, during the 1983 FA Cup semi-final against Arsenal at Villa Park. After going behind to a soft goal from Tony Woodcock, Robson fired the Red Devils back into the game before Whiteside scored a spectacular volleyed winner. This is what made an impact on Moran: 'The affinity I feel with the club now is very much in respect of the supporters who still, to this day, remember me. I got injured in the semi-final in 1983 at Villa Park and as I am going off the pitch I remember putting my thumb up to the crowd as if to say I was alright. The reaction I got from the supporters then was phenomenal and even to this day people still remind me of that moment at Villa Park.' But the bigger question for Kevin to answer is whether or not those same fanatical supporters contributed to the 26 lean years because they put too much pressure on the players to win the title. In Kevin's view, there was an element of truth in that: 'The way it contributed was in relation to the style of the game at that time and comparing it to the team now. Remember how Liverpool played in those days – they played a controlled game. Back passes, passing across the middle and all the rest of it, we couldn't do that at all. We found that at the back if you put the pass across the back you'd feel the crowd getting on top of you to knock the ball forward. They wanted it knocked forward, down the wings, get across the middle, let's have shots at the goals, let's have everything. It's all action they wanted then as well. So a lot of the time we were forcing the play, whereas now if you look at the United team that are playing now, they could put 15 passes together before getting out of their own half, make another five or six passes in the opposing half, they come back in to their own half and make another four or five passes and you don't hear a dickey bird from the ground – not a dickey bird because they're holding possession and now they've understood that. They've been educated now, the Old Trafford crowd. You could not have done that through the eighties when we played. Now maybe you could turn round and say that was the fault possibly of not winning the title for so many years, but success comes with the ability of being able to change the way you play.'

So from what Moran is saying, is it fair to extrapolate that there were occasions on the pitch when players knew it was safer to pass backwards but chose the risky attacking ball to give the crowd what it wanted? Kevin's answer is not convincing: 'No, you didn't consciously think that . . . if what was needed was a safe ball, you gave a safe ball. But you're all the time thinking, "get it forward". You're all the time thinking, full-backs would look forward, they wouldn't look to the side, we wouldn't be afraid to give away possession, you know what I mean. You put a ball in thinking you might get a second opportunity, something like that. But it wasn't the passing game we have now.'

Nothing wrong with Kevin's passing, I thought, as I left his office reflecting on his ability to field any question in an utterly discreet manner. A real tiger in the tackle – but a gentleman and a scholar in his new life as a businessman and former Manchester United star.

REASON TO BELIEVE: There was no debate or hesitation when it came to choosing Kevin Moran as one of the two central-defenders alongside his international team-mate and former United colleague Paul McGrath. This pair were stunningly efficient defenders together although their partnership never seemed to gel at Old Trafford. Moran became a Stretford End hero, mainly through his willingness to spill his own blood in the United cause. The bravery of the 'Blood Donor' in the tackle and his ability in the air were strengths that made him a formidable ball-winning defender and it was his ability to win the ball in crunching, uncompromising tackles that proved to be his greatest strength. When deciding on the defensive line-up for this team, Moran really had no competition!

KEVIN MORAN: THE QUESTIONNAIRE
BORN: **Dublin – 29 April 1956.**

Which junior clubs did you play for – and during what years?
Rangers Schoolboy Club – 1970–74.

Which club did you support as a boy?
Liverpool.

Was it always your ambition to be a professional footballer? Or did GAA take priority?
Yes Gaelic did, like it did for every kid, or schoolboy. But once 18, no, not really.

I seem to remember United giving you special permission to appear for Dublin in a big game – was it an all-Ireland final?
It was the All-Ireland Championship game of 1978.

Do you recall the moment you first realised you were signing for United, and describe your reaction to being taken on by such a big club?
Absolute shock. I did not expect to be asked.

Do you have academic qualifications? And did you deliberately set out with a plan to secure qualifications before committing yourself to life as a professional footballer?
I have a business and commerce degree but I had no plan to get them before signing as a professional.

You made your debut for United away to Southampton on 30 April 1979. Can you describe your feelings on that day? Did you know you were going to play?
Yes I did know I was going to play but I cannot remember my feelings.

Whilst at United you had something of a reputation as a player who would spill his own blood in the name of the United cause. Were you aware of this? And were you aware of the adoration among us supporters because of this bravery?
Probably not at the time. But later on I realised I had a great rapport with the supporters.

You played 283 games – which one stands out in the memory and why?
The Cup-Winners' Cup quarter-final game against Barcelona at Old Trafford which we won 3–0.

The best manager you played for at Old Trafford – and the worst?
N/A

The highlight of your football career? When, where, etc?
Playing in the World Cup in 1990 and beating England in a European Championship game in Stuttgart and of course the FA Cup win with United.

Your worst moment at Old Trafford and why?
Coming off injured with hamstring problems.

Which individual was the biggest influence on your career – first as a player and secondly as a manager?
No one in particular.

Your best game for United? (When, where and against whom?)
Don't know.

Your worst game for United? (When, where and against whom?)
Don't know.

The 1985 final. I was there with my son Steven (at ten years of age he was attending his first ever M.U. game) and we found ourselves among the Everton fans at the end where you were sent off. We were gutted. Nothing like your feelings, I am sure.
N/A

I read in Paul McGrath's book that because he was the one to give you the bad pass which led to that tackle he was prepared to give you his medal if they did not present you with yours? Were you aware of this?
No.

It must have been horrific not to receive your medal in the normal way. Can you begin to describe your emotions at this point?
It did not bother me because we had won the game and I just assumed I would receive the medal later.

Did you ever encounter that referee (Peter Willis) again? If so, can you remember when? And how did you regard him?
No!

It must have been difficult to sit and watch the game once you had been sent off?
Very difficult. I just felt numb until Norman scored.

Describe, if you can, your emotions when Big Norm scored a brilliant winning goal?
It lifted me out of the numbness I was in.

Pick your greatest ever Man Utd team. (And give a few comments to explain if possible.)
I played with too many great players to pick just eleven.

You were at Old Trafford at a time when there were many players from Northern Ireland and the Republic of Ireland. Did this add to the

enjoyment of playing at Old Trafford? Or did it cause difficulties?
No problems. We got on very well together.

Best player you ever saw in a United shirt? And why?
Bryan Robson. He had everything.

The most difficult opponent you ever faced? (Example of game – with year and competition if possible.)
Graeme Sharp of Everton and Peter With of Aston Villa.

You made your international debut in 1980 (30 April) against Switzerland. Describe your feelings on that day. (You won 2–0 with goals from Givens and Daly in front of 20,000 in Dublin.)
This was the proudest moment of my career.

The best game for your country and the worst?
Don't know.

How did you regard the Man Utd fans?
The best supporters in the country . . . by far!

Why do you think they remained so loyal throughout the years when they so desperately wanted a league title but had to watch for 26 years as Liverpool dominated?
Tradition and entertainment value.

Did the fans' desire for a League Championship ever put pressure on the players? Do you think it might in some way have contributed to the failure to win the title for 26 years?
Possibly . . . NO.

Your views on the team selected for this book?
Not a bad team. Would definitely hold its own.

SIX

Paul McGrath

(DEFENDER)

Manchester United: 1982–83 to 1988–89: 191 (7) games: 16 goals

DEBUT: **13 November 1982 v. Tottenham Hotspur at Old Trafford. (Won 1–0)**

TEAM: **Bailey, Duxbury, Albiston; Moses, McGrath, McQueen; Robson, Muhren (1); Stapleton, Whiteside, Coppell.**

HONOURS: **FA Cup 1984–85**
Republic of Ireland (83 caps 1985–97)

The sun was warming our beer faster than we could consume it in its chilled state on the street outside a small bar close to Lansdowne Road in Dublin. It was Sunday, 17 May 1998 and occasionally the light breeze brought the sounds of a football game to our street corner. Inside the stadium, around 40,000 Irish citizens were paying tribute to 38-year-old Paul McGrath for his contribution to making Ireland a footballing nation once again – an honour fit for a true Irish sporting icon. Had I not been busy trying to expose the dishonourable failings of another Irish sporting icon – triple Olympic gold medallist Michelle Smith – I would been at the match myself. But there we were – 'we' being me, the television crew and journalist Stephen Downes – all waiting for a call from Mary O'Malley of the Irish Amateur Swimming Association to say whether or not she would be interviewed for the UTV current affairs programme *Insight*. We had completed a programme a year earlier but UTV chose not to transmit it for fear of offending the woman who had betrayed her country and cheated those children of Ireland who had Olympic swimming ambitions. She had hidden, first of all behind her cheating husband and then behind her lawyer. But now, however, Michelle Smith and her drug-cheat husband Erik de Bruin were back in the news. A random sample given to persistent drug testers smelled very strongly of whiskey. It was the beginning of the end for Michelle Smith.

Fellow journalist Stephen Downes and I were still waiting for a telephone call from Mary O'Malley of the Irish Amateur Swimming Association when crowds of fans passed the pub on their way home, clutching match programmes and pictures of McGrath. They had long gone by the time Irish swimming had finished its crisis meeting. Yes, Mary O'Malley would be interviewed. By the time we met up with her along the shores of Dublin Bay, Paul McGrath had long since showered, changed and moved on to celebrate his retirement from international football among those who appreciated his sporting prowess. It was a missed opportunity.

Just five days earlier in Belfast I interviewed Norman Whiteside over lunch and he very kindly agreed to deliver to Paul McGrath my letter of explanation and a request for an interview. Since then I had heard nothing from McGrath, although Roy Keane responded to his letter – also very kindly delivered by Norman. Fast forward to December 1998 and still no word from McGrath. I am in Manchester for the Bayern Munich game and to interview McGrath's old playing partner Kevin Moran in Wilmslow. I explain my difficulty in getting to McGrath and Kevin immediately picks up his phone and tries to contact McGrath. There is no response and Kevin remembers that McGrath is moving house but he promises to get in touch and give him my numbers. By the time United play their quarter-final home tie against Inter Milan in March and then the semi-final tie against Juventus in April, I still had not received any communication from McGrath. On one of the match days Kevin Moran called me on my mobile as I was enjoying breakfast in a café next door to the Pelican Pub on the A56 leading to Old Trafford. He told me he had contacted McGrath and that I should receive a call soon. McGrath lives in the Altrincham/Hale area, my general neighbourhood, but I have adopted a policy all my life not to harass players. They play football and entertain me. What they do in their own time is not my business. I could have gone to the pubs in the Altrincham/Hale area frequented by Manchester United players but that, to me, would have qualified as unwelcome attention, and therefore harassment of a kind. Paul McGrath knows I want to talk to him but obviously he is not ready to make that commitment. The purpose of relating this tale of woe is to let you know that this chapter of the book may be considerably shorter than the others. There was an alternative, of course – drop him from the team. That would entail choosing a different player who might be more available – but every United Irishman would have screamed in horror at the omission of one of Ireland's best-loved football icons. And quite right too!

'Ooh, Aah, Paul McGrath's da!' The President of South Africa was on his first visit to Ireland and, as he travelled through the Dublin streets packed with well-wishers, he could be forgiven for being slightly confused at the words of welcome from Irish citizens. What he did not perhaps realise was that his arrival pre-empted by a matter of hours the return of the 1990 Irish World Cup squad from Italy. Manchester United fans had first given voice to the 'Ooh Aah Paul McGrath' chant and here were the Irish, delirious at the achievements of the Jack Charlton-inspired Irish team, adapting the same tune to give South Africa's first citizen a rousing if somewhat unusual welcome. In Italy in 1990, Ireland had reached their international peak. Paul McGrath was in his fifth year as an international and had long since departed Old Trafford in acrimonious fashion.

Republic of Ireland International (83 caps 1985–97)
DEBUT: **5 February 1985 v. Italy in Dublin. (Lost 2–1)**
TEAM: **Bonner; Hughton, Beglin, Lawrenson (McGrath), McCarthy, Brady, Sheedy, Waddock (1), Galvin (Whelan), Stapleton, Byrne (Campbell).**

The lovable rogue arrived on the international scene just a few months before gaining his only medal with Manchester United. It was the beginning of an impressive international career which was blessed with 83 caps – 31 with United, 51 with Aston Villa and one while at Derby County. His first cap came courtesy of Eoín Hand although the most important caps came during the reign of the Englishman who virtually became a saint in Ireland, Jack Charlton. Before his testimonial game in Dublin, McGrath was asked about the highlights of his career and he said it was the games against Italy that stood out. Now, to be clear on this, he was not referring to his debut game, although obviously that has its own special significance. No, he was speaking of the games in the two World Cups he graced – in 1990 and 1994. McGrath told the Irish football magazine, *Kickin'*, why these games mattered so much to him. He said: 'Playing Italy in Rome was a big game. It was a magnificent boost for us, especially with it being the quarter final. And then again in the Giants Stadium because we owed them one and we gave them one, so it was good to get a victory over them. Those two games internationally would stand out for me.'

World Cup quarter-final: 30 June 1990. Republic of Ireland v. Italy at Olympic Stadium, Rome. Attendance 73,303. (Lost 1–0)
TEAM: **Bonner; Morris, Staunton, McGrath, McCarthy, Moran, Houghton, Townsend, Quinn (Cascarino), Aldridge (Sheridan), Sheedy.**

This was the game that brought Ireland to a halt. Streets were deserted, entire families huddled around their television sets and pubs were packed with grown men behaving as badly as teenagers at a Boyzone concert. This was the tournament that raised the profile of Irish football, took it into orbit and gave it a legacy of youth for the future. Youngsters were suddenly turning to 'soccer' in their droves, turning away from the traditional Irish games of hurling and Gaelic football. Paul McGrath's status in Ireland had grown during the qualifying rounds of the World Cup but by the time they kicked off against England in the Italian finals, McGrath was a figure of worship throughout the Irish nation. Ireland drew against all three opponents in the group stage – England, Egypt and Holland. In the second round against Romania, the game ended 0–0 and went to a penalty shoot-out which the Irish won 5–4. Packie Bonner was the hero of the hour. So Ireland, against all expectations, had qualified for the quarter-final game against Italy. The Irish defended bravely but their forwards were not allowed to cause problems for the Italian defence, although Quinn frequently troubled them with his height. The difference between the two teams was Toto Schillaci, who had one goal disallowed for offside and then also hit the underside of the bar, before eventually ramming home the winner after a shot from Donadoni. It was hit with such power that it knocked Packie Bonner off his feet. The one man who almost prevented the little Italian from getting the winning goal was that man McGrath. On the television screen it seems as though Schillaci is on his own as the ball rebounds off Bonner into his path. But suddenly this figure emerges from the right to get tantalisingly close to blocking the shot. Seconds earlier McGrath was seen on the opposite side of the pitch.

Spearheading the Italian attack that night was Roberto Baggio who had just been transferred to Juventus for more than £8 million, at the time a staggering figure. He was substituted after 71 minutes. McGrath snuffed him out of the game. But then when he was playing for Ireland, it was not uncommon for Paul McGrath to stifle some of the greatest football talents in the world. When you look at the list of top-class players who have been rendered useless by McGrath, it is little wonder that at the end of the 1990 World Cup he was chosen for the International Select Eleven. Here is a list of 14 international strikers who have been mastered by McGrath: Roberto Baggio (Italy); Ruud Gullit (Holland); Alan Shearer (England); Jurgen Klinsmann (Germany); Emilio Butragueno (Spain); Gary Lineker (England); Gheorge Hagi (Romania); Jari Litmanen (Finland); Jean-Pierre Papin (France); Hristo Stoichkov (Bulgaria); Romario (Brazil); Ian Rush (Wales) and Paolo Rossi (Italy). In anyone's language that is an impressive list of notches to have on your belt. What is also worthy of consideration in this regard is his display against Maradona in 1987, when he was playing for the Football League in its centenary game against the Rest of the World. Of course, this was categorised as a 'friendly' but he handled the Argentinian so well that shortly afterwards his name was being linked to some of the top clubs in Europe. Thus it came to pass that on the day the Irish football team was coming home to a tumultuous welcome, President Nelson Mandela got the benefit of their hospitality as they warmed up for the real thing!

Paul McGrath was born in Ealing, North London on 4 December 1959. His mother was Irish, his father, whom he has never met apparently, was a doctor from Nigeria. At just six weeks of age he was brought back to Ireland and on the quayside at Dun Laoghaire harbour, Paul McGrath was handed over to a Protestant foster agency. From there he was placed in the care of a Mrs Donnelly whose home was in the Whitehall streets where a young Liam Brady had played football. Although he was raised as a Protestant, McGrath regards himself as a Catholic – his meeting with the Pope in 1990 during the World Cup ranks as one of the greatest thrills of his life. McGrath credits Mrs Donnelly, with introducing him to football. As a child his favourite football club was Chelsea, his hero their Scottish right-winger Charlie Cooke.

McGrath played for Pearse Rovers before moving on to Dalkey United as a 17-year-old and then St Patrick's Athletic. United's Dublin scout and former first-team goalkeeper, the late Billy Behan, had first identified McGrath as a potential Red Devil when he was playing for Dalkey. But in the end United paid £30,000 to St Pat's for his signature in April 1982. Ron Atkinson was the man who saw the enormous talent in McGrath. He recognised that even though McGrath was just over six feet tall, he had speed and strength, was naturally good in the air, and could use both feet. McGrath made his debut the season following his signing but, in truth, for the first couple of seasons he appeared in the side on a very intermittent basis. In his first season, 1982–83, he made 14 appearances and scored three goals. The following season he appeared just nine times in the first team and scored just once. It was only in the FA Cup winning season of 1984–85 that McGrath could truly say he had begun to establish himself with 23 League appearances.

FA Cup final: 18 May 1985 v. Everton at Wembley Stadium. Attendance 100,000. (Won 1–0)

EVERTON: Southall; Stevens, Van den Hauwe, Ratcliffe, Mountfield, Reid, Steven, Gray, Sharp, Bracewell, Sheehy.

UNITED: Bailey; Gidman, Albiston (Duxbury), Whiteside (1), McGrath, Moran, Robson, Strachan, Hughes, Stapleton, Olsen.

This game is remembered for two reasons – the dismissal of Kevin Moran and the marvellous Whiteside goal that gave United's 10-man team victory over the 'Blue' Scousers. Just as Jimmy Nicholl confessed that he had believed he was responsible for the winning Arsenal goal in 1979, McGrath was to make a similarly startling confession after his one and only winning FA Cup final appearance. In his book, *Ooh Aah Paul McGrath* (Mainstream, 1994), he had this to say about Moran's premature departure from the game: 'Wembley beckoned again for the 1985 Cup final. We beat Everton and Kevin Sheedy 1–0 in the decider, thanks to a Norman Whiteside goal. But everyone remembers that game for just one reason – Kevin Moran's red card. He became the first player to be sent off in a Wembley final. The referee's name is a great quiz question now. I couldn't remember it – until Joey Lovejoy of the *Independent* newspaper reminded me it was Peter Willis. A history-maker. I still feel guilty about that red card. It was my poor back pass to Kevin that let Peter Reid in to pick up the ball and sweep towards goal. I had given Kevin no choice but to go for Reidy after that hospital pass. The referee decided it was a sending-off offence. It was a harsh decision to say the least – and it caused uproar within football. There was consternation when Kevin was refused his medal after the match because he had been sent off. In fact somebody found it in the Royal Box afterwards and he did eventually receive it. Had they refused to give it to him point blank then I would have given him my medal – after all I was responsible for his dismissal.' As you will have read in the Kevin Moran chapter in this book, Moran says he knew nothing of this plan but it does offer an insight into the kind of team spirit that existed during what were the best years of McGrath's career at Old Trafford. In the following season, 1985–86, he produced his most consistent form in a United shirt when he appeared in a staggering 40 games. The next season he appeared in 32 games. United supporters were now beginning to think they had one of the best players in Europe who had also started to show some consistency. The team was beginning to shape up as potential League Champions. After all, since McGrath started playing under Ron Atkinson's management we had finished third, fourth, fourth and fourth in the League. One more push and McGrath would help us end the League title famine.

But we were wrong. Behind the scenes, McGrath was drinking along with a group of players – notably Robson, Moran and Whiteside. Big Ron seemed happy enough so long as it did not prevent them from either training or playing. But the climate changed when Ron got the sack and Alex Ferguson took control in November 1986. Fergie was not going to be so tolerant. Soon Moran, McGrath and Whiteside were history. For just £450,000 Aston Villa got a bargain – at least when considering the playing qualities of the

Irishman. What was far from clear was whether or not he could put his drinking to one side long enough to establish himself as the truly class player he really was. He did and eventually he managed to get some revenge on Fergie for his decision to sell him off. Nowadays the hatchet has been buried, the animosity forgotten between Fergie and McGrath. Fergie has admitted that McGrath was 'the most talented' player he had ever worked with. Praise indeed. Knowing now what we do about Fergie's ability to work with temperamental stars, for example Eric Cantona, it remains a mystery why he could not find the time to find the means of controlling 'the most talented' player he had ever worked with. At Wembley in 1994, Paul McGrath gave a masterful display – and in so doing exacted some revenge on Alex Ferguson.

League Cup final: 27 March 1994 v. Aston Villa at Wembley Stadium. Attendance 77,231. (Lost 3–1)
TEAM: **Sealey; Parker, Irwin, Bruce (McClair), Kanchelskis, Pallister, Cantona, Ince, Keane, Hughes (1), Giggs (Sharpe).**

Langdon is in North Dakota, located just about a dozen miles from the Canadian border. On 27 March it was f***ing cold – 36 degrees below is the way the locals put it when they argued that this was quite warm. It was so cold the tyres on the car bumped for the first mile or so until the frozen flat portion had been moulded back into shape by the heat of the movement. It had been a good day for me. We had filmed a service at a Catholic church in the small town with a population of a few thousand souls. We had interviewed some parishioners and the parish priest Father Dale Kinzler. We had established the facts about an Irish priest by the name of Father Brendan Smyth, who had spent a few years in the early eighties as a parish priest in Langdon. The reason for my interest in Smyth had been stimulated by interviews done back in Belfast over the previous three months when I discovered his secret. He was a paedophile. We found that he had abused children whilst in Langdon and that he had paid $20,000 to one of the young men he had abused. Then we discovered that his religious order, the Norbertine Order, had known about his paedophilia since 1958 and had managed to hush up every case of abuse – until now. Smyth was interviewed by detectives in Belfast in March 1991. He was charged and released on a personal and paltry bail of £100. He fled to the Republic of Ireland, to the abbey at Ballyjamesduff in Co. Cavan where the Norbertine Order was based. The police in Belfast did not see him again for almost three years while he remained on the run. Extradition warrants were served to the authorities in Dublin but never executed. The scandal of why they were never processed by the Dublin authorities was exposed in the television documentary I made about the priest. I also revealed that the Catholic Church hierarchy had covered up for Smyth's paedophile activities for four decades.

He was a figure of evil who abused his position of trust and everywhere Father Smyth went he left behind a trail of shattered lives – broken and humiliated individuals given a life sentence while the abuser led a comfortable life, protected by the Church. When the facts emerged about the failure of the Republic of Ireland to extradite this criminal to the North to face sex charges, the Southern Irish Government fell. Brendan Smyth had a lot to answer for.

On 27 March 1994 I was hanging around our hotel lobby in Langdon waiting for a call from a lawyer who would confirm an interview with the boy Smyth abused and to whom Smyth had paid $20,000 in the hope it would be kept hushed up as usual. The League Cup final was being played. There was no way of getting the score other than by telephoning a friend or relative. Time dragged by. Hours passed before I got the call that would take me south to Grand Forks for a meeting with the boy and his family. It was difficult to quell my desire to know how United were doing at Wembley against Villa. I felt guilty even thinking about United given the horror stories I was now asking people to relive. But when we had finished our work for the day, I could not wait to call home.

My son Steven gave me the bad news. United had been beaten. In the circumstances, I did not really give a toss. But once again Ron Atkinson had dumped on his old club. He had had the same success in the League Cup final two seasons earlier with Sheffield Wednesday. But this win by Villa was, in large part, due to the great performance of Paul McGrath. He had shown in a very tangible way just what it was about his play that United missed. As I have said, McGrath's views on Fergie and United have mellowed over the years and as he approached his Dublin testimonial he had this to say: 'I have a lot of respect for Alex and for what he has done for Manchester United. I mean, as a man . . . I don't think as a man we would ever have seen eye to eye. He has done a great job for them and I think he did me a favour really, letting me go, because I went on to have a good career myself so I have no bad feelings.' Manchester United fans have no bad feelings either – just regrets about what might have been!

REASON TO BELIEVE: Paul McGrath was an outstanding talent who could not only tackle but could distribute the ball accurately with both feet. He could read the play and anticipate the focus of the opponents' attacks as well as pack a punch in the tackle. Along with the 'Blood Donor' Kevin Moran, this should have been the dream partnership to dominate United's defence for the eighties. Should have been. Yet during their time together at Old Trafford, Moran and McGrath played surprisingly few games together. Injuries undoubtedly interrupted what should have been a winning partnership at the heart of the United defence, but by the time McGrath was reaching his peak events off the field took him in a new direction.

SEVEN

Sammy McIlroy

(STRIKER-TURNED-MIDFIELD MAESTRO)

Manchester United: 1971–72 to 1981–82: 390 (28) games: 71 goals

DEBUT: **6 November 1971 v. Manchester City at Maine Road. (Drew 3–3)**

TEAM: **Stepney; O'Neill, Dunne, Gowling (1), James, Sadler, Morgan, Kidd (1), Charlton, McIlroy (1), Best.**

HONOURS: **FA Cup 1976–77**
Second Division Championship 1974–75
Northern Ireland (88 caps 1972–1986)

The 'colours' lay in a plastic bag at my feet. It was about 4.30 p.m. on Saturday, 12 May 1979. The heart was low, the spirit as far back as three valium and a couple of pints of lager could take it – not that I had swallowed any valium. The body perspired profusely; a mixture of the fear of humiliating defeat at the hands of the Arsenal and the heat of the sunshine outside through the glass of the Wembley press box. At least it was not like facing the Scousers – I would not have to subject myself to the humiliation of facing a hoard of 'Gooners' at work on Monday. In Northern Ireland in 1979, Arsenal fans were as thin on the ground as intellects on the North Bank. The lunchtime pints in the Irish pub in Notting Hill Gate were beginning to die inside. Sleep was definitely trying to tempt me out of this miserable state. But then it happened. Not once, but twice. First it was Gordon McQueen who somehow pushed the ball into the corner of the Arsenal net past Pat Jennings. Four minutes left on the clock. Automatically my hands went up in the air, punching the steel girder above my head and sending pieces of rusting steel cascading down around my fellow reporters who were now scowling at me. I had broken the golden rule of the press box by displaying emotion for my team. At least mine was openly on show. Theirs is very faintly disguised in some of the garbage they write daily.

However, as a reporter on only his second mission to Wembley – the first was for the wondrous 1977 final against the 'Dirties' – and fearing retribution, I quickly sat down. As I did so, I tugged furiously at the sleeve of the other miscreant beside me, Peter McCusker. The previous Saturday from the press box at Windsor Park I had watched Peter win an Irish Cup medal with the unfancied Cliftonville – my uncle Bobby's old team. We met that Saturday morning on the airport tarmac as we prepared to board the plane for London. My eight-year-old son Jason was going to his first FA Cup final. I had four tickets for the game and Peter had none. Two for my son and brother in the stadium and two to the press box. The solution to Peter's problem was in my pocket. He was about to become a journalist for the day.

Back in the Wembley press box, worse was to follow our first indiscretion. Sammy McIlroy was the cause of our next misdemeanour and this is how Sammy remembered the moment nearly twenty years later: 'It was 2–1 with a minute and a half to go. I remember Jimmy Nicholl had the ball on the left side. He cross-fielded it to Arthur Albiston and then Arthur put it in the box . . . it got put out to "Nich" again and then "Nich" sort of miskicked it and it went to Sammy Nelson [of Arsenal] but he miskicked it back to Stevie Coppell. When Stevie Coppell had the ball I just decided to run forward into the box and he put me through. As I say, there were a couple of challenges from Walford and O'Leary and I thought I'd hit the ball too far in front of me, past O'Leary. I saw big Pat Jennings running out towards me and it looked at the time like he was favourite to come and get the ball. So I just got down, stretched the toe and it was a good thing I stretched the toe – gave it extra pace and it only managed to trickle in over the line. So that was it, trickled into the corner. But I thought then, go to extra time and we could win it.'

Like Sammy and the other United players down on the pitch, me and McCusker thought we now had this game won! We would have 'these' in extra time. We were on our feet hugging each other, rattling the roof of the press box and rapidly removing our 'colours' from our plastic bag! In that instant, we did not care if we were forever banished from the Wembley press box. What folly! Our celebrations were short-lived under the collective glare of the cream of British sports journalism, as a run down the left wing by Graham Rix, later to become the paedophile of Stamford Bridge, set up the winning goal for Alan Sunderland at the far post. The cream of British football writers missed the moment as they concentrated on their collective hatred of the defiant and partisan demonstration on the back row of their precious enclosure. We, however, were facing in the right direction and saw everything, which was just as well as I had to phone the story over to my employers, the *Sunday News*. Little did they know of the disgrace I had heaped upon them. In the space of four minutes we had experienced joy and despair. Now here I was reliving those moments with one of the men responsible for that rollercoaster ride.

It was the day 'King Eric' was back in Manchester to play in the Munich Memorial game, 18 August 1998. Somewhere in the city he was probably relaxing with some of his old friends over croissants and coffee whilst I was nursing a hangover and dodging rush hour traffic leaving Warrington on my way to Macclesfield. I was avoiding motorway madness by driving along leafy side roads while back at my son's house *Sunday World* football writer Steven Looney from Belfast was avoiding all contact with the outside world – including this opportunity to meet one of the Stretford End's favourite sons. As he nursed his hangover in bed, I was driving mine around Cheshire. The sun was splitting the heavens. My head was just splitting.

In the bright sunlight, the Macclesfield ground looked unexpectedly inviting. Players had begun to gather. Inside the club's compact office a very pleasant woman was dealing with an inquiry about tickets, a young lady was earnestly trying to locate what appeared to be the club's pet dog and I was informed that the 'Boss' had not yet arrived. The *Daily Mail* crossword occupied my mind for the next five or six minutes before I was called through and led down a passage, under the stand I think, to a corridor where I could immediately see the door marked 'Manager's Office'. The 'Boss', Sammy McIlroy, came along the corridor and asked me to wait outside for just a moment. He disappeared into his office. Two young apprentices were brushing the corridor and sharing jokes with some of the players as they emerged from the dressing-room ready to travel to the club training ground a few miles away in the grounds of a rather posh school.

The office door opened. Sammy Mac was ready to be interviewed. Inside there was a small desk with a phone and two chairs – the visitor's seat was covered with training gear. Avoiding the manager's chair, I knelt on the floor and rifled my shoulder bag for the Sony recorder, the appropriate notebook and the file on one of Manchester United's super-heroes of the seventies. McIlroy was also a Northern Ireland favourite who made appearances in two World Cup finals – the striker who scored against City on his debut at their midden, aided and abetted in the goal by that other Belfast boy, George Best. It has to be said, however, that Sammy's memory of his debut is not all that reliable as he had George Best playing in the reserve team that day! In any event, as I made my preparations, Sammy chatted away. He spoke of a recent interview with Ulster Television for a documentary called *One Night in Valencia*, which commemorated the finest night in Irish international football history during the 1982 World Cup finals when Northern Ireland beat the host nation 1–0 to qualify for the quarter-finals. Throughout this conversation, Sammy busied himself undressing. The tape recorder was running as he stretched his naked body directly in front of me to reach into a drawer on his desk that was packed with his underwear, jockey briefs. Having chosen a pair, as cool as you like, he proceeded to get into his training gear. It was as if I was not in the room. But then I suppose that is the matter-of-fact way it is with professional sports stars accustomed to changing-room nakedness. By the time he had completed this 'undressing-dressing' manoeuvre, the interview was well under way. The '79 Arsenal Cup final came up during our chat about the three finals Sammy appeared in those of 1976, 1977 and 1979.

FA Cup final: 18 May 1979 v. Arsenal at Wembley Stadium. (Lost 3–2)
TEAM: **Bailey; Nicholl, Albiston, McIlroy (1), McQueen (1), Buchan, Coppell, Greenhoff, Jordan, Macari, Thomas.**

For the second time in three years Sammy Mac experienced Wembley defeat. But given the nature of the astonishing conclusion to this game it was by far the most painfully taxing on the emotions. From the depths of despair at the very real prospect of impending defeat at 2–0 down with just a few minutes to go, and then the heights of scenting extra-time victory when the game was pulled back to 2–2. Then almost immediately the long plummet to the depths of despair again as the game is lost – again and this time forever! This was Bayern Munich 1999 in reverse. McIlroy remembers it all very clearly: 'Well, I do still have the tape. You look at the equalising goal and you think, we are back at 2–2 and I honestly thought, looking at them, that they had gone. They were shocked, absolutely bewildered and we had many a chance to stop Brady making the run. But that is the type of team we were. We didn't have that type of nasty streak in us when we should have brought Brady down. Mickey Thomas tried to win the ball fairly, little Lou tried to catch him, but a nasty streak in any one of us could have brought him down. It killed the game. We had just scored and the crowd was going berserk. We were really up in the air. We were 2–0 down, dead and buried. All of a sudden we were 2–2 and we were thinking we are going to win this bloody thing. You know it is close but you think, let's get the ball back and score again. But well, when the ball went up there the big goalkeeper, Gary Bailey, should have done better I think – but having said that it should have been stopped before the cross.'

Of course, this was not the first time Sammy McIlroy had experienced defeat and deep depression as a United player. There was the 1976 FA Cup final against Southampton and there was the relegation of 1974. 'That last game of the '74 season against Manchester City was very emotional,' Sammy Mac recalled, 'especially as we got relegated. It was a bad one. The Cup final of '76 was a bad one as well, but that is football. Mind you, the football in the Second Division was just unbelievable.'

Sammy McIlroy has good reason to recall the swashbuckling football of the Second Division campaign because he flourished in his new midfield role. The switch from striker undoubtedly lengthened McIlroy's career at Old Trafford. In Tommy Docherty's United, McIlroy was outstanding. His popularity reached new heights and it was a move that McIlroy fully appreciated: 'It was the Doc's idea to drop me back to midfield and it changed my whole career. As you say, it was a disaster going down. A disaster for the club, Manchester United going down was unreal. But in the long run, the next three to four years, it was unbelievable. Those FA Cup finals – OK, we didn't win them all but it was great to be at Wembley. We came straight back up from the Second Division and we came back a better team, the most supported club in the country with all records broken in the Second Division. The football was just unbelievable and I absolutely loved it.' With very good reason too! The Doc had created an exciting team, with as much excitement off the pitch in his clashes with some of the players. But McIlroy was not one of those to fall foul of the Doc and, in fact, he carries a torch for the Scotsman's style of play in his managerial role at Macclesfield. 'Tommy had difficulties with certain players,' McIlroy told me, 'but I got on alright with him, had no trouble whatsoever. Sometimes there would be a bust-up between Tommy and a player and it would have to be sorted out. But he was a jovial manager, very quick with great one-liners. He was great company, loved to play football himself – and played in the five-a-sides and when he did he made you want to play. On the pitch he played two wingers and I try to play with two wingers when I've got them. But there are not a lot of wingers around these days. I love to see wingers go down the line and cross the ball – that is great. Aside from that training has to be fun and you know he was one who wanted that as well.'

In the spring of 1974, Northern Ireland was being ground to a halt as the loyalist/unionist community embarked on a strike to show their opposition to the power-sharing executive set up by the British Government. Power cuts and petrol rationing became the norm as the Ulster Workers' Council controlled the protest action although, it has to be said, not without the support of loyalist paramilitaries who provided the muscle to intimidate anyone still inclined to go to work. On a personal level, I witnessed the intimidation first hand. As a journalist I did enjoy more freedom of movement than most other citizens at the time, in spite of losing my car briefly to masked men on a UDA barricade one night. But one Saturday afternoon our football team gathered as usual outside a bar opposite the Europa Hotel in Belfast city centre. Suddenly a car drew up and a bunch of heavies climbed out and entered the bar. Staff inside had been left in no doubt about the consequences if they remained open. Within minutes customers filed out and the doors were slammed closed and bolted. Worse still, however, was the prospect of having no toilet facilities at home. Things were getting that bad. For me, this was the last straw. Having just taught my four-year-old son Jason to use the bathroom rather than a potty, I felt it was going too far to have to talk him back on to the pot!

I travelled to England for a two-day trip, up and down the country organising interviews for jobs advertised in the latest issue of the *UK Press Gazette*. Of the four offers, Sheffield seemed the best – not least because it was closer to Old Trafford than Greenock, Rugby or Hereford. So I became a regular on the Stretford End terracing as the great Manchester United began the process of rebuilding their team in the Second Division.

Day one of life in Division Two began with a visit to Leyton Orient which was won 2–0. Sammy McIlroy came off the substitutes' bench to replace Lou Macari – but it was his only appearance as a sub because for the remainder of the season that saw United go straight back up as champions, McIlroy played in every game, scoring seven goals. United topped the League from beginning to end. When they were drawn against First Division 'Shitty' in the third round of the League Cup it was the beginning of a run of three games in that competition against teams from the top division. We beat City 1–0 thanks to a Gerry Daly penalty and then we were drawn against Burnley in the fourth round. Given our previous result against 'Shitty' we could not be certain that our team would live with First Division sides every week. 'Derby' games are notoriously fervent affairs, played with the kind of passion and at such speed as to negate their value when assessing the merits of the participants. Any United team will lift their game against that 'big' club from the bitter blue side of Manchester, so in that sense it could not be regarded as a measure of our pedigree. Now we were going up against another First Division side and we would soon find out if our boys had the bottle for the big boys.

Saturday games at Old Trafford were difficult for me because I played for a Sheffield team most weekends and playing football was more important to me at that particular period in my life than watching the professionals. However, midweek games in the League Cup were easier and more often than not one of two work colleagues at the *Sheffield Star* – either Dave Hand or Carole Freeman – would drive me over to Manchester. To be truthful,

I think Dave and Carole were fascinated by this 24-year-old father of one going to United games with such enthusiasm. Looking back, they must have found my whole disposition bewildering as this supposedly sane individual clambered into their cars dressed in the 'colours' of the day. This meant me appearing for a game with a scarf tied to each wrist, one hanging from the belt around my jeans and one around the neck. A pair of Doc Martens completed this ensemble. Then they were forced to stand on the Stretford End as this spectacle roared himself hoarse and behaved like a lunatic! On this particular occasion, for the Burnley game, it was Dave who drove through the Peak District and the moors to Manchester. The date was Wednesday, 13 November 1974.

Football League Cup. (Fourth Round): 13 November 1974 v. Burnley at Old Trafford. Attendance 46,275. (Won 3–2)
UNITED: **Stepney; Forsyth, Houston, Greenhoff B. (Morgan (1)), Sidebottom, Buchan, Macari (2), McIlroy, Pearson, McCalliog, Daly.**

At half-time it looked as though the First Division side was too good for us. It was not that they could match us for enthusiasm or our fearlessness in the art of attacking in waves. It was simply that try as we might we appeared to be incapable of breaking down their defence as often as we might have expected, given our forward momentum. After 45 minutes Burnley led by two goals to one. My memory is of Sammy McIlroy running the midfield, constantly probing their back line for an opening. He performed majestically. You knew when he had the ball it would not be wasted. Never renowned for his tackling ability, this was one of those nights when he seemed to regularly get himself between the Burnley players and the United goal. He skipped tackles like he was a gazelle, his lithe but fragile figure weaving its magic spell as he caused the Stretford End to miss heartbeats. We feared for his health every time as he faced big men who would gladly have done him harm as they lined him up in their sights – but almost every time he somehow managed to evade the pain of a collision, leaving his opponent lying bewildered on the ground. Sammy Mac never gave up the fight, never lost his faith or fervour and certainly never gave United and its fans anything but his all. In a previous round of the League Cup Sammy scored one of United's five goals against Third Division Charlton Athletic. But this was Burnley – a First Division team and although Sammy did not score and even though we needed a former Burnley player, Willie Morgan, to score our winning goal, it was a winning goal. We had demonstrated that we could play with the 'big boys'.

United were to get another opportunity to match their skills with Division One in the next round – this time the opposition was to be provided by Middlesbrough. We drew 0–0 away from home but in the replay at Old Trafford on Wednesday, 18 December 1974, we hammered them 3–0 and McIlroy was among the scorers. The passage of time has dimmed my memory and try as I might sitting here 24 years later, I just cannot recall that McIlroy goal. Anyway, his efforts were all in vain because in typical United style we lost in the semi-final against our Second Division promotion rivals, Norwich City – even though we actually outplayed them in both legs. Norwich were a bit of a bogey team for United that season – we played them twice in the League and twice in the League Cup, losing twice at their ground and drawing twice at Old Trafford. Not that the League Cup really mattered even then – our priority was to get straight back up to the First Division and that we accomplished in style!

Following promotion from the Second Division, the Doc took United to the third spot in the top league and to the FA Cup final against Southampton. After the shock of losing to Southampton, Docherty promised to be back to win it the following year – and he was. This time his team finished sixth in the top flight and beat Liverpool in the FA Cup final to deny the 'Dirties' the unique treble of League and Cup double along with the European Cup. It was clear that this Docherty side was showing potential to win a First Division title. Everything was indicating this possibility. Everything in the garden was rosy. Or was it? McIlroy picks up the threads of the 'Doc' story: 'What a team he created. Very exciting and then just when he appeared . . . the whole thing just disappeared. It was the Mary Brown affair. We didn't know anything about it and it was a blow really 'cos Tommy had that side really ticking. The fans were all for him and then next thing is he was gone.' Opposition fans were singing 'Knees up Mrs Brown' – at least that is what it sounded like! Willie Morgan put it rather candidly when he said Docherty as the 'Boss' was sending Mr Brown away on scouting missions all over the place while he was back at home 'giving his missus one!' Or words to that effect. The Doc's term of office at Old Trafford was over and it was not because he had failed the club in terms of the results on the pitch. He says his crime was to 'fall in love'. Dave Sexton moved into the top post and for the next four years McIlroy built on the midfield foundation stone laid during the Docherty years.

During the Sexton years McIlroy was virtually an ever-present in the side. In 1977–78 he made 39 League appearances with nine goals; 1978–79 – 40 League appearances and five goals; 1979–80 – 41 League appearances and six goals; 1980–81 – 31 League games (plus one as sub) and five goals.

During those years United finished tenth, ninth, second and eighth in the League. The season they finished runners-up, 1979–80, McIlroy played 41 out of the 42 League matches. Life was sweet for the East Belfast man who had supported United as a child when playing for Mersey Street Primary School and Ashfield Secondary School. He also supported Rangers and Linfield. It was always his ambition to become a professional player.

McIlroy left Northern Ireland in 1969 to begin his career at United. 'The troubles were just kicking off when I left,' he recalled, 'and I was very, very worried about my family. I decided to bring them over in the seventies. When I went back home during 1969 and 1970 the troubles were well under way with people marching the streets at night and my dad, who was no spring chicken, was having his door knocked at night by men who were calling on him to go on vigilante duty. I was worried sick and thought this was not for me. So I asked them if they would come over and they said yes, they'd like to come over.' What happened next is pretty much a secret to McIlroy's adoring fans on the Stretford End – he moved his family into a house located directly behind the Stretford End! Little wonder so many of his goal efforts worked at that end – the entire McIlroy family were behind the goal sucking the ball towards their back garden!

Sammy's parents died in 1986 but they were still living in Manchester when Sammy was sold to Stoke City for £350,000 in February 1982. He did not fit into the plans of the new United boss Ron Atkinson who was appointed in July 1981. McIlroy says he knew the writing was on the wall on the day that Big Ron paraded his new midfield signing, Bryan Robson. But if McIlroy was about to become surplus to Atkinson's requirements, he was determined to go out in style. On 3 October 1981, a crowd of 46,837 gathered at Old Trafford for the visit of Wolverhampton Wanderers. Prior to the kick-off a table was placed on the pitch with three chairs positioned around it. Then Big Ron emerged from the shadows alongside chairman Martin Edwards and the man who was due to replace McIlroy – record £1.5m signing Bryan Robson. The contract was signed in front of over 46,000 witnesses. Then play commenced. 'There was a lot of speculation that me and Ray Wilkins were going to be the first to leave,' Sammy said. 'So on the day that Bryan Robson signed on the park I went out and got a hat-trick, the only League hat-trick of my career at United. I got the ball and it was signed by all the players and Bryan Robson. Robson wrote on the ball, "Well done Sammy, by the most costly substitute in the game."'

There is no bitterness about the move away from United but with the benefit of hindsight McIlroy does feel it was perhaps a little premature, that he should have stayed and fought for his place. This is how he described his departure from Old Trafford: 'At the time Big Ron Atkinson came in and spent a lot of money on Bryan Robson and Remi Moses. United were a little bit stuck for money and there had been a few offers for Ray Wilkins and myself. United wanted to balance the books. Anyway, Big Ron told me that Stoke had made an enquiry and it was a good enquiry. They offered £350,000 and I had cost the club nothing so it would mean good business. The disappointing thing is that I knew Arsenal and Everton had enquired as well, but Big Ron didn't tell me that. No, that only emerged after the event. I went to Stoke. I shouldn't have gone – no disrespect to Stoke – but my pride was hurt and I just got into the car and drove down the motorway. My thoughts were that United didn't want me but I could and should have stayed and fought for my place. He [Big Ron] wasn't showing me the door but when he said he accepted the bid, well, my pride was hurt. My one regret is my hasty decision to leave United. But you have to do it sometime. Even the best players in the world, the people who have been there more than 13 years, have to move on. Maybe that decision was a little bit hasty.'

Sammy McIlroy left Manchester United after 390 games and 28 as substitute. He scored 71 goals. Born in Belfast on 2 August 1954, he was first approached by the famous Manchester United scout Bob Bishop at the tender age of nine. It was Bishop who discovered other United talents such as George Best and Norman Whiteside. Best was in the United team when McIlroy made his debut against 'Shitty' in 1971 at the age of 17 and 11 years later when United sold him, the 16-year-old 'man-boy', Norman Whiteside, made his debut. Whiteside and McIlroy were to play together before 1982 expired – and in the most extraordinary circumstances!

Northern Ireland International (88 caps 1972–86)
DEBUT: **16 February 1972 v. Spain at Hull. (Drew 1–1)**
TEAM: **Jennings; Rice, Nelson, Neill, Hunter, Clements, Hamilton (O'Neill), McMordie, Morgan (1), McIlroy, Best.**

English players dream of making their debut in front of their own supporters at Wembley. Scottish players prefer Hampden Park and the Welsh, well wherever. For Northern Irish players it is Windsor Park in Belfast. But in 1972, Sammy McIlroy's dreams were shattered by the violence of the times – and what violence. 1972 was the most bloody year in over three decades of conflict, with 467 violent deaths. It was the year of over 10,500 shootings; nearly 2,000 terrorist bombs and over 27 tons of explosives recovered by the security forces. It was the year of Bloody Sunday when 13 unarmed men were shot dead and 17 others wounded by the Parachute Regiment in Derry. It was the year the British government imposed direct rule from Westminster to replace the Northern Ireland parliament at

Stormont. It was the year of Bloody Friday when the Provisional IRA set off 26 bombs in Belfast, killing 11 people and wounding over 130 others. Getting to work was difficult and dangerous during these early years of the conflict. Personally, I witnessed buildings getting blown up in front of me as I walked to work and I was in the offices of the Unionist morning daily newspaper, the *News Letter*, when they were attacked in an IRA bombing. Six people died and over 100 were injured as they were lured towards the 100lb car-bomb by a cruel hoax call. Belfast was considered too dangerous to entertain visiting international football teams. As a consequence, during 1972, 1973 and 1974, Northern Ireland played their 'home' fixtures at English League grounds.

Sammy McIlroy's first appearance in front of a home crowd at Windsor Park was his eighth cap. It came in March 1975 against Yugoslavia – and, funnily enough, when McIlroy was making his 57th appearance for Northern Ireland in June 1982 alongside the 17-year-old Norman Whiteside, Yugoslavia were the opposition. The significance of the occasion was that it was Northern Ireland's first game in the World Cup finals in Spain. Northern Ireland had not appeared in the finals since the heroics of Harry Gregg *et al* in 1958. Group Five was made up of Honduras, Yugoslavia, Spain and Northern Ireland. Against Yugoslavia the Irish set out to gain a draw and did so quite efficiently, although they should have had a penalty when the youngest player ever to appear in the World Cup finals, Norman Whiteside (17 years 41 days,) was upended in the penalty box. In the second game, they drew with Honduras who had managed a draw with the host nation in their first match. The final group game for Northern Ireland was against Spain in Valencia – and many mistakenly believed it would be their final game of the tournament. The date was 25 June 1982.

25 June 1982. Northern Ireland v. Spain at Luis Casanova, Valencia. Attendance 49,562. (Won 1–0)

TEAM: **Jennings; Nicholl J., Donaghy, Nicholl C., McClelland, McCreery, O'Neill, McIlroy (Cassidy), Armstrong (1), Hamilton W., Whiteside (Nelson).**

This was pure 'Roy-of-the-Rovers' heroics out of a comic-book! It was theatre! It was the most dramatic game in the history of Northern Ireland international football. Out there on the pitch and in front of a partisan crowd of Spanish supporters, the bunch of no-hopers from the Emerald Isle conjured up the most majestic of performances and in the most dramatic style. Victory was achieved in spite of the loss of defender Mal Donaghy after 61 minutes, sent off for the most innocuous touchline push on Camacho, 'the

Commanche'. If he deliberately performed the dying swan routine with a view to improving his side's chances of putting one over on the Irish, then he scored only a partial success. Donaghy got the red card alright – but the ten-man Irish side fought like demons to frustrate part two of the Camacho plan. For half an hour Jennings performed wonders in goal as his defence battled with the frustrated Spanish forwards, taking great care not to throw themselves into careless challenges. Author Chris Freddi, in *The Complete Book of the World Cup*, published in 1998, described the Irish win over Spain as 'arguably the best performance by a British team in any World Cup'. Praise indeed, and from an impartial source. Of course, we Irish knew this already! The game was scoreless at half-time but just two minutes after the restart, Hamilton went on a long sweeping run down the right wing. He got to the goal line. His low cross was hit with considerable force and was curling away from the Spanish goalkeeper Arkonada. The Spanish keeper dived forward and got his outstretched right hand to the ball – but succeeded only in palming it into the path of the advancing Gerry Armstrong. The West Belfast man – a reserve player for Watford who had just won promotion from the Second Division – did not hesitate in smashing the ball low and hard past the still-recovering Spanish goalkeeper and into the net. The island of Ireland trembled, such was the scale of joyous celebration in homes and bars as an entire population bounced up and down on mother earth. Drink was spilled, strangers were hugged and hangovers next day were overcome by the communal sense of achievement. At work, my boss still declined to order up my travel tickets. 'If they win through the next round,' he said.

Sammy McIlroy was one of the heroes of a June night in Valencia. A few minutes after the Armstrong goal, Sammy was taken off – replaced by Tommy Cassidy. McIlroy had endured a series of heavy tackles that left him with scars down his legs. For the final 30 minutes of the game he was on the substitutes' bench watching his team-mates battle to take Northern Ireland into the quarter-finals for the second time. 'It was a marvellous night for us,' he recalled. 'I think we confounded all the experts with our determination and our ability to play together as a team and to achieve what we did. The Spanish were cutting up a bit rough as their own fans began to get on their backs. We were successfully defending everything they had to throw at us. Even after Mal was sent off we still held the line in defence as the Spaniards fought for an equaliser. There was one brilliant moment in the second half when big Pat [Jennings] managed to very skilfully avoid giving away a penalty by putting his hand out and flipping the ball over the head of Juanito. In the end I think the Spanish were happy enough to lose only by one goal – another goal from us would have put them out of the tournament.' As it was, history was made. This was, and is, Northern

Ireland's only victory over Spain. That 'night in Valencia' will forever live in the memories of the heroic players who did battle and who rarely had such a world stage upon which to demonstrate their abilities. Simply put, this was the zenith of international football for Northern Ireland and its memory for fans and players alike is a sustaining one for a football nation which has since struggled to repeat such a heady achievement.

Life after United was perhaps never as fulfilling for Sammy McIlroy but he played 133 games for Stoke before two spells with the 'bitter Blues', two spells with Bury, two spells abroad with teams in Sweden and Austria and finally concluding his playing career with Preston North End. After that he went into management with Northwich Victoria and then on to Macclesfield Town in 1993, where he succeeded in bringing them into League football and got them promoted into Division Two.

Watching him in action on the training ground with the Macclesfield players, it is clear he enjoys his work and that his players enjoy being with him. Macclesfield were part-time when Sammy arrived and trained twice a week. Today they have a reserve team and 46 players on their books. Like Leicester City's Martin O'Neill from the 1982 World Cup side, Sammy McIlroy is building something of a reputation as a manager, a good team motivator working with limited resources. In my estimation, one day one of the two of them will manage the Northern Ireland side. McIlroy says the past five years have been a wonderful learning curve and that, yes, he does have ambitions to go on to greater things and eventually when and if the right move comes along it will be given careful consideration. But what about the fact that an Englishman, Lawrie McMenemy, and a Scotsman, Joe Jordan, currently have control of the Northern Ireland team along with our own Pat Jennings? McIlroy was quite candid in his response: 'To be honest I never thought, and don't take this the wrong way . . . I never thought I'd see an Englishman manage Northern Ireland. In my time they were all Irish – people like Billy Bingham, Danny Blanchflower, Terry Neill and Dave Clemence. I always thought that would be the way but football has changed. It makes it that little bit like . . . well, put it this way, Lawrie McMenemy was assistant manager of England not that long ago. So that's a bit of a shock but I am sure he'll do his best and I wish him all the best.' But when I pressed him on whether or not it would have been preferable to keep the Northern Ireland manager's job 'in-house' the Macclesfield boss said: 'It's the way of society, the way everything is going. The way they [the IFA] have looked at it is that they have tried Brian Hamilton and Gerry Armstrong since the Bingham era and now they think Lawrie McMenemy is the man. He is experienced. And they have my old mate Joe Jordan there as well after years of knocking lumps out of us. Big Pat is there as the goalkeeping coach – I just hope they'll do well.' Perhaps one day, it will all be in Sammy's control. 'You wait and see,' he told me, 'there's plenty of time for that!'

REASON TO BELIEVE: Sammy McIlroy and Roy Keane make up the midfield. McIlroy enjoyed the best seasons of his career at Old Trafford in midfield, having replaced another Irishman in that position, Gerry Daly. He began as a striker, scoring a goal against the 'Bitter Blues' on his debut, his opportunity to score aided and abetted by his mentor, George Best. McIlroy overcame the media comparisons with Best to create his own individuality at United. Watching McIlroy from the terraces, you could have been forgiven for thinking that his slight frame risked mutilation against strong tackling defenders. That he seemed to be approaching these hatchet men in a somewhat cumbersome manner. Yet, again and again, just when you considered closing your eyes to avoid the dreaded collision, McIlroy's nimble foot skills would take him past opponents and into their 'danger zone'. For one of the best examples of the McIlroy footwork, study the wonderfully executed equaliser against Arsenal in the 1979 FA Cup final. It is a gem of a goal – unfortunately it is sadly lost to the memories of most people, who look back on the 'five-minute' Cup final because of the winning Arsenal goal moments after McIlroy's equaliser.

SAMMY McILROY: THE QUESTIONNAIRE
BORN: Belfast – 2 August 1954.

Which junior clubs did you play for – and during what years?
Mersey Street School & Ashfield Secondary 1966–69.

Which club did you support as a boy?
Linfield, Rangers, Manchester United.

Was it always your ambition to be a professional footballer?
Yes.

Do you recall the moment you first realised you were signing for United? Describe your reaction to being taken on by such a big club.
At first, very exciting. I told everyone that I was going to join Man Utd.

Tagged as the last 'Busby Babe', what was your experience of Sir Matt?
Great man to me. He *was* Manchester United.

United were relegated in 1974. Describe your feelings. Was there any doubt that you would stay, and did you have any offers from other clubs?
No offers. I had no thoughts of leaving. When we went down it was a horrible feeling of letting the fans down.

You made your debut against Man City in front of 63,000 supporters at Maine Road, aged 17. Did you know you were going to play? Describe your feelings on that day, especially when you scored.
I knew at eleven o'clock that morning [6 November 1971] of the game. I felt a bit nervous but once the game started, no problem.

You played 390 games – which one stands out in the memory – and why?
The debut, scoring and of course it was against Man City.

You were only 27 when Atkinson let you go. Were you suprised?
Yes. But I acted a bit hasty. I know I could have stayed – but my pride was hurt when he said I could go.

The best manager you played for at Old Trafford – and the worst?
Tommy Docherty, the best. Very hard to say who was the worst.

The highlight of your football career? When, where etc.?
First cap for Northern Ireland against Spain at Hull City's ground, due to the troubles back home.

You made your international debut in 1972 against Spain. Describe your feelings on that day.
Very excited – but I wished it could have been in Belfast.

Your worst moment at Old Trafford – and why?
Relegation – and leaving after 13 years.

Which individual was the biggest influence on your career – first as a player and secondly as a manager?
George Best as a player. Tommy Docherty as manager.

Your best game for United? (When, where and against whom?)
Perhaps against Wolves at Old Trafford. We won 5–0 and I scored three. [3 August 1981]

Your worst game for United? (When, where and against whom?)
Ipswich Town, away, when we lost 6–1. [Actual score was 6–0 and Gary Bailey saved TWO penalties!! On 1 March 1980.]

Pick your greatest ever Man Utd team. (And give a few comments to explain if possible.)
Schmeichel; Irwin, Pallister, Buchan, Dunne, Crerand, Robson, Charlton, Cantona, Law, Best.

You were at Old Trafford at a time when there were many players from Northern Ireland and the Republic of Ireland. Did this add to the enjoyment of playing at Old Trafford? Or did it cause difficulties?
There was a great spirit at the club then. We were all friends.

Best player you ever saw in a United shirt? And why?
George Best – he had everything!

The most difficult opponent you ever faced? (Example of game – with year and competition if possible.)
Kevin Beattie, Ipswich Town in 1975 at Old Trafford. [United won 1–0 on 20 September 1975 and Houston scored the winning goal.]

The best game for your country – and the worst?
Best, against Wales in the Home Championships. Worst, against Finland away in the World Cup.

How did you regard the Man Utd fans?
The greatest!

Why do you think they remained so loyal throughout the years when they so desperately wanted a League title but had to watch for 26 years as Liverpool dominated?
That's why they are the best. They knew it would change.

Did the fans' desire for a League Championship ever put pressure on the players? Do you think it might in some way have contributed to the failure to win the title for 26 years?
Yes. More because of the pressure on the players and the club to provide attacking football, sometimes at the cost of a more clinical approach to winning.

Your views on the team selected for this book?
Your selection is a very good side. Would win a lot of games.

How difficult was it for you to respond to the predictable comparisons with George Best? Before you established you as yourself, there was the 'new George Best' label – did it not really annoy you?
Yes. For me there was only one Best. I did not let it bother me.

EIGHT

Roy Keane

(MIDFIELD MAGICIAN AND CLUB CAPTAIN)

Manchester United: 1993–present: 215 (10) games: 25 goals

DEBUT: **15 August 1993 v. Norwich City at Carrow Road. (Won 2–0)**

TEAM: **Schmeichel; Parker, Irwin, Bruce, Kanchelskis, Pallister, Robson (1), Ince, Keane, Hughes, Giggs (1).**

HONOURS: **League Championship 1993–94; 1995–96; 1996–97; 1998–99**
FA Cup 1993–94; 1995–96; 1998–99
European Champions' Cup 1998–99
Republic of Ireland (43 caps 1991–present)

> Roy Keane's magic – he wears a magic hat
> And when he saw Old Trafford, he said I fancy that
> He could have signed for Arsenal or Blackburn – but they're
>   shite
> So he signed for Man United 'cos we're f***ing dynamite

The air was as blue as the 'bitters' shirts. At least it was in my living-room as I tried to come to terms with the fact that the 'bitter' bastards were 2–0 ahead at half-time in our first 'derby' game of the season – away at their midden. Niall Quinn had thus far contrived to ruin my Sunday afternoon enjoyment of Sky's 'live' television coverage. The Republic of Ireland international had bagged two goals. It was our 14th game of the Premier League campaign and in the previous 13 we had won all but two – one lost and one drawn. As United fans everywhere braced themselves for humiliation at the hands of our sworn enemy, I was on my knees, beating the carpet in utter frustration, as the players beat a half-time retreat to the changing-rooms to face what presumably would be a 'Fergie special'. In my rage I was unaware of what our players were having to endure as they trudged off Maine Road's 'theatre of nightmares', where the previous year

I had quietly relieved myself at a corner flag whilst filming on the pitch for the BBC2 investigative sports programme *On The Line*. I would like to say I thought it might bring them luck — but that would be stretching the truth to breaking point. Anyway, as it happens, it would take five years and a journey from Belfast to Dublin to get the inside track on the half-time scene at Maine Road on 7 November 1993.

It was on Monday, 9 February 1999 that I set off to meet Roy Keane and Denis Irwin at the Republic of Ireland's team hotel near Dublin airport — prior to their friendly two days later with Paraguay. The appointment to meet them was made the previous Thursday when Keano phoned my house — persuaded to do so the previous morning by my good friend Sean Connolly from Altrincham. I had lived next door to Sean when working for two years in Manchester and when I revealed my difficulties in getting in touch with Keane and Irwin he announced that he saw Keano most mornings as they dropped their daughters off at school. Salvation! I asked Sean to deliver a letter personally for me. To be truthful, I had been warned by some with previous experience that a direct and unsolicited approach to the Cork-born Keane could be injurious to my health. Consequently, I had some time earlier made my initial approach to Roy Keane by sending a letter explaining the context of this book and seeking his co-operation. Norman Whiteside very kindly offered to deliver it in person on my behalf. I knew he had received the correspondence because Keane completed and returned my questionnaire. But two letters to Old Trafford in an effort to arrange an interview had drawn no response — until Sean offered to help. It worked a treat. Keano was as good as his word. At the prearranged time he arrived in reception and we found a quiet corner for a chat.

He was charming, warm, friendly and nothing like the terrier who defends the good name of United with such vigour and passion on the field of play (some would have you believe corner-boy brutality). But if this was the wild man of football, then I was Ghengis Khan. There had been stories — the court case involving a girl from his home city of Cork, whom he allegedly called a 'whore', springs to mind. It was further alleged that he attempted to beat up her boyfriend. She sued. It was four years before a court ruled in Keane's favour. The incident was alleged to have happened in May 1991 when the 19-year-old Keane had returned to Cork following his first full season in professional football in England. It provided him with an unwanted and he would say unwarranted reputation.

At this point, it is only fair to point out that in Ireland there is a strange type of pastime. Those who advance out of their own community to become rich, famous and/or successful are all too often subjected to the distorted judgements and values of some of those they left behind — the culture of 'let us knock him/her off his/her pedestal' – no doubt motivated by jealousy or a need to feel important. The Irish refer to this breed of individuals as 'begrudgers'. Roy Keane was not the first, nor will he be the last, to suffer from such homespun petty hatreds. When such feelings are added to the goldfish bowl existence of top footballers, it is perhaps understandable why they might occasionally hit out and earn themselves a reputation for petulance. There is no doubt that Roy Keane had such a reputation for a time – even though there was nothing on the scale of Stan Collymore's very public beating of Ulrika Jonsson in Paris during World Cup '98. So, before going on to discuss his first 'derby' game against City, I put it to him that he appeared to have gone from wild man and pub brawler to family man, if not country gent. He fielded the question well.

First off, he said he 'would not go that far'. But then he explained: 'My first two or three years were great. Then I had one or two scrapes off and on the field and obviously the press had a new image for me. I was this new kid coming through and then I was the bad boy. But honestly, them things don't bother me. At the moment I am the goody two shoes I suppose, settled down and I've got a cigar and slippers at home – but nah, that's just the way the press build you up. I think maybe I have settled, but I think it's like any normal thing, I'm a lot wiser now than what I was ten years ago. I'm a lot wiser but that's not to say I'm not going to make mistakes or I'm not going to walk away from certain situations. I like to think I can do more and walk away and see things before they happen, whereas before if there was trouble I'd probably hit first and ask questions later. Now I try and look at the situation before I get involved.' Captain Sensible then. Certainly on the evidence of my meeting with the 'engine-room' of the United midfield, and bear in mind the dire warnings I had received about his volatile nature and deep distrust of reporters, it was clear there must have been a trip down the road to Damascus. That, of course, presupposes that his reputation was entirely justified. The Roy Keane I met behaved in an entirely rational and mature manner, thus creating the impression that here, indeed, was a worthy Captain of Manchester United. Here was a man at peace with himself and who was prepared to speak candidly about his career at Old Trafford and, more importantly, about his future there. Any suggestion that he still has a problem controlling his temper can be put to bed this current season because during the 1998–99 campaign Keano played a staggering 52 games, with two as substitute, and was sent off once during the FA Cup semi-final classic with the 'Gooners'.

But I digress. Back to his heroic deeds at Maine Road on 7 November 1993. His role in making history. His role in making my life bearable in a week of unbearable events. It was now that I became enlightened.

Apparently as Keano and the other United players left the pitch at half-time they were walking on a carpet of Turkish Delight so thoughtfully provided by followers of that really 'big' club. The 'Bitter Blue' supporters were reminding Peter Schmeichel, Paul Parker, Denis Irwin, Steve Bruce, Lee Sharpe, Gary Pallister, Eric Cantona, Paul Ince, Roy Keane, Mark Hughes and Andre Kanchelskis of the fact that four days earlier on 3 November, United had been put out of the European Cup by the Turkish champions. 'I'd only been at the club a couple of months,' Captain Keane told me. 'We had just been knocked out of Europe by Galatasaray the Wednesday before so we were obviously disappointed. But at least we did well to get back at City and that was a good game, but that was a few years ago to be fair, six years ago I think it was. But I remember that at half-time all the City fans were chucking Turkish Delights at us. But then at the end of the game to win 3–2 was great. I think, well, we've played a lot more important games since then but supporters actually keep bringing it up. I wouldn't mind if it was the European Cup final or something but it was just a league match if you look at it that way. But yeah, 2–0 down and to win 3–2 was great, to be fair.' Was great, to be fair? Jesus, that barely does it justice. Victory over the 'Shitty' is essential for the wellbeing of the good name of United. On such outcomes are peoples' lives enriched or devalued.

Normally, it is just the result of 'derby' games that counts – not the manner in which they were achieved. However, on this November day, it was the manner of the achievement as much as the result itself. We were on our knees in the first half and yet recovered in the second half with two superb goals from Eric the King, the leader of our football team and the greatest centre-forward the world has ever seen. Twice he stabbed 'Shitty' in the heart. As the game moved seemingly inexorably towards a remarkable 2–2 draw, Ince took the ball in midfield, drew a defender in before slipping a short ball to Sharpe. A neat back-heel lay-off from Sharpe took a couple of their defenders out of the game and put Irwin into space on the left wing. His left-foot cross curled its way through the Maine Road evening air, evading low-flying defenders and their goalkeeper to reach the rapidly approaching Roy Keane at the far post. Even moving at such speed, he was able to hit the ball first time as he stretched out his right leg, sending it low and hard into the bottom right-hand corner of their net. Ecstasy! It was the 87th minute. Keano's momentum threatened to take him into the first row of seats behind the goal. But as his body lurched downwards to the right he managed to recover his balance and set off on a run towards the very corner flag where I had 'done the business'. No way back for 'Shitty'. Life suddenly turned sweet, holding no fears for United fans next day at work. Lo and behold, the man who spurned Arsenal and Blackburn to become a favourite of the fans at Old Trafford used this 'derby' debut to signal his potential to become a genuine 24-carat M.U. gold nugget – someone shaping up in the Bryan Robson mould.

At this point, dear readers, if you are of the cynical breed, the type of person who has grown weary of listening to professional footballers spin lines of bullshit about their expectations, disappointments, abilities and influences on the rest of the team, then look away now. Otherwise you may find yourself being disappointed by Captain Keane's refreshing air of humility. In spite of the words of his anthem, it became clear he does not believe he is magic. When asked to comment on the amount of energy he puts into a game the Captain's answer was as follows: 'Well that's the kind of player I am. You see world-class players who have a quiet game but then just turn it on and do something brilliant but I'm not capable of doing that. It's a fact and I'm not being critical of myself, I'm not capable of doing something magical, so my strength is my work-rate and if I don't have that I may as well pack the game in. So I need to do that and that's one of my strengths – to keep going when maybe others don't.' It is pointed out that he is being harsh on himself and that he is ignoring the versatility he has displayed at Old Trafford, even giving a bloody good impression of a right-back when faced with that particular challenge not long after he signed. He recalled the occasion: 'That's when I had a hernia problem. I was actually supposed to play about two or three matches and it ended up being nearly the whole season. The operation was put off and off and anyway I ended up playing quite a few matches at right-back because I was having problems with my hernia and they said it wouldn't be as stressful playing right-back. I was supposed to have the operation, I think, in October. I ended up having it at the end of that season after we won the 'double', so it was worth putting off, don't get me wrong, because I felt if I played at right-back it wouldn't be as strenuous as in midfield and I quite enjoyed right-back. I could be a full-back until I was 45 I think!' Try telling that to poor Tony Dunne! In any event, it was clear from the outset Roy Keane was displaying the kind of qualities most appreciated by United fans – that he would go through any pain barrier and risk life and limb for the sake of the team.

Why, though, had he chosen to do this in the United cause, rather than for Arsenal or Blackburn? 'Do I really need to explain?' he replied. No, Roy, your answer says it all. Your predecessor Bryan Robson could not have put it better himself.

Suddenly this interview was proceeding with all the speed of a Keane run from defence to attack. Having established his depth of motivation as a player, it seemed natural to move on to his depth of commitment to the United cause given recent media speculation about his 'threat' to move on if a contract cannot be agreed. Captain Keane is very clear on his position: 'People keep bringing it up. The press ask me questions. I think there's a meeting due in about two or three weeks' time. I know contract talks can go on for weeks or months or whatever, or it can be sorted out in one afternoon, but fingers crossed, I'll probably see it go to the summer. The fans have been good to me, the club has been good to me, but then I'd like to think I've done well for United in my six years there so far. But as I said before, from another point of view, as happy as I am there, it's an important contract for me and I think the club know my position – my contract is up next year.' No one at United wants to lose Keane – although the speculation that he is seeking £45,000 a week has prompted some supporters to write to fanzines suggesting where he can stick that demand. The reality of the situation is that Keane sees this as his last negotiation before signing a contract that will keep him at United for the rest of his career. So naturally he attaches great importance to the new talks: 'I think if I do sign in the summer – I'm 27 and I'll be 28 in August, so I'm sure the club will be looking at four or five years, obviously, because of the Bosman ruling. I think generally, this would be it for me. It would be a contract to see me through to 32 or 33. You know there are very few players that are playing that little bit further. But I think the position I play in and the type of player I am, I think you're looking at 32 to 33 – so this is really my last contract. This is why it's important that it's right for me. I have said all along if it's right, you know I would have signed it yesterday, but these things take time. Contract talks can drag on but I won't be asking for the world. I know what I want. I know what players are getting and I'll try and be realistic and hopefully the club will be the same. I don't want to leave.'

Indeed, after our conversation I noticed in the official Manchester United magazine, *United*, manager Alex Ferguson had taken the trouble to go into print to say Keane will not be leaving Old Trafford! The answer will be known by the time this book is published – but my prediction is that the club will make sure that Captain Keane is still a United player for many years to come. It would not take a rocket scientist to work out the costs of replacing him on the open market compared to signing him up for the remainder of his career at a substantial wage increase. Not forgetting, of course, his contribution to the cause of winning trophies and securing United's future in the new Europe which is slowly, if somewhat regrettably, beginning to take on the back-door look of a European Super League. Of course, at the time of writing, it is the quest for European glory that dominates Captain Keane's perspective on life. The European Cup, the pursuit of the Premier League title and FA Cup are paramount. He wants to concentrate on making this the most remarkable season in Manchester United's history.

Our conversation moves on to the prospects of European success in general and to the forthcoming visit of Inter Milan to Old Trafford in particular. This tie has got fans salivating on one level, but fearful on another. Are the players frightened or confident? 'Frightened would be the wrong word,' Captain Keane responds. 'We obviously respect them. They have some world-class players.' So, come on Roy, what is going to be the score? 'Fingers crossed,' he said, 'it is important that we – and it is easier said than done – try not to concede a goal at home. We obviously want to win the game but it is important not to give them an away-goal. One– or two–nil would be a great result and would give us something to go over there to defend.'

Keano was not a bad judge. On 3 March at Old Trafford we won 2–0 and in the return two weeks later we qualified for the semi-finals with a tremendous 1–1 draw. These were two landmark European performances in a season already packed with some great Euro-results – 11 goals against Brondby, two drawn games against Bayern Munich and those fantastic, hard-on-the-ticker, 3–3 home-and-away draws against Barcelona. Mind you, while the rest of the football world viewed the tussles with Barca as two 'cracking' games, Captain Keane had a different opinion: 'People say that, but I don't think it was that great to play in because we didn't play that well, to be honest, in each game. We played well in the first half at Old Trafford but then we let them back into it. I'm probably being overcritical of the team. But conceding three goals over there – you have to remember they needed to win and I think they had about nine up front for the whole of the second half. So like a friendly match it's probably great to be neutral but personally I didn't think we played well, defensively anyway. Obviously it will go down as one of the great games . . . it doesn't matter at the end of the day – we got through from the group which obviously was the most important thing. If we can entertain along the way that's good.' Entertain? That does not do justice to the range of emotions we endured during these two epic games. But then United fans have become well accustomed to the pressures of trying to regain the European Cup.

Two years earlier we faced our quarter-final first-leg game against FC Porto at Old Trafford without Roy Keane. Porto had an awesome reputation that season and we were prepared for the worst as we walked to the ground. Such was the compelling presence of Keano on the pitch that we began to doubt our ability to dispose of the Portuguese team – and this was when 'King Eric' was in the side. But it was one of those nights when we surpassed ourselves. Along with my son Steven we stood before kick-off absorbing the atmosphere. My other son Jason was in a different part of the ground. The pub chat before our arrival at the 'Theatre of Dreams' was that without Keano the Portuguese side would make our lives hell. The game got under way. After 22 minutes

United went ahead with a David May goal. Our throats had no time to recover when the second goal came in the 34th minute, courtesy of 'Le Dieu' himself. The best player on the pitch got our third in the 61st minute – Ryan Giggs after a delightful 50-yard through ball from Cantona to Cole who then fed Giggs. Fortified with the pints from before the game we were by now in orbit. But there was another little surprise in store when Andy Cole completed a wonderful 4–0 rout of the champions of Portugal. From 'no Roy Keane' to 'who the f**k are FC Porto?' That was the mood of the moment. We even taunted our visitors with a couple of chants inquiring as to whether or not they were City in disguise. Now face to face with the man missing from that night's victory, I had to find out where he had been during the action on the pitch. Was he there at all? Or was he lying at home injured watching on television? He was there alright. 'I would have been at the match,' he recalls, 'but you just watch it in one of the boxes because you can't really go on the bench, especially in Europe since you're allowed so many substitutes. I actually watched it up in the Sharp suite and again I think we would have settled for 1–0 or 2–0, never mind 4–0, and lucky enough I came on for the second leg – but to be fair it was all over by then so it was a nice game to come back for.'

Talking of comebacks, it is clear to this writer, and United fans everywhere, that Keano's greatest ever comeback has been this season, 1998–99. After his damaging, career-threatening injury against Leeds United last season, we flattered to deceive as we pursued three trophies without Keano. History is marked by the fact that we won zilch, surrendering the League to Arsenal who then compounded our misery by winning the FA Cup as well against the greetin' Geordies. At first we did not seem to miss the Cork man – leading the League table by something like 13 points at one stage and heading for the European and FA Cup finals. But in the end, we had no teeth to bite in midfield. Without Keane to win our battles, we lost the war by succumbing in all three competitions. This season it is different – Keane has been an inspiration. No, not just an inspiration – but a leader of men, a sensational engine giving Manchester United strength and durability. At this moment of writing – 24 April 1999 – Keano has just given one of the performances of the season in Turin against the mighty Juventus. We went there with a 1–1 home leg draw. Not to mention a record of having scored just twice on Italian soil. The first time was in the eighties when Whiteside scored in a game against Juve that we lost. The second came earlier in this current campaign on 17 March when we travelled to Inter Milan with a 2–0 lead and Scholes got the goal in a 1–1 draw which sent us through to the semi-final against Juventus. At Old

Trafford Zidane and Davids ran the show for 25 first-half minutes and to be truthful, they were worthy of more than just one goal. With ten minutes gone of the away game, they were doing the same as Juventus strolled into a two-goal lead. But even at this point, I did not fear defeat because I just had this feeling we would recover just as the great 1968 European Cup-winning team did in the semi-final away leg against Real Madrid when they were 3–1 down at half-time and recovered to draw 3–3. The 1–0 home leg win gave us passage to the final. On Wednesday night past (21 April) Roy Keane and Nicky Butt took control of midfield and neutered the power of Davids and Zidane. Keano got our first goal – what better way to inspire as team captain than to put one into the opposition net? This colossus of a man ran himself ragged defending and setting up attacks as United fought back to win in sensational style, 3–2. Surely one of the greatest ever comebacks in European football history. Sadly though, along with Scholes he got a booking that puts both players out of the team for the European Cup final in Barcelona on 26 May. But because of the way the team is playing at the moment, there seems to be an attitude that if you kick one of them, you kick all 22 in the squad.

Captain Keano certainly believes the team spirit is tremendous at the moment and he views it as a crucial factor in shaping a side capable of winning championships and cups. It is, according to Keano, the spirit of the great 'double'-winning side of the 1993–94 season. 'That was the season Alan Hansen said "You can't win anything with kids",' he reflected with an enormous grin, 'and I think he's probably been reminded of that. I think that was the best United team I have played in. But the team we have now, squad wise, is probably a lot stronger. It has the potential to match the 1993–94 team. Normally it takes a few years for teams to prove themselves and we've had three or four new players and you have to give them a chance to prove themselves. I think the way we're playing at the moment, we are capable of achieving what the '94 team won but it's easier said than done. It is one thing having the potential but you've got to do it and, fingers crossed, we can do it this year.'

Those new signings – Dwight Yorke, Jesper Blomqvist and Jaap Stam – have proved to be essential assets to a team competing once again for a unique 'treble' of League and FA Cup 'double' along with the European Cup. 'Dwight Yorke has been fantastic,' said Keano, 'but to be fair so too have Jaap and Jesper.' Stam's United career got off to a very shaky start in the Charity Shield at Wembley where Arsenal tore us apart to win 3–0, a feat they repeated a few weeks later in the League at Highbury. At the time Alex Ferguson's purchase of Stam for just over £10m was being viewed as excessive for a player who did not have a good World Cup and who had been made to look positively donkey-like in his early games in a United shirt. However, as we all know now, Stam has been a star performer this season. As Keano puts it: 'He's done very well this season. But I think people were jumping on the criticism bandwagon. It was a lot of money – but that's been going on for years. But you shouldn't judge him so quickly. Judge him in four or five years' time, that's when I think you can judge a player at a club and I hope Jaap can do as well as the previous centre-halves Brucie and Pally. Remember Pally when he first came, he struggled for a while and Jaap's actually done quite well, so if he keeps going at the progress he's going, he'll go down as one of the greats – fingers crossed! But as I said, people were judging him after one or two games, even the Charity Shield, his first game, and it was unfair. I am sure he was expecting it you know, all big money signings are going to be criticised no matter how well they do and in the last few months anyway, he's definitely proved his worth.'

Any thoughts that the Wizard might have done better to keep Gary Pallister at United for another season to help Stam find his feet were quickly rubbished by Captain Keano. In his view, Pallister would not have been happy sitting on the bench as cover for Stam. 'Middlesbrough is his home team,' said Keano, 'and I think United wanted to reward Pally for his services. He deserves more than becoming a squad player, if you know what I mean. At this stage of his career Pally still wants to be playing. He had a few injuries last year and the club thought the offer of two million was too good to turn away. And how can anybody question our manager's judgements on the transfer business . . . well, I think in 25 years you can count on one hand how many bad buys or bad deals he's made. So I wouldn't question Pallister's sale if it is put that way.' Pallister's departure from Old Trafford was a mirror image of what happened to his old partner in defence two years earlier. Club captain Steve Bruce could see the writing on the wall when it came to the end of the double 'double'-winning season, 1995–96. He was dropped for the final League game at Middlesbrough and for the FA Cup final. Faced with the choice of becoming a 'bench' player, Bruce accepted the opportunity to leave United on a 'free' transfer and signed for Birmingham City. His place in the '96 Cup final went to David May and although this was largely a very disappointing game, it was one in which Roy Keane gave the type of performance that has become his benchmark. It was, undoubtedly, one of his best performances in a United shirt.

FA Cup final: 11 May 1996 v. Liverpool at Wembley Stadium. (Won 1–0)
TEAM: Schmeichel; Irwin, Neville P., May, Keane, Pallister, Cantona (1),
      Beckham (Neville G.), Cole (Scholes), Butt, Giggs.

Roy Keane collected the Man-of-the-Match award. But ask any fan what sticks out in the memory of this game and universally they will speak of the wondrous strike by 'Le Dieu' that brought United an unprecedented second 'double' in two seasons. It is certainly what Roy Keane remembers. 'I got the Man-of-the-Match but I think Eric deserved it just for that goal alone,' said Keano, adding: 'It was a great goal. He was the best player I have ever played with. Don't get me wrong, there were some other great players as well. But I think what Eric did for the club as an individual – and I know Robbo was a great player for 12 years or whatever, Brucie and Pally in their own right were great players for United. However, what Eric did with regard to winning trophies and the knack of scoring important goals stands out. He scored so many goals to win the 'double'. That goal against Liverpool at Wembley, I just don't think anyone else would have been capable of scoring that goal. So as an individual he was a legend, to be fair.'

Legendary performances are Cantona's legacy at United, but Keano is our living legend. Week in, week out, we have witnessed the Cork dynamo construct his own legendary status. The 1996 FA Cup final performance was one of sheer class. He patrolled the middle of the wide Wembley turf and seized control. It was clear from his crunching tackles in the opening minutes that he was determined to run the show. The Liverpool midfield of McManaman and Redknapp was rendered clueless by Keane's stamina, courage and ability to lead our attacks from defensive positions. The Scousers looked on from the safety of their seats as their so-called midfield heroes were shown up to lack the heart and courage to get stuck into Keano. The yellow streak still runs through their team today as Keano regularly scares the shit out of Scousers, usually winning his personal battle with former side-kick, Paul 'Big Time Charley' Ince. Keano regards himself as a defensive midfield player but we all know he is much more than that. He is 'cool' on the ball and has the knack of being so composed as to make it look as though he has time to slow the game down, time to look around and decide which option he wants to take.

Having taken over from his hero Eric as the club captain, Keane has shown signs of maturity that in turn has illuminated another key quality – inspirational leadership. Watch him closely during a game and he is constantly roaming all over the pitch, shouting at miscreants who yield possession and then encouraging others to concentrate and commit to the United cause. No one can doubt his commitment. Some doubted his temperament, with good cause. He is quick to point out that any attempt to tame his aggression will result in a less effective player. He is equally quick to point out that he has found a means of curbing his temper. Consequently, perhaps in this season we have begun to see the emergence of a natural born leader who will guide United to success for many years to come – and, of course, the Republic of Ireland.

Republic of Ireland International (38 caps 1991–present)
DEBUT: **22 May 1991 v. Chile in Dublin. (Drew 1–1)**
TEAM: **Peyton; Hughton, Staunton, O'Leary (McGrath), Moran, Townsend, Keane, Houghton (McLoughlin), Sheridan, Kelly D. (1), Sheedy (Cascarino).**

You always remember the first time you had sex. Even if you do not, because of extenuating circumstances such as an over-abundance of alcohol, remember who you scored with. But you certainly will remember the first goal you scored in a properly organised game. You know what I mean, the first game where you turned out in a proper team kit, smelling of liniment, high on the fumes and where there is a proper referee in the black tunic – and most important of all, where there are proper nets attached to the goalposts. My first goal in such a game was for Blairgowrie High School in Perthshire in 1964 – a thing of Bobby Charlton-esque beauty, a left-foot special from about 25 yards which hit the underside of the bar before sending the net billowing outwards – like a caged animal trying to escape. I can remember my trial at Dundee where I put two goals past their keeper on the Dens Park pitch from outside the area. I can remember my greatest-ever goal for an Aberfoyle team in 1968. This moment of pure soccer genius came after I had already hit one home from 25 yards. With my back to the goal, I received the ball on the edge of the area, just inside the 'D'. Turning to face their defence I deftly dribbled the ball at great speed from one foot to the other in order to avoid the tackles of three or four defenders – similar, I suppose, to Giggs's run and dribble against Arsenal in the FA Cup semi-final replay this season. Then, as their keeper advanced, a deft shimmy of the shoulders sent him down the road for a fish supper as I chipped the ball over his almost prostrate body for a sensational goal. It was very similar to one George Best scored during his spell in American football, a goal he describes in great detail elsewhere in this book. You just do not forget such moments. They are important in your development.

If I had gone on to represent my country, I would certainly have savoured the debut match – would recall every detail of every pass, every movement, every tackle and every foul. But the point of this history lesson about my failed football career is to report what Roy Keane told me about his international debut: 'Of course I was very proud but it was just another game to me.' This tells you a lot about the man and his approach to the game. For him, it is clearly one game at a time and as a professional player he simply goes out on to the pitch to do what he is paid to do. No sentiment. Little emotion. Just performance. And, of course, the result has priority because clearly, in Keano's thinking, the end justifies the means. Consider this comment about his heroic showing in the rather disappointing spectacle that was the '96 Cup final: 'It was a great match. People say to me it was a bad match but I thought it was a great match because we achieved what we wanted – victory.' Further evidence of a very single-minded approach that says so much about the man who has become the leader of our football team.

On Cup final day in 1996, his single-mindedness brought handsome rewards. Of course, boxers have that self-same attitude to life. You know what I mean. They have this ability to endure their own company for long periods as they run miles and miles every day doing battle with that part of the body and mind that wants to bring an end to the pain long before reaching the 'pain barrier'.

Growing up in Cork, the diminutive Roy Keane had a reputation among his peers of being fearless. The Brian Dillon boxing club gave him an opportunity to assert himself and in four fights and four victories he was on the verge of making a name for himself. Apparently his boxing idol was Mike Tyson. But football was his first love and after realising that he was too small to play centre-forward he moved to midfield to hone those skills that are so essential to Manchester United. Incidentally, he was a Spurs supporter as a kid although once again his admission to having a liking for the London club reveals a little more of that single-minded streak in his character. Recognising that many kids switch their allegiance from club to club, Keane said: 'As a kid of ten or eleven years of age I had an interest in Spurs. But not when I was a bit older, 'cause as you get older you tend to change and I was busy playing soccer myself and I didn't really support anybody when I got to be a teenager. But when I was a kid, yeah I did support Tottenham at the time because I used to like the way they played, but I wouldn't say I was a fanatical Tottenham fan, put it that way. And then obviously as you get older you just, well, I didn't really support anybody in particular but then when I got to Forest I thought if I did get the chance to go to a big club and it was United I would obviously take it.'

Around Cork, the story is that the young Keane wrote to all the English First Division clubs requesting a trial – all, that is, except Manchester United because he apparently thought he was not good enough. Nottingham Forest did not take him up on his offer at the time and later paid £10,000 to Cobh Ramblers for his services. Brian Clough soon had him in the first team and United's manager was not slow to recognise the strength of character Keane displayed in midfield for Forest. He played against United in the final of the League Cup in 1992 when the Red Devils won 1–0. But Fergie the Wizard saw much that he liked about Keane and set his sights on securing Keane's signature. That day finally arrived just over a year later, in July 1993, when the Irishman joined United for a then record British transfer fee of £3.75m. He collected medals for the first of United's three 'doubles' in his first season. United fans had been waiting for over a century for a 'double' – and then three come along in five years – and that includes this 1998–99 season's fantastic 'treble' of Premier League title, FA Cup and European Champions' Cup.

As I prepare to conclude this chapter on Captain Keano, I have just returned from Barcelona where United became the champions of Europe for the first time in 31 years in the most dramatic of fashions. In the space of around two minutes on the evening of 26 May 1999, the Manchester United team created one of those moments in history when everyone will remember where they were and exactly what they were doing – just as for the assassination of President John F. Kennedy. I was there as history was made by the following set of Manchester United players:

European Champions' League final: 25 May 1999 v. Bayern Munich at Nou Camp Stadium, Barcelona. Attendance 90,000. (Won 2–1)
TEAM: **Schmeichel; Neville G., Stam, Johnsen, Irwin, Giggs, Butt, Beckham, Blomqvist (Sheringham (1)), Yorke, Cole (Solskjaer(1)).**

Manchester United package their Old Trafford football ground as the 'Theatre of Dreams'. There is no doubt that the events of 26 May 1999 at the Nou Camp Stadium were just pure theatre. At the end the Manchester United-employed disc-jockey Keith Fane led the celebrating hordes of United fans in song – dictating the pace, for example, by spinning Queen's 'We Are The Champions' or playing the 1991 European Cup-Winners' Cup anthem after victory over Barcelona in Rotterdam, 'Sit Down'. The players savoured every moment in front of the mass of red and white shirts and scarves. Together with their fans, they created their own 'theatre' – not that ITV showed any of this half-hour of pure joyous celebration. Britain was watching ITV make millions from their advertisements by this time. But meanwhile, back in the stadium, the players on the pitch and the 50,000 United fans remaining inside the magnificent Nou Camp were at one as they made their own fun, eventually drowning out and rendering redundant the music from United's disc-jockey.

The players brought the European Cup down to the United end of the stadium and set it tantalisingly close to the supporters before sitting down a few paces behind the trophy. They formed a straight line and put their arms around one another's necks to get the crowd to sing along with them, 'Sit down next to me'. Then David May approached the trophy as it remained on the pitch close to the fans. He put his finger across his closed lips to signal that he wanted everyone to shut up – including that infuriating little shit Fane. The word soon spread around the United masses – as everyone went 'Shhhhhhhhh!' Now the stadium was completely quiet. Not a sound from anyone – even the remaining German fans seemed to be transfixed and intrigued by the sound of silence. David May stood over the biggest and most coveted prize in European football. For what seemed like a lifetime, the silence was maintained. Then the former Blackburn defender suddenly leaned over the trophy as if in a rugby scrum before grabbing the big handles and raising the trophy over his head. The crowd went wild. This act of creating a silence continued over and over again with a succession of United's players getting into the act. It was an awesome sight indeed.

Then without warning the mood of the crowd changed. They decided to set their own agenda. Fifty thousand voices united as one. Their cry? 'Keano!' Repeated over and over and over again. 'Keano!' Captain Keano was at this time nowhere to be seen. 'Keano!' The crowd was in no mood to be denied acknowledgement by the man who had led his team to this unique 'treble'. 'Keano!' The fans were determined to honour the contribution from the Cork man who, like Paul Scholes, was booked in the wonderful semi-final victory over Juventus in Turin which resulted in their bans from the final. 'Keano!' United supporters would not be denied. 'Keano, there's only one Keano,' they roared before settling back into the simple demand, 'Keano! Keano! Keano! Keano! Keano! Keano!'

Eventually, Keano appeared from the area of the players' tunnel, close to the halfway line. At first, it looked as though our hero seemed too shy to acknowledge the crowd down to his left. But then it became clear that the captain of the greatest club side in Europe, if not the world, was trying to tempt his team-mate Paul Scholes to come forward with him to face the adoring United fans. Still they shouted 'Keano!' The fact that they could now see him did not diminish their demands that he come to them to receive their plaudits for his efforts during an amazing campaign which yielded the 'treble'. Slowly Keano moved forward, looking back to the United officials and non-playing players to wave the reluctant Scholes forward. Eventually Scholes moved out of the group towards Keano. Together they edged forward towards the United end of the stadium. 'Keano!' The sound was deafening. 'Keano!' The United captain finally reached the celebrating United players – some of whom had joined in the crowd's enthusiastic rendition of 'Keano!' Now, with Scholes by his side, he approached the European Cup. The United players formed a guard of honour as they applauded their captain and Milan hero Scholes. Together they picked up the European Cup and held it high above their heads to an enormous roar of approval from the United faithful. Finally, the battle-cry of 'Keano' was ended as Captain Keano stood before his adoring army of fans, his contribution to the 1998–99 season acknowledged by those who hero-worship the Irishman. These are the people who appreciate the qualities he brings to United in terms of leadership, dogged determination to avoid defeat and ability to torment, tame and contain the opposition midfield.

At my meeting with Keane in February, I had asked him if he felt under pressure at Old Trafford to win the European Cup. He replied: 'I don't think there's pressure to win the European Cup. There's pressure to win every match playing for United and I mean every League match, even friendlies because every team we play against, it's their Cup final or whatever, so I personally don't feel this pressure. As I said there's pressure to win the League, there's pressure to win the FA Cup and I think the European Cup would be in the same bracket as that, that's my personal feeling. I don't go out thinking every season we have to win, we obviously want to but there are a lot of other teams all over Europe saying the same thing. But put it this way, there's no extra pressure, I don't think.'

After the famous semi-final victory over Juventus in Turin, Captain Keane was interviewed about the booking that would keep him out of the team in Barcelona. Keano demonstrated his maturity and determination when he told his audience that what was important was the team's qualification for the final, not his personal situation. We all know it must have hurt him not to have a place in the European Cup final and yet he buried that personal pain in order to promote the cause of the team. Such commitment to the 'team' would have brought tears to a stone! Hail Captain Fantastic!

REASON TO BELIEVE: The muscle in the middle comes from 'Keano'. There is no one to match Roy Keane's all-round ability in the modern game. His ball-winning skills and distribution. His ability to tackle and defend in the final quarter of the pitch when required. He is a one-man midfield, defence and attack . . . a human dynamo. When Keane first played for United it was alongside Paul Ince. Two hard men when it came to winning the ball – or delivering retribution for an opponent's misdemeanour. But without Ince, Keane still dominates the midfield. Nobody f**ks with Roy Keane – at least, not if they have the full complement of sandwiches for a picnic. When I enquired from Keane as to why he chose to sign for United rather than some of the other teams pursuing him, he simply said, 'Do I have to explain why?' So, as the Keane anthem reflects, 'he wouldn't sign for Arsenal or Blackburn 'cos they're shite . . . so he signed for Man United 'cos we're f***ing dynamite!' Yes, Keano is a Red through and through. No contest in choosing him to crucify the midfield opposition . . . and to captain this team of United Irishmen. A natural-born leader!

ROY KEANE: THE QUESTIONNAIRE

BORN: **Cork – 10 August 1971.**

Which junior clubs did you play for – and when?
Rockmount – 1980–89

Which club did you support as a boy?
Spurs.

Was it always your ambition to be a professional footballer?
Yes.

You could have signed for Blackburn or Arsenal instead. Why United?
Do I need to explain?

It took a British record fee of £3.75 million to swoop you away from Nottingham Forest. What did you think of your price tag? Describe your feelings on leaving Forest.
The price tag did not bother me. I was quite sad but it was a chance to play for United so that was that.

What were your first impressions of the club?
I always knew it was a big club but until you play for them you just don't really know how big.

You made your debut for United on 15 August 1993 against Norwich at Carrow Road. Can you describe your feelings on that day?
To be honest, it was just another game to me. I don't get nervous so that's that.

You have already played 150 games for United – which one stands out in the memory – and why?
Every single game for United meant something to me.

What has been the highlight of your career? When, where etc.
Signing for Forest. Playing for Ireland. Playing for United. Winning trophies and getting made captain.

Your worst moment at Old Trafford – and why?
Getting injured. especially snapping my cruciate ligaments.

Which individual has been the biggest influence on your career?
Quite a few. But I have to say Alex Ferguson and Brian Kidd.

Your best game for United? (When, where and against whom?)
You'd have to ask somebody else.

Your worst game for United? (When, where and against whom?)
You'd have to ask somebody else.

As the Club Captain with three League Cups and two FA Cups under your belt, what are your ambitions with United?
To win every trophy available to United to win.

Pick your greatest ever Man Utd team. (And give a few comments to explain if possible.)
First 'double'-winning team in 1993–94.

Do you wish there were more Irish players in the current squad?
Yes.

Best player you ever saw in a United shirt? And why?
Eric Cantona. He always did it when it mattered most for the team.

The most difficult opponent you have faced? (Example of game – with year and competition if possible.)
Zidane in the 1996–97 European Cup.

You made your international debut on 22 May 1991 against Chile. Describe your feelings on that day.
Of course, I was very proud but it was just another game to me.

The best game for your country – and the worst?
You'd have to ask somebody else.

How do you regard the Man Utd fans?
The best in the world.

Do you think the problems with Old Trafford stadium regulations during games has contributed to the reduction in atmosphere? Does this lack of atmosphere affect the players, and do you think the introduction of a singing section would benefit the team?

There is a problem with the atmosphere sometimes where the fans can be a bit quiet. But then again it should really be up to the team to get them going. As for a singing section, no. The whole stadium should be singing.

Recent success has given the fans an insatiable appetite for more. How do you and the others players deal with this pressure?

Personally, I don't mind the pressure because when you're playing for the best club, the fans expect the best. The club was starved of League success for 26 years so they are trying to make up for it. So I don't blame them.

Your views on the team selected for this book?

I think it would be a great soccer team, as well as a great drinking team.

NINE

George Best

(FOOTBALL GENIUS/SHAGGER OF MISS WORLDS/SUPERSTAR/
SCORER OF GOALS AND MASTER OF THE LAY-OFF)

Manchester United: 1963–1973: 446 games: 178 goals

DEBUT: **14 September 1963 v. West Bromich Albion at Old Trafford. (Won
1–0)**

TEAM: **Gregg; Dunne, Cantwell, Crerand, Foulkes, Setters, Best, Stiles,
Sadler (1), Chisnall, Charlton.**

HONOURS: **European Cup 1967–68; 1998–99**
League Championship 1964–65; 1966–67
Northern Ireland (37 caps 1964–77)

Cheyne Walk, Chelsea. It was somewhere around here – the place I was
looking for – located in the heart of an area that is home to the rich and
famous. Memory flashbacks to the years of Mick Jagger and Marianne
Faithfull cavorting around these very streets, if not in their bedroom
overlooking the streets, high as kites and looking down on ordinary mortals
like me – clinging to the earth's surface as we scurried about looking for
the next pay cheque. Walking down the King's Road in bright spring
sunshine you are made to feel inadequate – bloated and fearful of catching
a glimpse of your middle-age spread in the frontage of some of the grand
shops. The great, the good and the glamorous cock their noses in the air as
they meander about in pursuit of designer garb to match their designer lives.
Eyes straight ahead to avoid the unnecessary 'pane' of reflected images in
the highly polished glass.

My mission on this warm and sunny March afternoon is to seek out the
person who has lived his life by the rules of the good, the bad and the
bubbly. Eventually, the Phene Arms came into view. This is George Best's
local – the place where he comes to be among friends. I knew it was his
local because I had spoken to him on the phone here once before but had

failed to locate him on a number of calls prior to this visit. So I was taking a chance in sneaking up on one of the greatest ever footballers in the world – someone known to millions of fans around the globe even though he had long since hung up his boots. I had the place 'surrounded' as I entered the bar, noting that there was another door at the back of the bar leading into the beer garden outside – a potential escape route to keep an eye on if there was any 'funny business' from the bar staff. But there would be no escape. My pint and a packet of crisps had just been set on the counter as the great man himself wandered into the bar. To be truthful, he looked like I felt many a morning after a liberal libation or two the night before. His hair was still damp, suggesting he had just emerged from the shower. It was three in the afternoon and he was casually dressed in one of those dreadful shell suits so popular on housing estates and holiday camps the length and breadth of Britain. This was no time to be a fashion guru or, indeed, to be faint of heart. I moved swiftly towards the former United star, intercepting him before he could get to his favourite 'corner' at the rear of the front bar. He listened politely as I introduced myself and explained the concept of *United Irishmen*. Equally politely, he told me he could not spare any time today for an interview and suggested, as he moved off, that I contact the bar sometime in the future to arrange an appointment. Naturally, I was disappointed as I stepped aside to sip my pint and enjoy my crisps in the opposite corner.

George spoke to a couple of customers at his end of the bar as the barman produced a white wine and soda in a large glass goblet with heaps of ice. The Cheltenham race meeting blared out from the television set on the wall and George and his mates chatted animatedly about the racing. Inside my shoulder bag was the previous book I had written about United and my 40 years of devotion to the club. I signed a copy and waited for George to approach the bar for another drink. Before he did, his thin blonde wife turned a few heads when she made her entrance. George moved towards the bar and at that very moment I chose to step forward quickly to order a second pint and to present him with the book. As he took it, I gave him the page number for the section referring to him. As I sipped my second pint I could see Mrs Best reading the book and then George came over to say he could after all spare me a half-hour to do the interview – after the next race! As he moved off towards the television set, I reached for my notes and tape recorder. St Patrick's Day had come a day early for me!

George Best has lived his life in a goldfish bowl. What is there to say about the man that is new? Aside from the millions of gutter press words that have chronicled his 50 years on earth, George has been responsible for at least three books giving insights into most aspects of his life. In short, thousands of United fans like me could say we have known George Best all our adolescent and adult lives. But George Best didn't know us. To put this another way — Raymond Gilmour was a Republican terrorist who was also an informer, a supergrass, for the security forces in Derry and on the strength of his word, a large number of Republicans found themselves behind bars. It has been said a local wag was quick to pinpoint the irony of the situation when he, or she, wrote on a Derry wall: 'I knew Raymond Gilmour — but thank God he didn't know me!' Having such thoughts did me no good at all as I waited for George and by the time he sat down at my table I feared the interview would go badly because he would regard my questions with disdain, having had to answer them so many times before. But if he felt that way, he did not show it at all as we quickly got into our stride, talking about those moments in his life which had some impact on my life.

As he spoke, I realised that he was just the same lad I had interviewed in the summer of 1970 at his family home in Belfast when he was at his peak of form and stardom. Of course, much had changed since our first encounter — but his manner, his apparent ease with any question pushed in his direction and his willingness to display his enthusiasm for the game he graced so magnificently clearly had not diminished with time. I began by asking George about a recent readers' opinion poll in the official Manchester United magazine which put Eric Cantona at No. 1 in the Top Fifty all-time greatest players. 'Everyone has their own opinion,' he said, rather defensively given that this was probably the first time he had not topped such a poll. 'Many of those who voted did not play football as professionals. It would be hard to judge. We all know by word of mouth what players from the past were like. Sir Matt always said Duncan Edwards was a massive player, one of the greatest ever and what Sir Matt said was alright by me. You accepted it because you could take his word for it.' At this early mention of the great man, I put it to George that he was a great fan of Best: 'Sir Matt never said a bad word against me — even through the bad times. And he would not let anyone else away with saying a bad word about me. Sir Matt had two great sides — and when you consider he lost more than half of one of those sides at Munich and then rebuilt the second side within ten years and go on to win the European Cup — it was a hell of a feat!' Indeed, he did seem very tolerant of the enigmatic genius that was George Best. The kind of genius who in his youth had little regard for tactics, even of the limited kind contemplated by the genius of Sir Matt.

European Cup quarter-final: 9 March 1966 v. Benfica at Stadium of Light, Lisbon. Attendance 90,000. (Won 5–1)
TEAM: **Gregg; Brennan, Dunne, Crerand (1), Foulkes, Stiles, Best (2), Law, Charlton (1), Herd, Connolly (1).**

Ninety thousand fans looked on as Eusebio received his European Footballer of the Year award before the kick-off. Then they sat back expecting the great man to snuff out United's slender 3–2 lead from the first leg at Old Trafford. But just 12 minutes after the kick-off the new 'King of Europe' emerged in the form of the Irish wing-wizard who by then had scored twice! Manchester United's reputation was as an attacking team, but this was an incredible display given the circumstances. Had Sir Matt sanctioned such bravado? Not according to George: 'He said, "Wait for 20 minutes to see how you go." But after a quarter of an hour we were three up. I never thought anything about tactics. It was the start of the "Fifth Beatle" stuff for me. What an achievement – to go there and beat one of the best sides in Europe at the ground where they had never before lost a game in Europe was just a little bit terrific! And we didn't just beat them. We slaughtered them.'

Indeed we did. This was a game I was forbidden to listen to on radio because of the late hour and the parental declaration that sleep was important to teenagers and their studies. Bollocks! I simply listened on my tranny hidden beneath my pillow – although my screams to celebrate the goals and alert my brother in the other bed in the room also drew some unwanted attention from my father.

It could be argued that Best's performance in Lisbon brought him the kind of public attention which ultimately placed him under the kind of pressure that led to his difficulties and eventual early departure from his beloved Old Trafford. But you will not hear that argument from Best. No sir, he will say his ten years at United were the 'best' of his life and he doesn't even regard victory in the 1968 European Cup as the peak of his career. This is how he put it: 'Every game for Manchester United was the pinnacle for me but winning the European Cup in 1968 was the pinnacle for the club. Sir Matt was brilliant.' As he had when we first met in 1970, Best admitted that the star of the '68 Euro show was John Aston. 'John Aston was just brilliant,' he reflected, 'and for the first 20 minutes their full-back was gasping for breath. God knows how he felt after extra time!' Best will be remembered for his goal in the '68 final that set United on their way to victory. However, he has been known to complain that television replays tend to cut to the crucial moment he rounded the goalkeeper to put the ball in the net rather than show the whole move. But there is another little known game for which George Best will forever be remembered by those lucky enough to be present at Windsor Park on 21 October 1967.

Northern Ireland International (37 caps 1964–77)
DEBUT: **15 April 1964 v. Wales at Swansea. (Won 3–2)**
TEAM: **Jennings; Magill, Elder, Harvey (1), Neill, McCullough, Best, Crossan, Wilson (1), McLaughlin (1), Braithwaite.**

George Best was just over a month short of his 18th birthday when he pulled on the green shirt of Northern Ireland for the first time. It was his first season in the United first team and he had played 15 times for them and scored four goals for them. Given the fact that he had youth on his side and the span of 13 years at international level, it has to be said that just 37 caps is an extremely disappointing return. Of course, by the time he took on the Welsh in 1964, his reputation had grown into almost legendary proportions already. Looking back at the first sighting of his genius on the pitch, it is easy to recall why he was so pleasing to the eye. Here we had a kid who was showing the men that football was not about brawn alone. He may have been a skinny little runt who took the piss out of Irish international goalkeeper Harry Gregg, but he appeared not to have a nerve in his body.

They verbally assaulted him, kicked him from behind without mercy and they engaged in attempted murder with tackles aimed at cutting his spindly body in two. But he was too smart, too quick for them. Grown men were made to look foolish. Perhaps the only way to convey the impact the impish Irishman had on the game is to get you to cast your mind back to your childhood. The chances are there was always one boy who stood head and shoulders above the rest in the school playground or in the street at home. He would always be the first choice when it came to picking teams. This guy could dribble around opponents with disarming ease. He was not afraid to beat someone and then just for the sheer hell of showing off, pause to allow the poor sucker he had just beaten time to recover for yet another humiliation. This was a player who could dribble the ball from defence and beat the entire opposition before taking it around the goalkeeper to score a sensational goal. His feet moved like lightning speed and yet still enabled him to have total control of the ball. At my school, it was me. But the startling realisation for English First Division defenders during the 1963–64 season was that in George Best, Manchester United had found a youngster who had the confidence and ability of the playground show-off. A show-off who was not afraid to use this talent to belittle the efforts of seasoned international players who tried to stop him. With a wiggle of his hips and a sudden drop of his shoulder, he could send defenders to the local shop for a packet of cigarettes and by the time they returned with the change he would have either scored himself or set one up for a team-mate. Every time he received the ball wide on the wing the hairs on the back of your neck suddenly stood to attention. You were already savouring the acute embarrassment about to be caused to their defence and you were not alone in preparing your body for such inspiring pleasure because his every touch set the whole crowd breathing rapidly in anticipation.

This then, was the waif who came out to torture Welsh full-back and hardman Graham Williams at the Vetch Field in Swansea on his international debut. If I am not mistaken, Williams had already been tormented by the teenage Best when he made his debut against Williams's club, West Bromwich Albion, the previous September. Things did not improve for the full-back on this occasion. But for me, the icing on George Best's international cake came three years later when he tormented and tortured the entire Scottish nation for 90 exhilarating minutes!

21 October 1967: Northern Ireland v. Scotland at Windsor Park, Belfast. (Won 1–0)
Northern Ireland: Jennings; McKeag, Parke, Stewart, Neill, Clements (1), Campbell, Crossan, Dougan, Nicholson, Best.
Scotland: Simpson; Gemmell, McCreadie, Greig, McKinnon, Ure, Wallace, Murdoch, McCalliog, Law, Morgan.

In May 1967, Tommy Gemmell scored a fantastic goal to help Celtic become the first British team to win the European Cup. He had also helped them win the Scottish League title, the Scottish Cup and League Cup. But for 90 minutes at Windsor Park he was made to look like Sadie Gemmell from Sauchiehall Street. Not just poor Tommy, but hard man Eddie McCreadie too. For at one stage in the game they tried swapping their full-backs to contain the rampant Best. It was a useless exercise. This was the greatest ever one-man show on a football pitch – and what a pitch. It was a damp day, the pitch was slippy and cut up but it was just one of those days when George Best took the ball past four or five defenders before sending magnificent 20 to 25-yard drives towards the Scottish goal. In truth, he might on any other day have scored a hat-trick or more. But Celtic's thirty-something goalkeeper Ronnie Simpson chose this day to match Best's form and he prevented an embarrassing slaughter.

Poor Tommy Gemmell was humiliated. Eddie McCreadie as well. In fact, no one in the Scottish team had the answer to George Best's jinking and weaving. 'It was just one of those days,' Best remembered when I mentioned the name of Tommy Gemmell. 'Everything went great and if it hadn't been for Ronnie Simpson I might have got four or five goals that afternoon. He was absolutely brilliant that day and he was 36 years of age. But everything I hit at him he somehow got to. But we got a result at the end of the day. Davy Clements got a goal. Yeah, it was a special game because they were a good side. Apart from winning, it was just one of those days that everything I touched just worked. It was brilliant, yeah.'

Windsor Park was also the setting for another major talking point in Best's all-too-brief international career. The other Windsor Park talking point came in a game against England in 1971 and the 'goal' Best scored – or, should I say, did not score. What happened was this. Gordon Banks was preparing to clear the ball upfield from open play. He threw the ball up into the air with the intention of kicking it when it eventually dropped to the appropriate height. Quick as a flash, Best is in there – he raises his foot to lob the ball, which he regards as having been thrown into play, over the England goalkeeper. He runs around him and as the ball bounces he gets to it first with his head to put it into the England net. Goal? Not according to Scottish referee Alastair MacKenzie and it was a decision which incensed not only the entire crowd, but Best most of all: 'I still to this day say it was a goal. The ball was in the air and was in play. The referee's excuse, eventually, when he tried to come up with an explanation, was my foot was too high. His foot was the same height as mine, so what's the difference? It was a goal no doubt because I did the same against Pat Jennings at Old Trafford and blocked him as he went to kick it, tackled him actually and it [the ball] broke and I scored and they allowed it. So it was a brave referee not to give it, especially at Windsor Park.'

At this point George wants to return to the television set to watch the next race in which he clearly has a stake. I take stock. I also take to my heels and run to the nearest newsagent's to buy new batteries for my tape recorder that has died, causing me no end of embarrassment. The race round to the shop returned some colour to my pale, embarrassed cheeks by the time George had finished with his race.

It was time to approach the subject of the views of Tony Dunne, given during an interview for this book, that there came a time when Best stopped being a 'winner' and instead became an 'entertainer'. This development, according to Dunne, rendered George useless to forwards like Denis Law and Bobby Charlton who were pulling their hair out because George was busy playing to the crowd by beating players many times over. It is a view that George very quickly makes clear he does not agree with. 'I think it was the opposite,' he said, rather more sternly than had been the norm up to this point. Then he added: 'I was like that as a kid, hogging the ball, but the more I played, the wiser I became. As a matter of fact, if you watch the videos – and there is one on me, Bobby Charlton and Denis Law – you will see not only did I score goals, I set up most of them for Bobby Charlton and Denis Law. I was surprised myself about how often I made goals for them.'

Mention of Bobby Charlton brings me to the next question about the truth of the relationship between Best and Sir Bobby. It has been well documented that there was a great deal of animosity between the two, even to the very noticeable way in which they refused to pass to each other on the pitch. Best has admitted to this period in their lives and has even stated that it was a childish way for the two of them to mark their personality clash. 'He was great while we were winning,' George said assertively, 'but when we were losing I became disillusioned. And if you are losing week in, week out you cannot be happy. I started to miss training. The sense of achievement began to fall apart very quickly. Think about this – four years after we won the European Cup we were relegated. I thought the club started playing players who were not good enough to be Manchester United players. They had some average footballers, but they were not good enough. I did not get much help from the club where I had help previously. If only they had signed some good players. They had the chance of getting Alan Ball and Mike England – players who wanted to play for United – and if they had then we might have kept winning games and I may have taken a different direction in life.'

The thought occurs, although I do not express it to him, that this was typical alcoholic logic – passing off the responsibility for failure on to the shoulders of someone else. At least that is very much what it sounded like to me. But who am I to speak? As we say in my drinking circle, if truth was to be told, the only difference between the alcoholics and us is that they go to the meetings. One thing is for sure, George's drinking and bars have played a very important role in his life, resulting in one very highly publicised period of time behind bars rather than propped up in front of them. In 1984, when he was sent to prison for a motoring offence, I took it upon myself to write to him enclosing a prison poem by Oscar Wilde, 'The Ballad of Reading Gaol'. At the very least it would give the greatest player the world has ever seen something with which to occupy his mind during the lonely hours in a prison cell. My wife Fiona thought I was mad, but to me it was one of those ideas that once conceived was never going to let go until it had become a reality. It seemed vital to communicate with the man, who had given us United fans so much pleasure, at a time when his life may have been at its lowest ebb, when he possibly felt more lonely and vulnerable than ever. Perhaps it was simply to illustrate that another

Irish genius had found a means of making his stay in an English jail creative and memorable, that something lasting and good came out of adversity. Whatever it was that stirred inside me, I just wanted George Best to know he was not alone. Of course, I had no way of knowing if Best ever received the letter. I think I sent it through his then manager and friend, Bill McMurdo.

I mention the letter and the poem as we progress through the interview in his local. He admitted receiving the letter and poem – informing me that he had always been a great admirer of Oscar Wilde's Irish genius and had 'read everything he'd ever written'. So it was not a complete waste of time after all.

As we were chatting on the eve of the second leg of the European Champions' League quarter-final against Inter Milan in the San Siro Stadium, it was time to catch up with George's thoughts on the 'new' United built under the careful guidance of Alex Ferguson. As a child Best supported Wolverhampton Wanderers. Would he describe himself as a United fan nowadays? 'Oh yeah,' he answered without hesitation. 'Not much . . . you ought to see me in here when the games are on. I take all their money. We have all sorts in here, Chelsea, West Ham, Arsenal and Tottenham.' He mentioned particularly enjoying the replayed Chelsea FA Cup game the previous week when United went to Stamford Bridge and stuffed them 2–0.

How did he think United would play in San Siro the night following our interview, 17 March – St Patrick's Day? He had this to say: 'Going back to the game with Benfica [March 1966], being told to keep it tight. They will have to keep it tight. If they get to half-time with a clean sheet you gotta fancy them. If the Italians score early then it is a big struggle for them. Yorke and Cole have the pace up front to hit the Italians on the break although it is always difficult to hit Italian teams on the break. They have been in the defensive business for a long time.' Spoken like the Sky TV pundit he is. Of course, United kept it tight and the game was scoreless at half-time. Even after the Italians scored, United kept the faith and Paul Scholes managed to get the crucial equaliser which guaranteed United a place in the semi-final of the European Champions' League.

It is during the next part of our conversation that I become aware of another thought, a rather unsavoury one at that, but one that does not find audible articulation in front of the great man. I keep it to myself but I will explain it to you shortly. The focus for the question is the unavoidable comparisons being made between the 1968 team and the Wizard's present collection of nineties stars. It is a question George Best is often asked and it is one that he has written about regularly over the years. On a number of occasions he has deliberated it in the *Daily Mirror*. On 18 March 1997 he chose the 'Best team of all time'. The team he chose was as follows: Schmeichel; Brennan, Irwin, Stiles, Pallister, Cantona, Keane, Giggs, Charlton, Law and Best. Clearly George is still very much attack-minded. His substitutes were Beckham, Crerand, Dunne and Foulkes. But on each occasion he has addressed the issue of 'which team is the greatest' George has always tempered his remarks with the thought that the 1968 team had won the European Cup and so the nineties teams could not stand comparison until they had proved themselves in Europe. Fair enough. This is how he put it to me during our chat: 'The thing is, if an English team wins it now they are going to say it is not the European Cup. It is not the Champions' League because the teams at second and third were not the champions. So even if Manchester United win it, you are going to get people who are going to say, well, it was not a proper European Cup because they let three teams from each country in. So you can't call it the Champions' Cup. They are after money. A European League will come one day, but at the moment, it's money they are after because they are playing on the league basis first before they get in. In the old days it was knock-out, two legs and the best team went through . . . most of the time. But now, of course, you gotta play so many games, and they are complaining about too many games in a season and yet they are adding games almost every year now. I don't know. I am a little bit old-fashioned, I think it should be the way it used to be.'

This brings me to my unsavoury thought. In my view perhaps not just old-fashioned, but perhaps is there just a hint of jealousy about the threat Fergie's team posed to the unique achievement of the '68 side? I wondered if there was a part of George that really did not want the achievement of his European Cup-winning side to be matched by the new kids on the block. After all, that would in some way reduce the marketable value of the 1968 European Cup winners, take away from the status of the members of the '68 team. Perhaps I am being unkind. Who can really fault him if, and I accept it is a big *if*, George wants to retain his special place in the history of Manchester United? Oh, God, I wish I had not had that unsavoury thought. I withdraw it immediately.

Back to George and the pressure on him to make those comparisons between the '68 and '99 teams. Two days after the Wizard's team beat Juventus 3–2 in Turin to clinch a place in the European Champions' League final in Barcelona, the *Daily Mirror* got George to do another comparison. He scored the individuals in both the '68 side and the '99 side by giving them marks out of ten. This is the way it looked to him: Stepney 8, Schmeichel 8, Brennan 8, Neville G. 7, Dunne 7, Irwin 8, Foulkes 9, Stam 8, Sadler 8, Johnsen 7, Stiles 9, Keane 9, Crerand 8, Butt 8, Aston 9,

Beckham 8, Best 10, Blomqvist 7, Charlton 8, Cole 9, Kidd 8, Yorke 10. So the 1968 team scored 102 and the 1999 team had a total of 99. George gave Fergie and Busby 10 each.

Occasionally George has rubbed the United fans up the wrong way – but believe me, he is still one of the most popular heroes ever to wear the red shirt. He enjoys cult status among all the fans – even those not even born when he was strutting his stuff all over Europe. Jesus, they still occasionally go into the 'Yellow Submarine' song, 'And Number One was Georgie Best, And Number Two was Georgie Best', and so on right through to number eleven. He knows just how popular he is because of the reaction he gets at Old Trafford. 'I went on to the pitch a few weeks ago to do the draw and the reception was just fantastic,' he recalls with undoubted pleasure. But, I wondered aloud, did he not find the atmosphere at Old Trafford more subdued than in his day, given the lack of singing fans and the extended periods of almost total silence. But he did not agree at all. 'No, I think it is brilliant,' he said with conviction. 'It's just that people always said you lost the atmosphere when it is all-seater, but you don't. I think it is amazing there. I take friends there and people just freak out. They think it is brilliant. I still find it terrific and I love going there. The whole place, for me, is buzzing. The fact that when you go there – Denis is there, Bobby is there, Paddy Crerand is there, Billy Foulkes is there – the club doctor still goes there. We meet up for a drink in the directors' lounge after the game and then I pop down to say hello to some of the new lads. I love it.'

Which of the new lads does he rate as players? George, an open admirer of Eric Cantona, had this to say: 'Eric was a terrific player, an exciting player but he did not do it for United in Europe. You have to do it in Europe as well. Giggs started off looking like a great, great player but what with injuries he has been kept out of the side for long periods and to me he has not yet delivered all that he can or that he promised. But Giggsy on his day is better than anyone. We know what a good player Roy Keane is . . . they've got so many. I think Solskjaer is a good player, Nicky Butt is a good player. Beckham has come out of the World Cup and is playing out of his skin and has just stuck two fingers up at them all. I did a dinner recently near Manchester and his dad was at it and I was chatting to him. I was saying to him how well he has done considering all the stick he has taken. I think Stam has got better and better. Schmeichel – we all hope they can talk him into staying maybe for another couple of seasons. He has been outstanding in the last couple of games.' I tell George about my friend's idea for a campaign slogan to keep Schmeichel at Old Trafford – 'The Dane must remain!' He laughs heartily but as we both now know, Peter the Great played his last game in the European Cup final at Barcelona. This was the game where I missed the winning goal because I was still celebrating the first and the prospect of winning in extra time.

George missed seeing both those goals because he was escaping early to avoid being surrounded by United fans. But such thoughts do not trouble the Irish wizard when it comes to attending games at Old Trafford. 'I do not have a season ticket,' he told me, 'but I have a friend who has a box, although I mostly go in the directors' box. I was up at the Fulham game [FA Cup] and Mr Al Fayed flew me up in his private plane. Obviously working for Sky I don't get up to the Saturday games, but midweek and Sundays I get there.' Fulham, for those of you too young to remember, is one of the clubs where George enjoyed his football after leaving United. He struck up a partnership with Rodney Marsh and seemed to bring a smile to many faces as they went about the business of winning games and entertaining at the same time. But did he regard his time there as serious football? 'I always played serious football whether it was five-a-side or at Fulham, Stockport or Bournemouth,' he said. 'It was great at Fulham. I played with Rodney Marsh and I played with one of the great, great, great footballers – Bobby Moore. We had a great time. We just enjoyed it. They were getting big crowds, the cameras were there and it was great for us as we were all getting towards the end of our careers. So it was just a nice way of easing ourselves out of the game. We all loved London and the club was a great little club with a terrific chairman. It was a nice couple of years.'

But not, apparently, the best years of George's life after United. Those were spent in America. George has very fond memories of his years there and totally rejects any suggestion that he was past it when he played there. He is also rather sensitive when he comes to suggesting that the game failed in the United States. Very assertively he said: 'It didn't fail when we were there. It was massive. When you have players like Cruyff, Beckenbauer, Pele and Alan Hudson, Gordon Banks, Gerd Mueller and Eusebio . . . you had some of the best players in the world. Everybody thought it was just that we had gone there because it was the end of our careers. But I was just 29 when I went there and I was there for seven years. I had a business there, got married there, my son was born there. I had a great time. Then they stopped bringing in the foreign players and the Americans then had no idea. They had improved but they had coaches who didn't know what they were talking about trying to coach the kids. So the league basically collapsed overnight and it's a pity because if they had kept going I think I would never have come back because I had a good business in Los Angeles. And so I got bored because I was sitting around doing nothing. Sounded great – the business going well and hanging around the beach all day, but after six months I just was so bored I came back in 1981. I started to get into the television side of the game here and radio and wrote a couple of books, remarried, just bought a beautiful new home – so all of a sudden, when you think back how it could have been, I could have sitting on a beach doing nothing, becoming a cabbage.'

Then there was that great goal he scored in America. You know the one where he took on the entire defence and with his fast footwork managed to get past about five defenders inside the penalty box before he slotted the ball home. It was just fantastic. What I did not know was the significance of the goal. George took great pleasure in explaining it: 'The American TV companies showed it . . . and trying to sell football to them was impossible. But . . . they were showing it and reran it, and for the league it was great because they never got any coverage. It was a little bit special and it was against some good players. It was against my old team, Fort Lauderdale. And I had moved from Fort Lauderdale to San Jose so it was even more special. I had fallen out with the coach at Fort Lauderdale the year before when they should have won the title and he messed up with a couple of substitutions leading up to the shoot-out. He didn't know that the players in the shoot-out had to be on the pitch at the end of the game so he took three of us off who were the main penalty-takers. And of course we couldn't come on and take the penalties and so I went nuts. We lost on the final penalty to get to the final. Also we played New York in New York once and there were something like 60,000 there and they had a terrific side. But we had a really good team and we were beating them 2–0 with about a quarter of an hour to go and the crowd were getting on their backs because they had never lost at home and we were toying with them. Cubillas the Peruvian and a lad called Ray Hudson who had played at Newcastle and a lad called David Irving who had been at Everton. We had a terrific side. And he took David Irving off and Ray Hudson – two of our best and most experienced players. And he brought on a triallist and a young Yugoslavian kid and the whole thing went, well, they beat us 3–2. I went nuts. And he was clapping us and saying, "Well done boys, we only lost 3–2."

'That was it, I decided I was not playing for him anymore and so I moved to San Jose. So this was the first time I had played against Fort Lauderdale and that's when I scored the goal. I scored another one in the game. We went into overtime and a minute into overtime I hit the crossbar but our centre-forward knocked the rebound in and so we beat them 3–2. So it was lovely justice!'

Justice indeed and the memory of it is not the only legacy from George's years in the United States. His son Calum was born there, on the 33rd anniversary of the Munich Disaster, on 6 February 1981.

George is very proud of his son who has now taken on the father's mantle as football star. George does not hesitate to sing his son's praises: 'He plays in America. We were thinking of bringing him over here and letting a couple of clubs look at him. At one stage I was going to send him to Old Trafford and let them have a look but then I thought about it, and I didn't want him living here with all the hassle and pressure. He has a great life in California. Here he would get all the comparisons. He plays over there. He wins 'Player of the Year' every year. His team have just won the State Championship, so he loves it. He is only interested in football.'

I left George Best to his wife and the next race at Cheltenham, happy that I had taken the chance to meet the man who at his peak was the best player in the world. Even Pele agreed with that thought. The last thought from the genius in the Phene Arms concerned player power. He believed things had gone too far in favour of the players. As I walked away from the pub, his thoughts about loyalty were still in my head.

'It is wrong,' he said. 'In the days of Bill Nicholson, Jock Stein, Bill Shankly and Sir Matt, any player behaving the way players do today would get a kick up the arse as they were being shown the door. In my days, you negotiated for a new contract and if you could not agree terms, then the player moved on. That is still more or less what goes on today. Mind you, in those days players had more respect for managers. You didn't have one-man strikes like Pierre van Hooijdonk – what was all that about? To start off with he said he thought the team wasn't good enough. Why did he go there in the first place? There's not too much loyalty these days. I mean, the number of players who are in and out. Look at Old Trafford in my years. There were players there for years and years and they never thought of playing for anyone else. So it was not down to money, it was down to loyalty. People think I had only a couple of years there, but I was there for 12 years.'

Twelve glorious years during which time world football was greatly enriched by the 'Belfast Boy'.

REASON TO BELIEVE: This team will score goals. Up front we have the greatest player in history, George Best. This man was the complete footballer and the idol of millions throughout the world who admired him for his ball skills on the pitch – and off it as well. I had the privilege of watching Best develop into a world-class performer – and he was a performer. An entertainer who could tackle, score goals, make goals and single-handedly turn defeat into victory. Best was making United great again alongside Charlton and Law. He was winning League Championships and building towards victory in the European Cup final in 1968. But then, as

Tony Dunne put it, Best turned from being a winner to being a performer. Dunne was in awe of the man but knew that once George began beating the same player nine times before attempting to pass to a team-mate, the game was up. By the time he crossed the ball Law and Charlton had already made four unfulfilled runs up front and had just given up. Dunne said they had taken to screaming at Best to pass the bloody ball, even dropping back into the defence to collect it so that Best wouldn't get it. Dunne said Best had them tearing their hair out in disgust. Sir Bobby obviously took these violations of good team play very seriously indeed! Pele described Best as the greatest in the world. That'll do for me.

TEN

Frank Stapleton

(STRIKER/SPECIALIST WEMBLEY CUP FINAL DEFENDER)

Manchester United: 1981–82 to 1986–87: 265 (21) games: 78 goals

DEBUT: **29 August 1981 v. Coventry City at Highfield Road. (Lost 2–1)**

TEAM: **Bailey; Gidman, Albiston, Wilkins, McQueen, Buchan M., Coppell, Birtles, Stapleton, Macari (1), McIlroy.**

HONOURS: **FA Cup 1982–83; 1984–85**

Sunday morning, 16 August 1998. As soon as I wakened I knew I just did not want to function. This was not the result of self-abuse the previous evening in Billy-Andy's, my local watering hole. No, the problem was much deeper and more fundamental than self-inflicted pain. Put simply, it was a day for denying one's claims to 'earthling' status due to the burden of carrying all the guilt of the human race in the immediate aftermath of an event that so suddenly and sickeningly deprived a bewildered world of 29 innocent lives. I got into a hot steaming bath at 8.15 in a daze. My eyes were tight shut and did not want to open ever again. I struggled out of freezing water at 9.10.

My mission that day was to travel to Manchester for a series of interviews with former United heroes for this book and to attend the Munich Testimonial match at Old Trafford featuring, just one last time, 'King Eric'. Even thinking of the pleasures that lay ahead induced a cloud of depression, making movement almost impossible. It seemed disrespectful to those who had died or had suffered horrific wounds. Those for whom life would never, ever, ever be the same again. It is difficult to pick up the threads of normality after you have lost a loved one – or a limb. As I reluctantly left home, tears threatened to make driving impossible as I continued listening to the radio coverage of the aftermath of this horrendous event. It really felt as though I was betraying the dead and wounded. To make matters worse, as I drew up at traffic lights in Belfast I noticed a nurse in uniform in the car next to me. She was signalling right in the direction of the Royal Victoria Hospital. Our eyes met for just a second and I had to look away. Here I was setting off to enjoy myself and she was about to confront the consequences of the actions of the cowards who so callously butchered Saturday afternoon shoppers in Omagh. But why should I, or for that matter, any of us non-combatant civilians, carry the burden of guilt for these faceless fascist scumbags? I determined to carry on with my mission. But there was to be no escape from the events back home as I discovered when I met former United hero Frank Stapleton in the Four Seasons Hotel near Manchester airport early on the morning of Monday, 17 August. For, as it happens, Frank Stapleton has had personal experience of exploding bombs and mass murder.

The conflict in Ireland first impacted on the life of a 17-year-old Arsenal apprentice centre-forward during a visit home in the spring of 1974, he remembered, as we chatted about the awful, final brutality of the Omagh bombing. On 17 May 1974 three bombs exploded in Dublin city centre during the evening rush hour – killing 22 people outright and wounding over 100 others. Then a short time later that same day, five died in Monaghan, 80 miles north of Dublin and close to the border with Northern Ireland. The bombs were the work of the UVF and/or elements of the British secret services, depending on whom you believe. For the teenage Arsenal apprentice, it is a day he will never forget: 'I was at home and actually heard one of the bombs go off about five or six miles away in the city centre. What we heard was not a big bang, it was more like a motorbike backfiring and all of a sudden – well, it was just unbelievable. It was a Friday afternoon and people were waiting for family or friends to get off work when three bombs went off. It was horrifying. I was watching television news about Omagh last night and it brought back memories of the Dublin bombings and I just couldn't understand the mentality of the Omagh bombers when a child of one-and-a-half years is killed. I just sat there and could have cried.'

Stapleton reflected on the fact that later in 1974 IRA bomb attacks in Guildford and Birmingham left 24 dead and resulted in some nasty experiences for Irish people on British streets. 'Liam Brady got attacked on a tube train in London,' Frank recalled, 'he was 17 at the time and was with his girlfriend when he was beaten up by a group of lads because of his accent.' There's a strange paradox in the manner in which the conflict back home made an impact on the Irish living in Britain. Unlike Brady, Stapleton never suffered any racial prejudice from the English but when the IRA brought their 'war' to the mainland it served to remind everyone in Britain – British and Irish citizens alike – that the 'war' had not gone away. Of course, as the 'luck of the Irish' would have it, the two parts of Ireland were drawn in the same qualifying group for the 1980 European Championships, a group that also included England.

In any event, as the Irish bombed and shot each other in the six counties of Northern Ireland, Stapleton and his Republic of Ireland team-mates headed for Belfast in November 1979. 'Yeah,' said Stapleton, 'it was really tense in Belfast. It was the first time we'd ever met. Gerry Daly was playing and someone threw a coin and it hit him on the head and he thought he'd been shot. At the time it was pretty serious but afterwards, at least a month later, the lads were laughing about it. But it was a very tense situation going to Belfast to play, with the security situation there. I think that was the worst of it, realising people had to live with that every day, people who don't know anything else. I don't know how they could live with that. But then came the ceasefires and you could just see the whole place kind of lifting. People were being interviewed on television and they felt good about everything and there was a lot of belief in the country again with people starting to invest and you could just see the cloud lifting off the whole place . . . and then the Omagh bomb goes off . . .' Stapleton's voice trails off in disgust at this latest threat to peace in his homeland. Before the dark clouds of depression engulf us in the futility of Irish politics and Irish inhumanity to fellow Irish citizens, we return to the agreed agenda. That is to say, we talk about my memories of Frank Stapleton, Manchester United centre-forward and scorer of 78 goals in his six seasons with the greatest club side in the world.

Frank Stapleton grew up in Dublin supporting Manchester United but never actually saw his favourite team play until he arrived at Old Trafford for a trial as a 15-year-old in 1972 and, as it happens, what he witnessed was typical for the times. 'United were at home to Liverpool,' he says, 'and they were stuffed by three goals to nil. George Best was playing, and Bobby Charlton and Denis Law so it was a United team four years past its glorious peak of victory over Benfica in the European Cup final. The atmosphere was fantastic, as usual, but the United team was well beaten on the day.' That was Stapleton's brief introduction to a team five years into what was to become 26 barren years. He had his trial but was not considered suitable material for United until nine years later when he cost the club £900,000 from Arsenal. Naturally enough, his favourite club was still rummaging around for points among the 'nearly men' when he returned – although he became a member of a squad of talented individuals never quite capable, collectively, of delivering the league under the direction of Ron Atkinson.

Stapleton acknowledged the creativity and individual skills of the players gathered at Old Trafford but like so many before he had no definitive answer as to why they failed. 'We should have won it twice,' he told me, 'and we were close on other occasions. I think under Big Ron we used to get a little too relaxed. That's what really frustrates me given the quality of players we had at the time – Robson, Wilkins, Coppell and Norman – creative players. It should have really happened for us. But sometimes I think Ron was too relaxed, behaving as if we had won it already. Arguably the quality of player in our team was as good as today but because we did not win any League titles people do not regard us as being one of the great teams.'

That can hardly be considered surprising given that the League Championship trophy never got out of Merseyside in the time that Big Ron was in charge – going four times to Liverpool and twice to Everton. But then if you scratch a little deeper with Frank he begins to articulate some thoughts on these years of misery and the word to unlock this train of thought is 'discipline'. 'Ron's relaxed atmosphere is not something I would agree with,' Frank explained, 'I think it was probably half his problem.' Whereas Big Norm, Robbo and Paul McGrath might have enjoyed the 'freedom' of Ron's reign, clearly it did not inspire Frank. 'He [Atkinson] would say to the players, "Go and do well" and he did not tie people down to a routine and discipline. If you look at the top teams in the world today, there is a real discipline inside the team and a discipline outside the team. If you look at Arsenal at the moment they monitor all their players' diets and weights and control everything they eat. Strict regimes are used to help the coach keep the players on a tighter rein. You just can't leave players to their own devices, I have never believed in that. Alex Ferguson certainly did not believe in that either because when he came in he changed the whole thing and he kept tabs on players. The players know if they are out drinking, there are people who will call in to let Alex know.' You can tell simply by looking at the healthy sheen emanating from the man 11 years after he quit United that Frank Stapleton did not succumb to whatever temptations would have been permissible under Big Ron.

Behind every good team is a quality goalkeeper. According to Stapleton the United side of his era did have the foundation of 'greatness' in Gary Bailey, the blond-haired South African-born English international. 'Gary Bailey was a great keeper for us,' Stapleton told me, 'he was very underrated I think. He will always be remembered for a mistake he made in the 1979 Cup final. If you ask Peter Schmeichel today, he will tell you that his idol was Gary Bailey. And you have to say that Gary Bailey was a great goalkeeper who was brave as anything, someone who would come for crosses. He made mistakes, but then so did Bruce Grobbelaar, who was a great goalkeeper for Liverpool. Yet everyone remembers him for his mistakes. But I tell you what, you ask the players who played with him and they will tell you he was committed, they knew where they were with him when it came to coming for crosses. Of course, he'd come for stupid things but at least they knew he was coming and then they could drop off. How many times did you see the ball being cleared off the Liverpool line? Yes, there were occasions when Grobbelaar conceded goals but I think more times he killed off very dangerous situations. I think Liverpool in their days of success always had great goalkeepers – Ray Clemence was another. Look at United today, with Schmeichel. Think of the number of times someone has broken through and Schmeichel keeps them in the game with a wonderful save. It has happened so often and instead of being a goal down he has kept you in the match or he has made these saves to defend a lead. You need a top-class goalkeeper like that.'

As we sit chatting I become aware I am about to broach a paradox with our former centre-forward because one of my greatest memories of the man is not in the role of a Scouse-busting goal scorer but as Scouse-defying defender – twice in Wembley finals.

Milk Cup final: 26 March 1983 v. Liverpool at Wembley Stadium. (Lost 2–1)

TEAM: **Bailey; Duxbury, Albiston, Moses, Moran (Macari), McQueen, Wilkins, Muhren, Stapleton, Whiteside (1), Coppell.**

As Frank Stapleton and the rest of the United team were preparing to do battle against our principal adversaries, I was travelling due north from Belfast to a wedding in Harry Gregg's present home town, Portstewart. Prior to the formal part of the proceedings in the church, I managed to get my Liverpool-supporting wife Fiona into a pub to view the opening exchanges. Manchester United had never been to the final of this competition before. Sir Matt tended to regard it then in the same way as Alex Ferguson today, that is to say, as a Mickey Mouse tournament currently referred to by many fans as the Worthless Cup. Nevertheless, the Scousers were the opposition – and games against them are always taken seriously, especially during the 26 'wilderness' years when our Cup finals were the matches against the 'Dirties'. Now we were in a genuine Cup final against them – the first since we beat them in the 1977 FA Cup. We hadn't finished our first drink when Big Norm put us ahead with a magnificent turn against Hansen and shot into the bottom right-hand corner past Grobbelaar. There was almost an involuntary spillage as I celebrated the goal. Before my body had time to absorb the total pleasure my mind was disseminating, there were groans of disappointment as I was dragged away screaming from the television to go to the wedding. By the time I sneaked back to the action, we were playing extra time and I watched in horror as Ronnie Whelan accepted the luck of the bounce as the ball rebounded off Frank Stapleton's shin on the left edge of the penalty box. Without hesitation Whelan bent a fantastic shot beyond the sprawling reach of Bailey and Liverpool had secured a victory which, by all accounts, they deserved. My confusion about Stapleton being in our penalty box instead of theirs (where he had in the past been very successful in helping us to beat them) only became tolerably understandable when I discovered we had been plagued by a series of injuries. Kevin Moran had to leave the battlefield to be substituted by Lou Macari and Gordon McQueen struggled on with an injury that effectively nullified his brave efforts to contribute to our cause. 'I had to go back to defend,' Stapleton recalled. 'McQueen got injured. I ended up playing centre-back with Mike Duxbury, I think, and Lou Macari was playing right-back. We had to battle away because there were so many injuries. Ronnie Whelan got a great goal but was lucky it came back off my foot.'

Two years later and Stapleton was back in our defence again at Wembley in the FA Cup final against Everton when Kevin Moran was sent off. It should not surprise anyone with a passing interest in the 'beautiful game' that a poacher might just make a good gamekeeper given that he knows all the moves and dodges his erstwhile opponents might make. Indeed, one might ponder on the fact that more attackers should become defenders when they lose the sparkle up front. But hold on. 'Not so fast,' says Frank, 'I suppose if I had got to play there on a more regular basis to come to terms with what was needed, it would probably have prolonged my career at a higher level but it did not work out that way. Everybody said to me, "You will probably end up going back into defence." But I never really did. When I went to Bradford my intention was to play at the back, but team needs come first and I had to play in midfield.'

He did manage a couple of games at centre-half at Bradford but that was long after I admired his abilities in this position for Manchester United.

Although I missed the live action on the day of the 1983 League Cup final, I was fortunate to be present at Wembley when Moran got sent off and Stapleton found himself back alongside McGrath as Everton piled forward. It was impressive. Andy Gray and Graeme Sharpe chased, harried and moaned a lot – but there was no way through our makeshift defence. Stapleton was good at holding them up, staying on his feet and ignoring any temptations to launch himself into premature tackles of the defence-splitting kind. Our ten men held out to secure a memorable victory. As Stapleton recollected, the fact that we had been reduced to ten men was a significant factor in itself: 'It wasn't a great game but it was pretty tight. There had been one or two incidents but nothing special and the game wasn't going anywhere and then something like Kevin being sent off happens and it totally galvanises the whole match. Then we had to find that extra bit of determination and on such an occasion as a Cup final, that kind of thing does make the ten men work hard to find that bit extra. The crowd were really brilliant. Up to that point, they were probably thinking this game could go any way but then because they thought it was an injustice, they became more vociferous and they were louder and from then on we were all half a yard quicker.

'Everton were, they said, a little bit fatigued. Did you ever speak to any of the Everton lads, Andy Gray in particular? They always say they were totally bombed out, they were tired, and I think that's a bit of an excuse. I mean, they were saying they'd played a lot – they'd won the European Cup-Winners' Cup a few days earlier and they'd won the League just before that. I don't really believe they were fatigued. When you are on a run like that, the Cup is a daisy – you don't feel the fatigue. We got an extra bit on the day. That's why it's so hard with Cup finals to predict who's going to win them, regardless of how much favour you have, because there's always that little bit of something else that you can't put your finger on.'

Standing in the 'blue Scouse' end with my ten-year-old son Steven we made the acquaintance of a few Scousers who knew exactly where to put their fingers at the moment Big Norm struck with such devastating accuracy at the opposite end of the stadium. As we celebrated his wonderful strike in proper fashion, the kind Scousers behind us were busy with their fingers – pulling their cocks out to piss all over our overnight bag which lay at our feet on the terracing.

Still, it was another FA Cup final victory – another mere morsel to satisfy our hunger for the 'big one' – the Football League title. Big Ron's team all too often flattered to deceive. Stapleton has acknowledged that by stating that the side should have won the League at least twice during his reign as centre-forward. With 78 goals in nearly 300 appearances for United, it might be easy to criticise his strike rate which never rose above 14 in a season. But that would be churlish and would not take cognisance of his other attributes.

Stapleton was a tremendous leader of the forward line. A man who had an uncanny instinct of being able to somehow tell where his playing colleagues could be found on the pitch – even though they were behind him or extremely wide and therefore out of his line of vision. But when he scored, he scored important goals. Who can forget his winners against Liverpool? The right foot shot from ten yards at Old Trafford on 24 September 1983 in front of 56,121 fans. Then the superb winning header at Anfield during a televised game on 31 March 1985 (a Sunday I think). Sadly, at this stage of our 26 years in the Championship wilderness, these games against Liverpool were our 'Cup finals' – in much the same way their games against us in the '90s have become their 'Cup finals'. There is no better feeling than beating the Scousers and singing, as we did when I was at Old Trafford a few weeks ago (24 September 1998) for the Premier League home game. 'Two-nil in your Cup final,' we sang at the Scousers with total abandon. (NB: There was even more joyous celebration on 24 January 1999 when we brought about a late but nevertheless abrupt end to the Scousers' season with our stunning 2–1 win in the fifth round of the FA Cup at Old Trafford. I had to give up my ticket for this memorable occasion on the Friday evening before the game because of work commitments thus missing out on a real treat! Cathal, a friend of my son Steven, gleefully took my seat at the game. I have never looked at him in the same light since!)

However, Stapleton did not always save his best for the Scousers. No, indeed. Picture the scene at Old Trafford on a night of European glory against another old enemy, Barcelona. The date was 21 March 1984 – my son Steven's ninth birthday. What an occasion!

European Cup-Winners' Cup quarter-final. (Second Leg): 21 March 1984 v. Barcelona at Old Trafford. (Won 3–0)
TEAM: **Bailey; Duxbury, Albiston, Wilkins, Moran, Hogg, Robson (2), Muhren, Stapleton (1), Whiteside (Hughes), Moses.**

Diego Maradona and Barcelona arrived at Old Trafford with a comfortable 2–0 lead from the first leg of this European Cup-Winners' Cup quarter-final in Spain on 7 March 1984. United had a mountain to climb two weeks later in the return leg on 21 March. To be truthful, even the Stretford End faithful must have harboured doubts about our chances. But in an incredible atmosphere 'Captain Marvel' (Bryan Robson) scored two goals to level the tie. The second came just a minute before Stapleton screwed the cork into the finest Spanish rioja and scored the winner. I was still doing somersaults in our living-room to celebrate the aggregate equaliser when Robson got the ball near the centre-circle.

'Captain Marvel' took a couple of strides forward. The crowd crowed with anticipation every time he touched the ball. With the outside of his left foot 'Robbo' sent it wide to the left where Arthur Albiston was running into position. Albiston pushed it forward and then put over an excellent cross that was met by Big Norm at the far post. His header travelled back across the Barcelona goal, agonisingly for them, hanging in the air for what seemed like a slow-motion minute whilst at the same time wrong-footing the Spaniards. The ball bounced perfectly, four or five yards out from the goal, to allow Stapleton to volley it into the net from just a couple of feet away. I took off. From the edge of my seat I jettisoned myself into space in a star-shaped jump – towards the ceiling separating us from the landlord, a scream of utter delight emanating from my mouth. Unfortunately, my heels caught the underside of the chair. The impact sent the chair tumbling over onto its back and brought me crash-landing onto my face in front of the television. I left the air and the air left me as I crashed down on re-entry. Now I was gasping whilst trying to absorb the celebrations on the screen above me. I would not have thanked you for the thought at the time, but this was a supreme moment for the psyche of any United supporter. Suddenly the trap of European failure had been sprung and in the instant Stapleton lashed the ball into the Barcelona net we had become European favourites. That sadly, as we were all to discover so often in our more recent years, was also our European death knell. A repeat of the season when our hopes were raised with the 5–1 thrashing of Benfica at their Stadium of Light. Nevertheless, and I want you to think carefully about this, especially if you are unfortunate enough to recall the dreadful night in 1995 when the Spanish giants stuffed us 4–0. The true significance of the Stapleton winning goal was we had completed one of the most compelling turnarounds in European football history – and that, surely, is a much better feat to be remembered for than the 4–0 mauling we received 11 years later in Barcelona. This was one of the *great* European nights for British football and, more particularly, for Manchester United – a nine on the Richter scale.

Naturally, of all the memories in Stapleton's memory bank inspired by 286 games in a red shirt, this is *the* richest of all. 'This was a truly tremendous night for us because we were given little chance of coming back from 2–0 down,' he recalled. 'The crowd was fantastic. The noise they made from beginning to end was uplifting and there's no doubt it helped raise the team to one of the greatest ever European performances by a United side.' Tragically, our traditional European semi-final jinx struck again when we lost to Juventus. We drew 1–1 at home and lost 2–1 in Italy.

Strangely enough, it's only the excitement of European nights at Old Trafford that can still tempt Stapleton back to the stadium. Such has been our domination of the League, he finds little to inspire him: 'I go to European games. I go down and buy my tickets and entertain visitors from Ireland to a night at Old Trafford. I like European nights because they are so different. I've seen a few League games and most of the time United dominate them and it all becomes a little boring. You know, you expect them to win every time. When a good team comes to Old Trafford you think, "great", but you can tell from the first minute that they're just sitting back and you know they've just come for the draw and they're never going to get anything out of it. Eventually the goals come and the goals are the highlight of the game but the team just grinds and grinds out the results. But when you get European football, you see a different style and the visitors will always have something to offer – something spicy. The Liverpool and Arsenal games offer this feeling of uncertainty and maybe Chelsea as well, but the European games have that something special.'

It is easy to empathise with Stapleton here. Manchester United plc may have become the richest club in the world but many fans feel that success is at the expense of Manchester United Football Club. One manifestation of the profiteering from the fans is the dreadful lack of atmosphere inside Old Trafford on most match days. With 55,000-plus guaranteed at every game, you might be forgiven for thinking during a match that you have come to the wrong venue, that you are seated at a tennis tournament where silence is required during play. Aside from home fixtures against the likes of Chelsea, Arsenal and Liverpool, the Old Trafford crowd seems to raise itself only for the European nights. There is considerable debate about creating a singing area to try to generate the kind of atmosphere that in the past terrified opposition teams before a ball was kicked. Frank Stapleton was fortunate enough to experience life at Old Trafford in the days before the overemphasis on corporate hospitality.

'The atmosphere was special,' said Stapleton enthusiastically. 'Looking at it from an opposition point of view, when I played for Arsenal, we always knew that a game against United at Old Trafford was a big game and we used to look forward to going there. It was one of the highlights of the season and obviously when we played them at Highbury that was always the biggest of the season, apart from the Tottenham game. But when you are playing at Old Trafford for United and when you are out there you get a real feeling that you have to do something special for the supporters. They expect it, it is not enough to just go out there and play but you have to produce some level, some sort of skilful touch or something and that in many ways was probably a downfall for so many MU-ers until they won the League for the team. Everybody was trying to perform and probably didn't play as much as a team as they should have done. It kind of brings out the creativity in everybody, particularly the midfield and the forward players. You would try things and sometimes they should be more pragmatic.'

Stapleton seemed to be suggesting that in his days United played their football to satisfy the supporters' demands for attacking play, rather than play the game in a manner that would have given them a better chance to compete for the points necessary to end the League hoodoo. He acknowledged the change in attitudes with the arrival of Alex Ferguson when he told me: 'What Alex brought to the club was a certain way of playing and it was a little like the Dutch way – you play this way from the back, you play through the middle and then the forwards can try things. Forwards are always trying something. Too often in the past the defenders were trying things at a time when United did not win anything at all. I think this was probably the downfall when everybody wanted to try creative things and instead of Ron saying, "No, I don't want you to do that", his philosophy has always been to attack. The supporters liked that. They liked us going away and playing to win, not to draw. That never entered into our thinking. Everybody was trying to do things which sometimes did not come off and that is why when you have had so many failures over the years, particularly among the forwards, there was a lot of pressure exerted, not the verbal kind, but pressure for people to do something special. At United they were always looking for something special.'

Taking this argument a little further you wonder whether the fans' demands for success, and for success in a particularly pleasing-to-the-eye attacking manner, heaped an unspoken pressure on the players which in turn hampered the team effort to win the main prize, the League title.

Stapleton is quite clear about this aspect of life at United during the barren years. He was quite emphatic: 'I think that is a fair point because I know when I see the team playing today and there are times when the ball goes across the back four and back across again and people accept that. They wouldn't have accepted that in our day. When he played the ball back because we were forced to go back sometimes, we were booed by our own supporters at home because they wanted the team to go forward. But then what happened while Alex has been there, he has warmed the supporters to that style of play. Liverpool played that way as well when they started to win things in the seventies and eighties. They always built things from the back. In the days of Keegan and Toshack up front, everything used to go just straight to the front. Ian Callaghan pushing straight up to Jimmy Case with Keegan always buzzing about. Liverpool changed the way they played, the philosophy changed and they played out from the back with Neill, Lawrenson, Hansen and Kennedy. They played through Souness and the midfield and they got their success from there. United started to play like that. But initially the supporters would not accept it. Get the ball forward, we want it in the box, was their attitude. Now it has changed people. They see a bit more, there's a bit more knowledge of the game because of the television coverage and people are starting to see and they're explaining more to people. So it is a good thing that people are getting more educated about the game and today I don't think supporters get enough credit for what they pick up on the game. There's not too many supporters who will accept the ball just being whacked forward – even Wimbledon don't do that now. The game is more sophisticated now and the fans have grown more sophisticated as well.'

For players, sophistication comes with the experience of playing at European and international level. Frank Stapleton earned his European spurs with Arsenal and United. His international career covered a period of 14 years during which time he was capped 71 times. He made his debut in a Republic of Ireland side that included four others who at one time were on United's books – Giles, Givens, Daly and Martin.

Republic of Ireland International (71 caps 1976–90)
DEBUT: 13 October 1976 v. Turkey in Ankara. (Drew 3–3)
TEAM: **Kearns; Waters (1), Mulligan, Martin, Holmes, Daly (1), Giles, Brady, Conroy, Stapleton (1), Givens.**

It took Frank Stapleton just three minutes to make an impact at international level. In front of 40,000 spectators, mostly Turks, he marked his debut with a goal. His nerves disappeared in the instant the ball struck the Turkish net. 'Scoring so early in the game allowed me to settle down to enjoy the whole experience,' Stapleton recalled about the first of his 71 caps. Like so many other quality Irish players he suffered greatly from the inferiority which for so long prevented the Irish from putting together a team that collectively could make progress in the big competitions. The tragedy for Stapleton was that by the time his home country had found a means of providing a team strong enough to make it to the World Cup finals in 1990, he was 34 years of age and his international career was near an end. In fact, he made his final appearance in an Irish shirt during a World Cup warm-up game in Malta on 2 June 1990. He came on as a substitute nine days before the Irish played England in their first game of the 1990 World Cup finals in Italy. The Republic got through the group stage and the second round before losing to Italy in the quarter-finals. Stapleton did not make an appearance in Italy but he marked his final game in the Irish shirt in Valetta with a goal as the Irish cruised to a 3–0 victory. But when he looks back on his international career, Stapleton remembers his contribution to the Irish World Cup cause with pride.

'Without doubt my best game for Ireland was against the French in Dublin in 1981,' said Stapleton. 'We won 3–2 in front of 53,000 and I managed to score a goal.' France qualified for the 1982 World Cup finals in Spain as runners-up to Belgium. The Irish were third on the same points as the French but with an inferior goal tally.

Naturally, Stapleton was disappointed to miss out on successive World Cup finals – 1982, 1986 and then, most cruelly of all, in the Jack Charlton-inspired era which got the Republic of Ireland to the World Cup finals of 1990 and 1994. However, in a career which saw him play at the top level for United, Arsenal and Ajax, Frank Stapleton has many happy memories to sustain him in retirement. Such good memories, in fact, that even with the knowledge he has of today's game and the benefit of what he learned during his playing career, if someone was to offer Frank Stapleton the chance to relive his life, he would do the same again.

'I would still go into football,' he said without hesitation, 'because the knowledge and the things I have learned over the years I would use to my advantage. Of course the system is completely different today. We as players were very restricted when we first came to Arsenal. We were venturing for the first couple of years and to be truthful we didn't get our rewards. It seems there's a complete set of people today getting rewards now for doing nothing and I think the management need to balance it up. I think what's missing is that feeling about the game. It is not the same because of the money involved today. It has become a big business.'

When pressed to explain what he means when he refers to 'that feeling about the game,' Stapleton reveals that he means the kind of schoolboy enthusiasm to play the game for the game's sake rather than just as a means of making megabucks. As he put it: 'It is the enjoyment of playing, what it gives you inside and what it gives you when you are playing. The best times – the most enjoyable times for me – were when there was nothing at stake. When you are a junior and you are playing at 14 or 15 years of age and you lost – it was not the end of the world. You enjoyed the game, you enjoyed playing. When you get into the professional game that goes out of the door quite a bit – but there is still a little bit of the good feeling there. When I was a player, the first question you asked when you were going to a new club was, "Are we going to win the League this year? Or are we going to win the FA Cup or League Cup?" We were looking to win medals, we wanted to play for the sake of playing and we wanted good rewards for it, but nowadays those questions are way down the list – maybe even fourth or fifth. The first question asked today is, "How much are you going to pay me?"

'Football is an instinctive thing, it is a feeling, it is a game of feeling but what is happening now is that the financial side is taking over and it has squashed everything else. Football is becoming business, it is just business first and foremost. Now it is a real commercial business. It is just like the City of London . . .'

Indeed it is. Indeed it is. Stapleton still exudes that schoolboy enthusiasm for the game he once graced and he clearly blames the influence of America for the development of this commercial greed in football. He should know what he is talking about as he spent a frustrating year attempting to coach Major League 'soccer' in Boston whilst trying to breach the American sporting culture exemplified by American football, baseball and basketball. In his humble opinion, this has proved to be a futile exercise thus far. But he also saw another side of life there which he believes has been brought into Britain. 'When I lived there,' he said ruefully, 'everything was about the money. If you get a service you pay for it. That is the American philosophy and although we are not as bad as them we are getting a little bit more like that. I don't think we'll ever get fully like that because people here still care, they still care about the neighbourly things. Sometimes I think it is not like that anymore because you live in houses and you don't even know your neighbours. But years ago when we grew up the neighbours were in all the time, doors were left open, the keys were left in the doors – even at night. You went to bed and your keys were left in the door. Now it is all alarm systems and that's not the way to live . . .'

We finished our tea in the bar of the Four Seasons Hotel on this philosophical note. Frank Stapleton was the second player to agree to be interviewed for this book. My wife made an approach on my behalf when she met him in a Dublin hotel. She was working for Sky Television at the time and he was over in Ireland for an international game. From the outset he was more than willing to take part. He said he understood from the experience of writing his own book just how difficult it could be to get others to participate and share your enthusiasm. He gave my wife his home telephone number and told her I should give him a ring. Frank Stapleton was as good as his word in helping this United fan kick-start *United Irishmen*. Not only was he a brilliant Scouse-busting star of the eighties, but Frank Stapleton is a gentleman who has not lost the common touch when it comes to dealing with his public.

REASON TO BELIEVE: With George Best running defenders ragged, scoring goals, tackling back to win the ball and entertaining the crowd, who is going to benefit from any passes he does care to make? Frank Stapleton for a start. Now here was a leader of the line who could be dominant in the air and surprisingly fleet of foot on the floor. Stapleton was a gifted centre-forward who could read the play and anticipate the move that would provide him with a shot at goal or create a chance for a colleague with his running off the ball. With superb control, Stapleton could hold play up until he could see that little chink of light that would put a player through on goal.

Once when travelling back from collecting an award at the 1996 Celtic International Film Festival in Wales, I was compelled to listen on a car radio to the United FA Cup semi-final with Chelsea. The passenger terminal at Holyhead had no television set to entertain us during the one-hour delay in sailing. Bloody disgraceful if you ask this frustrated punter. Anyway, the car owner, Michael Beattie, knows as much about football as I do about snipe shooting. The commentator got excited during a passage of play and once normality was restored Michael burst forth with: 'What did he say there? A deaf little prick?' I buckled in laughter. But I knew what he meant, what the commentator actually said was 'a deft little flick'. Frank Stapleton was a master of the 'deaf little prick!'

FRANK STAPLETON: THE QUESTIONNAIRE
BORN: Dublin – 10 July 1956.

Which junior clubs did you play for – and during what years?
St Martins and Bolton Athletic, 1969–72.

Which club did you support as a boy?
Manchester United.

Was it always your ambition to be a professional footballer?
Yes.

Do you recall the moment you first realised you were signing for United and describe your reaction to being taken on by such a big club?
As negotiations were going on for quite a time, I had quite a lot of time to think about the move I was making. I was very pleased when it happened.

You were at United as a youth in the seventies – what years? And describe your feelings when you decided to leave there and move on to Arsenal. Reasons for the change?
I went to United in 1972 for a trial but they did not sign me. I then went to Arsenal that summer and signed for them.

What were your views when eventually United came back for you at nearly £1m? Did you have any doubts given your earlier experience at Old Trafford?
I had no doubts about going to United as it was nine years since I had been there and things had changed, as well as managers. I was coming for a lot of money and the situation was different.

You played 234 games – which one stands out in the memory – and why?
I think it is hard to pick out one particular game but the FA Cup finals are memorable and also European games.

The best manager you played for at Old Trafford – and the worst?
I only played under two managers at United. Ron Atkinson and Alex Ferguson, and both are good managers.

The highlight of your football career? When, where etc?
Played in Euro '88 for Ireland and the FA Cup finals I played in.

Your worst moment at Old Trafford – and why?
I think when I had to have a knee operation in 1984.

Which individual was the biggest influence on your career – first as a player and secondly as a manager?
I think people influence you when you are progressing and at all stages of your career. Suffice to say everyone I played with and under had an influence on my career.

Your best game for United? (When, where and against whom?)
Hard one, but I remember playing well against Spartak Verna/Bulgaria in the Cup-Winners' Cup at Old Trafford and scoring both goals in a 2–0 win in 1984.

Your worst game for United? (When, where and against whom?)
Again, a hard one but more of a choice here – but probably against Bournemouth in the FA Cup in 1984–85.

Pick your greatest ever Man Utd team. (And give a few comments to explain if possible.)
Schmeichel, Keane, Best, Law, Charlton, Giggs, Cantona, Edwards, Robson, Hughes, Taylor (Tommy). Best 11 players.

You were at Old Trafford at a time when there were many players from Northern Ireland and the Republic of Ireland. Did this add to the enjoyment of playing at Old Trafford? Or did it cause difficulties?
There were no problems whatsoever between players from north and south. In fact, it added to the banter in the dressing-room.

171

Best player you ever saw in a United shirt? And why?
George Best – self-explanatory.

The most difficult opponent you ever faced? (Example of game, with year and competition if possible.)
Too many difficult opponents.

You made your international debut in 1977 against Turkey. Describe your feelings on that day.
Very nervous and not sure how it would go but as I scored after three minutes I settled down and enjoyed the whole experience.

The best game for your country – and the worst?
Best against France in Dublin in 1981, qualifer for the World Cup. We won 3–2. Worst against Israel in 1984. I had a bout of 'flu but played and I had no energy and was substituted in the second half.

How did you regard the Man Utd fans?
I have the highest regard for United supporters who always treated me well and even forgave me that goal in the 1979 FA Cup final!

Why do you think they remained so loyal throughout the years when they so desperately wanted a League title but had to watch for 26 years as Liverpool dominated?
I think because MU is very special and has an attraction for people all over the world. They stayed with the club when they went down to the old Second Division and always believed the club would get back to the top.

Did the fans' desire for a League Championship ever put pressure on the players? Do you think it might in some way have contributed to the failure to win the title for 26 years?
I don't think so. I believe the media made more of it than the fans. I think they just wanted to watch attractive football and felt the honours would come by playing that way.

Your views on the team selected for this book?
I think it would be hard to better the team selected. But it is all a matter of opinion and you will never get two people to agree on the same 11. Still, a hard team to beat.

ELEVEN

Norman Whiteside

(STRIKER/MIDFIELD/DEFENDER OF THE FAITH)

Manchester United: 1981–82 to 1988–89: 254 (18) games: 67 goals

DEBUT: **24 April 1982 v. Brighton and Hove Albion at Goldstone Ground.
(Won 1–0)**

TEAM: **Bailey; Gidman, Albiston, Wilkins, Moran, McQueen, Robson,
McGarvey (1), Stapleton, Grimes, Duxbury (Whiteside)**

HONOURS: **FA Cup 1982–83; 1984–85**

The eyes, previously so quick to the smile, suddenly retreated to the more
menacing look which once sent shivers of fear coursing through opponents
– although more often than not, his glare would inspire full-bodied attacks
of the 'involuntary defecations'. Nowadays, the fearsome look which used
to be aimed at an offending defender in Scouse colours is more likely to be
directed at some disagreeable individual failing to deliver the promised
'service'. When we met at a Belfast restaurant overlooking rowers on a
decontaminated stretch of the River Lagan, it was a wine waiter who was
on the receiving end. Having twice returned an Australian Chardonnay to
be properly chilled, with justification in my humble opinion, the former
Manchester United hit man was less than impressed when the said careless
waiter delivered the next bottle in a totally frozen state! Norman
Whiteside's years of attending wine-tasting courses told him not to be
amused by this attempt to serve 'wine-pops'. He tackled the waiter in the
same uncompromisingly determined style which epitomised his performances
as a Manchester United player. A true swashbuckling 'Defender of the
Faith', whose stature took on 'Roy of the Rovers' proportions to the hero
worshippers on the terraces of Old Trafford, of which, by the way, I was
one. He was not rude to the waiter. He was firm. But then he would say
he was never 'rude' in the manner of his tackling. Hard – but fair! That's

what he would say. Try telling that to Steve McMahon! Picture the scene. Anfield. 4 April 1988. United 3–1 down. McMahon the hardman kicking seven shades of shit out of our midfield. Whiteside. The sub replaces McGrath midway through the second half. Two minutes later, McMahon felled. McMahon f***ed. No more hardman. United score twice. Result: 3–3 draw. Sublime! Surreal! Sir Norman!

Norman Whiteside was born in Belfast on 7 May 1965. Before he had reached his teens he had a 'reputation'. As a schoolboy international, this Shankill Road skinhead towered above his peers, a kind of Gulliver displaying his vast array of talents and imposing his will on the 'little people'. Belfast was a city of divided religious loyalties, where murder and mayhem was part of every citizen's daily diet. It was a place where rumour replaced reason, perception gripped so tightly to reality it was nearly impossible to sift out the truth. Sports reporters side-stepped the 'conflict bullshit' to report the daring deeds of one Norman Whiteside.

My first memory of Big Norman was on a local television report of a Northern Ireland schoolboys' game in 1978 or 1979. The whisper was that he was to join United. With his close cropped hairstyle he stood head and shoulders above the other boys as he blasted the ball goalwards in the fashion that was later to become his trademark at Old Trafford. He looked big, strong and exceptionally skilful. In 1979 the Northern Ireland schoolboys won the European Championship, beating Wales 2–1 in the final. Naturally, Norman scored one of the goals. Then in 1980 he appeared for his school, Cairnmartin, in the Northern Ireland Schools Final – scoring six of his side's seven goals!

By now, of course, he was already under the scrutiny of the late Bob Bishop, legendary Manchester United scout who sent George Best, amongst others, to Old Trafford. Scoring achievements such as the one just mentioned were not exceptional where Big Norm was concerned. Bob, fighting hard to hold back his laughter during a BBC interview in 1986, recalled one special match: 'I remember this trial game for Norman one time . . . they took him off after 20 minutes because he had scored seven goals!' This event was to be the benchmark for Whiteside's progress in the world of professional football. He gathered an impressive list of 'firsts' as his career developed – youngest to play in World Cup finals, youngest to score in an FA Cup final and also in a League Cup final in the same season.

As any youngsters from Belfast who have gone to Old Trafford in the post-Best era will tell you, there is one annoying consequence of being 'spotted' by Bob Bishop and then sent across the sea to follow in the footsteps of the great 'El Beatle'. Newspaper reporters make constant references to the latest protégé becoming 'the new George Best', thereby denying these young individuals their own identity. No matter how flattering a comparison with Best might have been, these young players – Sammy McIlroy, Norman Whiteside and Philip Mulryne immediately spring to mind – were at Old Trafford to make their own names. Sammy used to deal with this question by firmly informing anyone who cared to listen that there was only one George Best and that he, Sammy McIlroy, was setting out to make Sammy McIlroy's name. Fair enough! The benchmark for the man who discovered these three players with potential suited to United's brand of attacking football was George Best, and he was asked this same question many times over. When it came during the BBC interview, this is how Bob responded: 'You could not compare them, they had two different styles. George was an artist as well as a footballer – Norman is more direct.'

For 'more direct' in Whiteside's later career, read 'hardman'. But in his early days and as he himself will tell you, 'more direct' was the physical embellishment of the Whiteside mindset, even as a small boy. 'The most important thing in my life as a kid,' he explained enthusiastically over a well-done steak, 'was that I had tunnel vision . . . a stubborn belief that I was going to be a professional footballer and nobody was going to get in my way.' Those who tried, like McMahon, found Norman to be a formidable opponent who was blessed with such tremendous self-confidence, allied with an equally powerful determination to win, that he could make things happen to repel or remove undesirable obstacles.

Stormin' Norman remembers his first competitive game for a Boys' Brigade team attached to a church on the Crumlin Road in Belfast. At the time his primary school had no organised team and it wasn't long before his prowess on the pitch introduced him to games against older boys. He was soon playing for an East Belfast outfit – with a name to strike horror into the hearts of all true Reds – a junior team representing a Liverpool supporters' club. Norman takes up the story, first explaining about how he even refused to allow considerations about his academic future to cloud his single-minded determination to succeed as a professional footballer.

'When I got to the age for secondary school, my two brothers – Ken (a year and nine months older) and Hugh (five years younger) – both went to the Boys Model school. But I was always worried because I knew the Boys Model was a rugby school so I went to Cairnmartin because they played football in first year. So I started playing for the school. At that time there were a few boys' clubs who wanted me to play for them and in East Belfast there was a club called Clara Boys. Next I knew, I was playing for EBLSC (East Belfast Liverpool Supporters' Club) which is in Templemore Avenue. It was amazing because I was going to United then, this was when I was about 12.'

As a schoolboy Norman did not favour any football club. He's a 'Red' now though. But he wasn't then, when he was playing for the Scouse supporters' club side. It was left to his entire family to uphold the good name of Whiteside as United fanatics! Naturally, they were delighted to learn of United's interest in Norman.

Norman went to Old Trafford in August 1978 and even though his trial was specially shortened by a day to allow him to go on a school trip to the United States, it was an impatient Norman who walked the streets of Boston with his school friends. He just had to find out what impression he had managed to make on the United coaching staff. So, against the school rules, he sneaked off to use his hosts' telephone to call home. Then, unable to contain his glee upon hearing the news from Belfast, he proudly announced his news to an assembled group of friends. The teachers, too, shared in the joy of the moment, so much so that they did not invoke any 'penalty' for the illicit call. Norman was just 13 years of age! A boy playing among men. The American trip was useful experience for what was to become a globe-trotting career in professional football. 'The lovely thing I remember about that trip was that I went to the White House to meet President Carter,' he recalled. 'He welcomed us into the White House and the Oval room and all that . . . so that was quite a good experience for a kid from the back streets of Belfast. That trip to America gave me the confidence to be independent, to start my life. I went to America as a 13-year-old and was away from my family for four weeks, living with other host families. It was my first time away from home. In fact, the first time I was on an aeroplane was to make the trip to Manchester on the Monday and then on the Thursday I left United and on Friday flew to America. That was the start of my life.'

But not quite the end of his schooling, such as it was, given that the young Norman's mind was not on academic achievement, but on pulling on the red shirt of the famous Manchester United. During his three remaining years at school, Norman continued making regular trips to Manchester. There were many at Old Trafford who marvelled at his skill. Among his admirers were two former international stars from the Busby Babes era. One was Bobby Charlton, who paid the young Norman a telling compliment when he stated: 'He would be classed as a Busby Babe in the old sense. We had really skilful young players that suddenly had to play with men and that is exactly what Norman Whiteside has done.'

The other admirer was Harry Gregg, a coach during Dave Sexton's reign when the young Whiteside arrived from Belfast. As we have already learned, Gregg regarded his former club and international team manager Peter Doherty as his mentor and inspiration. 'He [Doherty] used to say the great player, the true genius sees a picture,' Gregg recalled, adding, 'bad players do not see pictures. And I found it was true. When I had my spell as coach at Old Trafford, there was one young lad who shone through and who was truly a genius. That was Norman Whiteside. Norman as a 15- or 16-year-old kid was a great player. Great is not a word I would use very often. He may have lacked a bit of pace, but there's no doubt he could see pictures. Inside his head he saw the image of what it was he wanted to do and he was one of the most gifted young players I ever saw in my life.'

At 16 Norman quit school to give full vent to his conviction that he was going to make the grade at United and he remembers Gregg. It was Gregg who put Norman through his paces during his trial and later when he was pitted against the most competitive centre-backs in trial games. These matches ultimately shaped his future. They determined the minds of those who mattered at Old Trafford as to whether or not a particular individual had the makings of a good player. According to Norman, Sexton and his coaching staff liked what they saw: 'Dave Sexton would have been looking out his window. I was a skinhead and he liked the look of me straight away. They liked my attitude, my approach to the game. People like Harry Gregg were watching. Deep down while you wonder if you are good enough, these coaches knew after a day or two I was going to be alright.'

Norman has another, more painful, reason to remember Harry Gregg. When he was 15 he attended the club doctor with a stomach pain following a Northern Ireland under-18s game in Glasgow. The pain was diagnosed as acute appendicitis and Norman was immediately admitted to hospital for surgery. During his recuperation Norman received two visitors: 'Dave Sexton came up to the hospital as did Harry Gregg and other players which, for a 15-year-old who nobody knew anything about, was quite encouraging. And Dave Sexton brought me some football books and magazines to read. When you have had appendicitis, anyone that's had it will know you don't want to laugh. Harry Gregg was calling me all the bloody names of the day and was cracking jokes to be hilarious, and I was saying, "Don't make me laugh, Harry, don't make me laugh." And I had this big tube sticking out of my stomach with poison flying out of it every time I had a chuckle . . .'

Mild-mannered Dave Sexton might have signed Whiteside during his four-year reign at what became known as 'Cold Trafford', but it was left to his colourful successor, Big Ron Atkinson to set a teenage Whiteside on the road to fame and glory. Norman thinks of Big Ron as his best manager because he 'really knew how to look after his players in terms of man-management'. He remembers very clearly the day about two weeks before his 17th birthday when he was summoned to Atkinson's office. He told me: 'I was out training with the juniors at Old Trafford, the usual with the youth team and I got word from one of the coaching staff that the boss wanted to see me in his office and so I went up to see him in his office. And he said: "Have you got a suit?" I said I think I've got one. "Well," he says, "go and get it, get a taxi home, the club will pay for it. You're travelling with the first team to Brighton." So I went and got me suit and travelled with the first team to Brighton and there was a lot of speculation in the media that this young kid might get a game. I was 16 years old. And I must add I was on £16 a week at the time and there was all this speculation. But when he named his team on the morning of the game, I was substitute. We went for a walk along Brighton beach and I was told I was to be substitute. I was absolutely delighted. Then the game started and Ray Wilkins, who never scored a goal in a month of Sundays, scored this unbelievable goal from outside the box. I came on for Mike Duxbury, 12 minutes to go. Think about this. The way the United bonus system worked was that as you go through the season you accumulate points, so you get more win bonus.

'So if you are on 35 points you are getting £100 a point; if you are on 45 points you get £200 a point. So at the end of the season it accumulates . . . we were on £800 win bonus. I got £800 for 12 minutes . . . for coming on the park in 1982 . . . 24 April. And then I was in the first-team panel and I got £3,200 in the next three weeks at a time when my wages were actually £16 a week. And I became the third youngest player to play for United after Duncan Edwards and Jeff Whitefoot.'

Norman did not know it at the time, but he would soon be back in Brighton that year even though he did not manage a goal in the final few minutes of the League fixture against Brighton, those precious first 12 minutes of his all-too-brief Old Trafford career. However, he put this right when next given a first-team shirt. The date was 15 May, just eight days after Norman's 17th birthday and it was the final game of the season at home to Stoke. United won 2–0. The scorers were Whiteside and Robson. Thanks to Big Ron, Big Norm had arrived!

But there was to be no time for the 17-year-old to dwell over the summer on his newly found fame which began as a 16-year-old star of *Match of the Day* on BBC television. While driving Norman to training one day United's youth team coach Eric Harrison made a prediction which was to be as startlingly accurate as one of young Whiteside's volleys. 'Eric Harrison turned to me in the car,' recalled Norman, 'and said if I kept playing the way I was I would have a chance of playing in the World Cup that summer. And I am thinking, I do not think so . . . but a month later I was there, in Spain.'

The English team opened up that World Cup finals campaign against France on 16 June 1982 – with Bryan Robson, one of Norman's heroes and close buddies scoring the fastest goal of the tournament – in just 27 seconds. The following day, just by walking on to the pitch, Norman grabbed his own piece of World Cup history!

Northern Ireland International (38 caps 1982–89)

DEBUT: **World Cup. 17 June 1982 v. Yugoslavia in Zaragoza, Spain. (Drew 0–0)**

TEAM: **Jennings; Nicholl, J., Nicholl C., McClelland, Donaghy, McIroy, O'Neill M., McCreery, Armstrong, Hamilton, Whiteside.**

Northern Ireland team manager Billy Bingham had no plans to play the 'Man-Boy' in the World Cup finals. According to Norman he was preparing to go on tour with United in America and Canada immediately after the end of the season. That was until he got a phone call to say he had been selected to travel to the World Cup finals in Spain with the Irish squad. He was to report for training back to where it had all begun just a few weeks earlier . . . at Brighton. This was real 'Roy of the Rovers' stuff. Barely believable. Two months before the World Cup got under way, few outside of Manchester or Northern Ireland had even heard of Norman Whiteside. He had been playing for the junior teams, a member of the Youth Cup final team that lost to Watford. Then he was thrust into the first team – twice! Now here he was heading for Spain. It was nothing new to Whiteside. All his life he used his build and determination to force his way into teams made up of much older players. He was just 13 when he played for the Northern Ireland schools team that won the European Championships. He was two years younger than the rest of his team-mates, according to one of them, QPR's Alan McDonald. Norman arrived at Old Trafford at around the same time as Mark Hughes who was to later describe the Irishman as two feet bigger than everyone else with a haircut that made him look like a US GI. In 14 games for the Northern Ireland schoolboys (1978–79 and 1979–80) he rattled in 12 goals. Now, the boy who had just left school at 16 was about to become a man at the World Cup. At 17 years and 36 days he became the youngest ever to appear in the World Cup finals, taking over the mantle that Brazil's most famous export, Pele, had held since his astonishing performances in winning the trophy in 1958.

From school to the World Cup finals in less than a year. Norman's driving ambition had taken him away from the bloody conflict back at home. By the time Norman was making his debut as a 'Red Devil', Northern Ireland had witnessed the extreme violence associated with the hunger strike and Britain had battled with Argentina over the Falklands. Of course, he was always aware of what was going on back home. It was natural that he would be concerned that his family was not caught up in the destructive sectarianism which afflicted so many teenagers born into the violence of the times, including some of his own teenage friends. 'To be fair, a few of them were in prison,' Norman told me, his face suddenly exploding into laughter at the memory. 'I know because I have been back since and have coached them in prison.'

This encounter took place in a packed room at H.M. Prison Maghaberry, 20 miles from Belfast. Among those present were a number of dignitaries. After Norman had spent a couple of sessions coaching the inmates a question-and-answer session was set up. 'When we are gathered for the question-and-answer session,' Norman recalled, 'someone says, "Any questions for Norman?", and one of my pals stands up and says, "Norman do you remember that time me and you robbed that Post Office up the Shankill and you got away with it?" You wanna have seen the faces of the prison staff! Classic!'

So it was from behind bars that some of Norman's childhood friends watched him play his first World Cup game against Yugoslavia. My abiding memory of seeing this precocious 'Roy of the Rovers' is his early run down the left side of the penalty box. Their right-back, Gudelj, looked big, strong and nastily efficient at stopping upstart wingers. But he underestimated our Norman. Cool as you like, Norman put the outside of his left foot under the ball as his body tried to sell a dummy to the right. In the very moment he did that, Norman scooped the ball into the air by a few inches, moving it forward along the wing in the direction he now intended to follow. The full-back lunged but missed because the ball had cleverly been shoved into the airspace above his boot . . . and Norman was now skipping over his boot on his way to putting over an early cross! His skill was never in doubt. I read recently in the *United World* magazine, on the occasion of Eric Harrison's retirement after 18 years as youth coach at Old Trafford, that he thought Big Norm had 'all the attributes of a world-class player when he first came to the club'. He remarked on his terrific pace and his strength and balance which should have made him an even greater player. But then he disclosed that – in his opinion – Big Norm never had the same pace after a knee operation when he was just 15. Nevertheless, Big Norm's skills during combat were compelling enough to get him into an Irish side which was to bring such glory back from Spain . . . even though the manager never really intended to use him . . . that is, until he saw him in training in Brighton. Billy Bingham has admitted candidly that he had no intention of playing a 17-year-old lad in the World Cup.

The Northern Irish lads excelled themselves. Against all odds they faced one of the favourites in the tournament, host nation Spain. One night in

Valencia nearly 50,000 looked on in amazement as the minnows of Northern Ireland flexed World Cup muscle and beat Spain for the first and only time ever. Gerry Armstrong scored the only goal two minutes after the interval and the Irish defended their goal like terriers for the most famous victory in their history. This in spite of the fact that Mal Donaghy was sent off in the second half. Whiteside, the 'Man Boy', played his part in what he now regards as the outstanding memory of his international career. 'I didn't play that well,' he said candidly, 'but obviously we got to the quarter-final stages which is unbelievable for us and I was part of it. I just remember all the Northern Ireland supporters, about 2,000 of them, in the corner. In Europe there's always a moat around the ground but this ground didn't have one and it was like they were on top of you. There are bits I remember and other bits I don't. I was a kid then and we were all drinking about ten pints of water before, during and after the game because of the heat and exhaustion. You remember things like that and then you don't remember things you're probably supposed to. But beating the host nation in the World Cup and getting to the quarter-final stage must be up there!'

As a measure of Big Norm's impact on the game, BBC Northern Ireland produced a half-hour documentary on his amazing career which was to be transmitted the night before his 21st birthday as he prepared for his second appearance in the World Cup finals, in Mexico in 1986. Producer and presenter Mike Nesbitt spoke to the Northern Ireland team manager Billy Bingham about the previous World Cup. Bingham told him: 'I had no plan to play him. We trained for a couple of weeks in Brighton and I remember he was *the* outstanding player in all the practice games we had. In fact, he could bend the ball and Pat Jennings was absolutely amazed by the skill of it and so he was more than impressive. By the second week I had decided he was going in the team but I did not mention it to anyone else.' Bingham regarded Norman as having the maturity of a 25 or 26-year-old. Whatever his 'playing age' in the '82 World Cup, Norman remembers little about the build up to his first game: 'All I can remember is the team being announced and I do not remember Billy pulling me to one side or anything. I just remember being in the team and all of a sudden there is an influx of world media around me because I was about to beat Pele's record.'

It was a different Norman Whiteside who returned from Spain. The 'Man-Boy' was now very much a man with a blistering hot desire to display his skills. Rested after the heroics of beating the host nation in Spain to reach the quarter-finals, the 17-year-old 'Roy of the Rovers' was about to tear through defences in the football league. Just as Michael Owen emerged as a frighteningly good prospect during France '98, Whiteside had shown sufficient skills in Spain to attract the attentions of other clubs. He confirmed his ability in the season that followed (1982–83). He appeared at Wembley twice, becoming on each occasion the youngest ever to score in Wembley finals. The first was in the Milk Cup final against Liverpool and then in the FA Cup final replay against Brighton. In total he played 56 games, scoring 14 goals. United finished third in the League as Big Ron galvanised an entertaining team suitably adventurous to be regarded as an outfit which played the game in the United style we had become so accustomed to during the '60s – and briefly in the '70s when the Doc was around. Defeat at Wembley in the Milk Cup final, losing 2–1 to Liverpool, was a defining moment for Norman.

When I asked him about his worst moment at Old Trafford, he replied: 'Leaving. Simple as that. I don't remember any bad games or disappointments . . . well, losing to Liverpool in the Milk Cup final. I scored the opening goal and I cried my eyes out.' What, Big Norm the hardman has a soft spot? He continued: 'On the park, I cried because when you are so determined you always want to be a winner, don't you? To lose was just . . . I had never come across losing before, in the B.B., when I played for Liverpool Supporters' Club and with the United youth team, we won everything to that date. I had played in the World Cup finals to the quarter-final stages, so I mean, that was my first big defeat, so, I mean, I cried my eyes out. I thought I do not want any more of this. That was probably one of my worst moments.'

But what a goal he scored that day. I saw it in a pub in Portstewart just before going to a wedding. McQueen to Whiteside on the edge of the Scousers' penalty area. Ball controlled in a piece of fantastic skill. Shielding it from Hansen, Big Norm turned him inside out and with an immaculate right-foot shot actually placed the ball, with pace, into the bottom right-hand corner of the net past Grobbelaar. A few weeks later and at the same end of the Wembley pitch Norman scored a superb headed goal in the 4–0 FA Cup final replay victory over Brighton to become the youngest scorer in a final. In the following season, 1983–84, Norman made 50 appearances in the United shirt, scoring 16 goals in all competitions, as the team finished fourth in the league with early exits in the two domestic cups. By now Norman was considered a 'seasoned' first-team regular who was beginning to enjoy the company of a small group of players – Paul McGrath, Bryan Robson, Kevin Moran to name just a few. This group 'hunted' in a pack. That is to say, they enjoyed their pints together. According to Norman, these were happy days under the leadership of Big Ron: 'He didn't care what you did off the park, well, I wouldn't say didn't care but he was more determined about what you did on the field. Another thing I liked about Big Ron was that he didn't care about the opposition. If you were Manchester

United, let them worry about us, that was his philosophy. We're the biggest, we're the best . . . let them worry about us. We are Manchester United. If we go out and do our business, we'll beat anybody. That was his attitude and I liked it.'

Of course, the highlight of the 83–84 season was United's progress in the Euopean Cup-Winners' Cup. 'Stormin' Norman' shook Europe with his cavalier performances as the Red Devils reached the semi-finals against the mighty Juventus following one of the 'great' European football nights at Old Trafford against Spanish giants Barcelona. Having lost the first leg 2–0 in Spain, and in front of a home crowd of 58,547 spectators, the excitement was at fever pitch as a magnificent performance of passion and commitment saw United through with a superb 3–0 victory. Two goals from Robson and one from Stapleton saw the departure of Barcelona, Maradona et al. Before being taken off, Norman played his part in this fantastic night. Bring on Juventus. After a 1–1 draw at home, Norman came off the bench in Italy to score in a 2–1 defeat. United had been knocked out of Europe but Norman had impressed a number of Italian teams. They began to show an interest. Lazio offered £1.4m for the Belfast man. However, with Hughes now pressing for the striker's role up front with Stapleton, Norman was about to switch from front-man to midfield. Once again Wembley was to be the theatre for one of those special Whiteside performances which lives long in the memories of all United fans – especially for a certain ten-year-old boy named Steven, my second son attending his first-ever United game!

FA Cup final: 18 May 1985 v. Everton at Wembley Stadium. Attendance 100,000. (Won 1–0)
Everton: Southall; Stevens, Van den Hauwe, Ratcliffe, Mountfield, Reid, Steven, Gray, Sharp, Bracewell, Sheehy.
United: Bailey; Gidman, Albiston (Duxbury), Whiteside (1), McGrath, Moran, Robson, Strachan, Hughes, Stapleton, Olsen.

For just a few seconds 100,000 people fell silent. It reminded me of the 'loud fart' scenario. You know, those occasions when in a packed and noisy classroom when your innards are in rebellion and you know you are not going to be able to prevent yourself from letting your flatulence sneak away. Then just at the very moment of release there is total silence – except for the eruption from your backside. Deep red cheeks reveal your utter embarrassment. This was one of those occasions at Wembley, except that the noise which initially broke the sudden silence was of Norman Whiteside's left boot making contact with the ball. It was a remarkable moment for me. It was as though time stood still and I just knew that this was the shot that was going to bring us a goal. Even though I was watching the game from the opposite end of the stadium, I clearly heard the thump of boot on ball and then waited for the bulge in the net. It was not until much later that night that I appreciated the very special nature of his winner against Everton in the 1985 FA Cup final. But at the very moment this magnificent banana-shaped left-foot shot eluded the touch of one of the world's greatest goalkeepers, a couple of Scousers of the 'blue' hue were busy pissing all over me and my son Steven. Fathers do things for their children. Steven was too young in 1979 to go to the Arsenal final, so his older brother Jason got to that one. In order to fulfil a promise to Steven, tickets were obtained on the black market. Hence our presence in the Everton end of the ground. Thirteen years later Steven and I were sitting in a Belfast restaurant chatting to the man who made our Wembley 'piss-up' worthwhile. You have to appreciate just how momentous this victory over Everton was. We were 18 years into what turned out to be a 26-year term of misery, inflicted mostly by the 'dirties', the 'red' side of Scouseland. But just as we had destroyed the unique 'treble' prospects for Liverpool in 1977, so we did the same for Everton in 1985 – and we did it with ten men! Scouse-busters supreme – with the supreme Scouse-buster in Big Norm.

If nothing else, United fans had become accustomed to FA Cup finals. Such was our staple diet of success in the absence of 'real' achievement in the League – even though Big Ron provided an entertaining side in the true tradition of Manchester United and even though his sides never finished out of the top four. Everton came to Wembley in 1985 as the League Champions (won at Goodison on 6 May with a 2–0 win over QPR) and winners of the European Cup-Winners' Cup following a 3–1 victory over Rapid Vienna in Rotterdam just three days earlier. What would Fergie have made of playing a European final so close to an FA Cup final at Wembley? Who cares? The fact is that the 1985 final received a poor press – mainly because the focus of attention was the first-ever Cup final sending-off. However, you ask any United fan about that day and he/she will tell you that it was a day to linger over in the memory for a variety of reasons. There was the unfair sending-off of Kevin Moran after a piece of over-indulgence in the drama department by Peter Reid. There was the spirited performance of our ten surviving players. But most important of all, there was the exquisite assassination of the Everton 'treble' dream by our executioner-for-all-seasons, Norman Whiteside. The Shankill Road sharpshooter pulled the trigger and gave United both victory and justice. It seemed to take forever for the ball to travel from his left boot to the net and in that short space of time Wembley seemed to go silent in anticipation of either a great goal or a magnificent save. Mercifully Neville Southall's world class was unable to read Whiteside's intention – just as helpless as Pat Jennings during the Brighton training for the '82 World Cup finals – and it seems it was an intentional moment of inspiration which Big Norm had rehearsed over and over again. At least, that is what he is now busy telling us over lunch. The conversation goes like this:

Norman: I don't remember a thing.
Author: Why is that? This goal. Neville Southall. Even at the opposite end I heard the thump of your foot hitting the ball for some reason and you knew it was going into the back of the net. Did *you* know it was going into the net?
Norman: Yes, of course.
Author: Did you practise that?
Norman: Well, I'm going to show you. You can't see it on the video, but I'll show you what actually happened. I'm going to do it with your beer.
Author: Is that Mountfield?
Norman: No, he wasn't playing was he?
Author: I think he might have been.

Norman continued: 'He wasn't involved. People say it was a cross and if the truth be known I was stuck out on the right wing 'cos I was getting back from the attack before. If you watch the video, I had missed a chance. If I had dummied it Robbo was in behind me to tap it in and I was like absolutely knackered, so I went out and stuck out on the right wing to just get out of the way. Sparky found me with this great ball and it was Stevens who played me onside, their left-back, if you look at the video.

'When I got the ball – one thing that I used to do a lot in training was [enthusiastically moving beer bottles and salt cellars about on the table] myself here, defender here, keeper there. And what my idea was to get the ball back to here. So to get the defender in a perpendicular straight line, so if you're looking at that line, Neville can't see the ball. And when I got the ball on the right wing and I went near the box – and I used to practise this in training – I looked up and Pat van den Hauwe was there and I could see Neville holding on to the post. So I threw my leg over the ball. Pat van den Hauwe at that particular time came in to obstruct Neville's view and something in the back of my mind said, "hit it". So I used him as a screen and when I hit the ball I'd have that distance there [pointing to the table-top mock-up] before Neville could first see it. That's the distance Neville's hand was away from the ball when it went into the goal. So I bought a half a yard off that defender. You see what I'm trying to say. People say it was a cross. But that's the theory behind it. I used to do it every day in training. Bergkamp does it every week. You see when he bends it around a defender? The keeper can't see it. Anyone who played with me will confirm that.'

Confirmation that Big Norm did indeed practise this shot in training came from his team-mate Frank Stapleton. Whiteside was the master of unexpected and truly breath-taking goals and there is no way he 'rehearsed' them all. Take for example the winning goal against Arsenal in the FA Cup semi-final at Villa Park in 1983. The 'Arse' were 1–0 up at half-time but a goal from Robson levelled it five minutes into the second half and then – and then – the 'boy wonder' struck! Moving down what is now referred to as the 'left channel', but is what we used to know as the inside-left position, Whiteside watches a high ball from Albiston travel 35 yards through the air. He continues to move forward as he watches the ball travel virtually directly above his head and drop, clearly anticipating exactly where it is going to land. The ball bounces once and having glanced over at Wood in the Arsenal goal, Big Norm volleys it home with great relish, not to mention accuracy. It is just one of the many stunning goals he hit home for United in a career which brought 67 goals in a red shirt.

He should have been around to make that total 167 goals but his Old Trafford career came to an abrupt end with the arrival of Alex Ferguson to replace Whiteside's mentor Big Ron. At the time Whiteside was a 'boozing' buddy of Paul McGrath and Bryan Robson. It was widely reported that Ferguson wanted to break up the Whiteside-McGrath-Robson drinking cartel. If McGrath's departure from Old Trafford was laced with a bitter sideswipe at Ferguson, the departure of Big Norm was positively friendly.

The night Big Ron got the sack, it was Whiteside, Robson, Strachan and McGrath who went to Atkinson's house to party. No other players turned up. 'Ron told us that night that Alex Ferguson would be our manager the next morning,' Whiteside recalled, 'so you can imagine coming back the next morning from Big Ron's party to greet our new manager. We weren't in the best condition. So when we met Fergie his first words were, after he got us all into the gymnasium, "Norman," and now he said this not to me but to everybody, "I don't care who you are – Norman Whiteside, Bryan Robson, Gordon Strachan, I am the boss . . ." And that is the way he started the conversation with the 60 pros who were there. So he gave me a mention in his opening line, I was quite chuffed!'

Whiteside may have been chuffed at the time but reality dictated that this was the beginning of the end for Norman Whiteside. In August 1989, he and McGrath slung their hooks and headed off to pastures new. Fergie had sorted out the 'booze brothers'. But while McGrath reacted bitterly and lashed out at Fergie in a very public manner, Norman Whiteside maintained a dignified silence — and it *was* dignified. According to Whiteside it was Fergie who helped him sort out a good deal at Everton where, he claims, he earned more in two years than he had in all his career at United. That's one thing you notice about Whiteside — his loyalty to his colleagues and former playing and drinking partners — about whom he does not speak. As you can see he even feels some degree of loyalty to the man who sold him to Everton.

The loyalty characteristic is reflected in Whiteside's personal life as well. Even though he was nearly ten years younger than one of his socialising partners, Robson, the young Whiteside had from an early age found a partner for life in Julie Dalglish — and before you even think it, the answer is, no relation! He met her when he was 16 or so. She came from a United-mad family and had been a Stretford Ender — where most of Big Norm's admirers were to be found.

But when it comes to persuading Whiteside to say who it is he admires most, you discover a sudden reticence to speak his mind. He refused to engage in the fantasy which entertains thousands of football fans all over the world — to pick their 'greatest ever' elevens. However, when pushed to name the players he has most enjoyed playing with, Whiteside finally succumbs and lists Bryan Robson, Mark Hughes, Gordon Strachan, Kevin Moran, Paul McGrath, Frank Stapleton, Arnold Muhren and 'unsung hero' Arthur Albiston. While we were on a roll, I managed to extract a few names from him of the most difficult opponents he has faced. He starts by naming Jimmy Case — but then corrects himself to say that Case was the 'hardest' opponent. The most difficult were Mark Lawrenson and Alan Hansen of Liverpool. I pushed my luck and asked about superstitions. His answer took me by surprise. See what you make of it. Denying he had any pre-match rituals, Big Norm told me: 'The only thing I ever did — and some people said it was a superstition, although I don't think so — was that I played the first half with a long-sleeved shirt and the second half with a short-sleeved shirt and that is only because of the kits we had at the time. But what I did at Man United was to change my full kit at half-time, even my jockstrap . . . everything. I stripped naked, dried myself down with a towel and had a brand new kit every single half-time because I wanted to feel fresh for the second half. I didn't notice this long-sleeve, short-sleeve thing until someone told me about it, someone who had picked up on it. Now, it could have been the other way around. But that was my routine every half-time at United.' Collectors of trivia may feel compelled to fetch all their United videos off the shelf to check this out for themselves. Me? I only look at United videos for the sheer pleasure and rush of adrenaline generated by watching players like Whiteside whack the ball into the back of the Scousers net!

REASON TO BELIEVE: No Irish team would be complete without the 'Man-Boy'. Norman Whiteside was the incarnation of comic character 'Roy of the Rovers'. He was training at Old Trafford from the age of 12, made his first-team debut at the age of 16 and was playing in the World Cup as a 17-year-old. Before his 17th year had expired, Big Norm had scored in two Wembley Cup finals to become the youngest player to do so in both the FA Cup and the then Milk (League) Cup. Whiteside is recognised by Harry Gregg and Ron Atkinson as a player with great vision. Big Ron said Whiteside instinctively knew the exact location of every player on the pitch even as he was waiting for the ball to arrive from a 40-yard pass. It was also Big Ron who said Whiteside was never a child, he was 'born a man'. Whiteside had tremendous skill on the ball and aside from packing a lethal shot, he could cover the pitch and strike fear into the hearts of opponents with his lethal tackling. A true defender of the Old Trafford faith. A player who was hero-worshipped by the United faithful. Alongside Best and Stapleton, Whiteside gives *United Irishmen* their cutting edge up front.

The United Irishmen

ANDERSON, Trevor: b. Belfast 3.3.51: Forward 1973–74: Games 13 (6) Goals 2.

BAIRD, Harry: b. Belfast 17.8.13: Forward 1936–38: Games 53 Goals 18.

BEHAN, Billy: b. Dublin 3.8.11: G/keeper 1933–34: Games 1 Goals 0.

BEST, George: b. Belfast 22.5.46: Forward 1963–74: Games 466 Goals 178.

BLANCHFLOWER, Jackie: b. Belfast 7.3.33: Defender 1951–58: Games 116 Goals 27.

BRAZIL, Derek: b. Dublin 14.12.68: Defender 1988–90. Games 0 (2) Goals 0.

BREEN, Tommy: b. Belfast 27.4.17: G/keeper 1936–39: Games 71 Goals 0.

BRENNAN, Shay: b. Manchester 6.5.37: Defender 1957–70: Games 355 (1) Goals 6.

BRIGGS, Ronnie: b. Belfast 29.3.43: G/keeper 1960–62: Games 11 Goals 0.

BYRNE, David: b. Dublin 28.4.05: Forward 1933–34: Games 4 Goals 3.

CANTWELL, Noel: b. Cork 28.2.32: Defender 1960–67: Games 144 Goals 8.

CAREY, Johnny: b. Dublin 23.2.19: Defender 1937–53: Games 344 Goals 18.

CAROLAN, Joe: b. Dublin 8.9.37: Defender 1958–61: Games 71 Goals 0.

CONNELL, Tom: b. Newry 25.11.57: Defender 1978–79: Games 2 Goals 0.

DALY, Gerry: b. Dublin 30.4.54: Midfield 1973–77: Games 137 (5) Goals 32.

DONAGHY, Mal: b Belfast 13.9.57: Defender 1988–92: Games 98 (20) Goals 0.

DUNNE, Pat: b. Dublin 9.2.43: G/keeper 1964–66: Games 66 Goals 0.

DUNNE, Tony: b Dublin 24.7.41: Defender 1960–73: Games 529 (1) Goals 2.

FEEHAN, 'Sonny' John: b. Dublin 17.9.26: G/keeper 1949–50: Games 14 Goals 0.

GILES, Johnny: b. Dublin 6.11.40: Forward 1959–63: Games 114 Goals 13.

GILLESPIE, Keith: b. Larne 18.2.75: Forward 1992–95: Games 7 (7) Goals 2.

GIVENS, Don: b. Dublin 9.8.49: Forward 1969–70: Games 5 (4) Goals 1.

GREGG, Harry: b. Tobermore, Co. Derry 27.10.32: G/keeper 1957–67: Games 247 Goals 0.

GRIMES, Ashley: b. Dublin 2.8.57: Defender/Midfield 1977–83: Games 77 (30) Goals 11.

HAMILL, Mickey: b. Belfast 19.1.1885: Forward 1911–14: Games 59 Goals 2.

IRWIN, Denis: b. Cork 31.10.65: Defender 1990–Present: Games 415 (13) Goals 28.

JACKSON, Tommy: b. Belfast 3.11.46: Defender 1975–78: Games 22 (1) Goals 0.

KEANE, Roy: b. Cork 10.8.71: Midfield 1993–Present: Games 215 (10) Goals 26.

KENNEDY, Patrick: b. Dublin 9.10.34: Defender 1954–55: Games 1 Goals 0.

LYNER, David: b. Belfast (date unknown): Forward 1922–23: Games 3 Goals 0.

MARTIN, Mick: b. Dublin 9.8.51: Midfield 1972–75: Games 36 (7) Goals 2.

McCREERY, David: b. Belfast 16.9.57: Midfield 1975–79: Games 57 (52) Goals 8.

McFARLANE, Noel: b. Bray 20.12.34: Forward 1954–55: Games 1 Goals 0.

McGIBBON, Pat: b. Lurgan 6.9.73: Defender 1992–97: Games 1 Goals 0.

McGRATH, Chris: b. Belfast 29.11.54: Midfield 1976–81: Games 15 (19) Goals 1.

McGRATH, Paul b. London 4.12.59: Defender 1982–89: Games 191 (7) Goals 16.

McMILLAN, Sammy: b. Belfast 29.9.41: Forward 1961–63: Games 15 Goals 6.

McMILLEN, Walter: b. Belfast 24.11.13: Defender 1933–35: Games 29 Goals 2.

McILROY, Sammy: b. Belfast 2.8.54: Midfield 1971–72: Games 390 (28) Goals 70.

MORAN, Kevin: b. Dublin 29.4.56: Defender 1978–88: Games 283 (5) Goals 24

MORRISON, Tommy: b. Belfast 1874: Forward 1902–04: Games 36 Goals 8.

MULRYNE, Philip: b. Belfast 1.6.78: Forward 1997–99: Games 2 Goals 0.

NICHOLL, Jimmy: b. Hamilton, Canada 28.12.56: Defender 1975–82: Games 234 (13) Goals 6.

NICHOLSON Jimmy: b. Belfast 27.2.43: Defender 1960–63: Games 68 Goals 6.

O'BRIEN, Liam: b. Dublin 5.9.64: Midfield 1986–89: Games 11 (19) Goals 2.

O'CONNELL, Pat: Dublin 1887: Defender 1914–15: Games 35 Goals 2.

PEDEN, Jack: b. Belfast 11.3.1865: Forward 1893–94: Games 32 Goals 8.

ROBINSON, James: b. Belfast 8.1.1898: Forward 1919–22: Games 21 Goals 3.

ROCHE, Paddy: b. Dublin 4.1.51: G/keeper 1974–82: Games 53 Goals 0.

SCOTT, Jackie: b. Belfast 22.12.33: Forward 1952–56: Games 3 Goals 0.

SLOAN, Tom: b. Ballymena 10.7.59: Defender 1978–81: Games 4 (8) Goals 0.

STAPLETON, Frank: b. Dublin 10.7.56: Forward 1981–87: Games 265 (21) Goals 78.

WHELAN, Anthony: b. Dublin 23.11.59: Defender 1980–81: Games 0 (1) Goals 0.

WHELAN, Liam/Billy: b. Dublin 1.4.35: Forward 1954–58: Games 96 Goals 52.

WHITESIDE, Norman: b. Belfast 7.5.65: Forward/Midfield 1981–89: Games 254 (18) Goals 67.